The Praeger Handbook
of Special Education

The Praeger Handbook of Special Education

Edited by Alberto M. Bursztyn

Westport, Connecticut
London

Library of Congress Cataloging-in-Publication Data

The Praeger handbook of special education / edited by Alberto M.
Bursztyn.
  p. cm.
  Includes bibliographical references and index.
  ISBN 0-313-33262-2 (alk. paper)
  1. Special education—United States—Encyclopedias. 2. Children with
disabilities—Education—United States—Encyclopedias. I. Bursztyn,
Alberto, 1952– II. Title: Handbook of special education.
  LC3957.P73 2007
  371.90973—dc22   2006029523

British Library Cataloguing in Publication Data is available.

Library of Congress Catalog Card Number: 2006029523
ISBN-10: 0-313-33262-2
ISBN-13: 978-0-313-33262-3

First published in 2007

Praeger Publishers, 88 Post Road West, Westport, CT 06881
An imprint of Greenwood Publishing Group, Inc.
www.praeger.com

Printed in the United States of America

∞™

The paper used in this book complies with the
Permanent Paper Standard issued by the National
Information Standards Organization (Z39.48–1984).

10 9 8 7 6 5 4 3 2 1

In memory of my father,
Valentin Bursztyn

Contents

Policies and Practices

Foreword

As you are about to learn in this book, special education is a dynamic field that holds great promise and faces many challenges. Special education today is based on the delivery and careful evaluation of a specially designed and coordinated set of comprehensive, research-based instructional and assessment practices and related services intended to address the strengths and challenges of individuals with disabilities and to promote their educational, social, behavioral, and physical development (Heward 2006). As a result, it has evolved into a field that is an integral part of the educational system in the United States (Salend 2005).

While one of the central goals of special education today is to foster equity and inclusion in all aspects of society, the education and treatment of individuals with disabilities has undergone many changes that have been shaped by an amalgam of historical, political, philosophical, and sociocultural factors. Prior to 1800, the lives of individuals with disabilities were characterized by isolation, fear, ridicule, and abandonment. In the late 1700s, educational methods were developed that showed the success of a range of teaching strategies, and society began to become more tolerant of individuals with disabilities. However, the nineteenth century saw the development of institutionalized placements for individuals with disabilities, which added to their isolation from the larger society. The early twentieth century brought special schools and classes for students with disabilities, although segregated institutionalized placements remained an integral part of our treatment of individuals with disabilities as late as the 1970s.

The movement away from the segregation of individuals with disabilities and toward their inclusion into society was fostered by the philosophical and political factors associated with the 1960s and 1970s, which ultimately led to judicial and legislative actions that provided greater access to society and public schools for individuals with disabilities. During this time frame, the normalization principle, which originated in Scandinavia, called for society to restructure educational, housing, employment, social, and leisure opportunities for individuals with disabilities to parallel those enjoyed by their friends, relatives, and neighbors without disabilities (Wolfensberger 1972). Motivated by and learning from the successes of the civil rights movement, individuals with disabilities and their families banded together to inform the public about and advocate for policies that would allow individuals with disabilities to become full and equal members of society. Based on the Supreme Court decision that *"separate but equal is not equal"* in *Brown v. Board of Education* (1954), families initiated court action to obtain a free, appropriate public education for their children with disabilities (Blanchett, Mumford, and Beachum 2005).

The interaction of these factors culminated in congressional passage of several landmark education and civil rights laws that provided greater access to all aspects of society for individuals with disabilities. More than any other law, the Education for All Handicapped Children Act (PL 94-142), now known as the Individuals with Disabilities Education Act (IDEA), has fostered the inclusion of students with disabilities in the educational system. Before it was enacted into law in 1975, more than a million students with disabilities were denied a public education, and those who attended public schools were segregated from their peers with disabilities. Since its initial passage, the IDEA has been amended and reauthorized numerous times to enhance the educational performance of students with disabilities and provide them with greater access to the general education curriculum.

Today these factors, aided by the technological advances of the 1990s and early 2000s, have continued the movement toward greater inclusion of individuals with disabilities. However, while the field of special education can be proud of its many accomplishments in enhancing the lives of individuals with disabilities and their families, many challenges that need to be addressed still exist. The impact of inclusion on all students, educators, and family members and the costs associated with special education continue to be debated. Studies on the effectiveness of special education programs indicate that, progress aside, students with disabilities still have high dropout and incarceration rates and low employment rates (Sinclair, Christenson, and Thurlow 2005; Unruh and Bullis 2005) and those who graduate high school are less likely to attend college than their peers without disabilities (Wagner et al. 2005).

In addition, the field of special education has struggled to address the overrepresentation of African-American and Native American students, particularly males, in terms of their classification as students with disabilities and their placement in more restrictive segregated placements. Given the strong connection between special education and the civil rights movement, the disproportionate representation of students of color in special education ironically raises concerns about special education being a separate program that segregates students of color, hinders their educational and social performance, and limits their access to the general education curriculum and success in society (Ferri and Connor 2005).

While we know about special education's past and present, how will it continue to evolve and address these challenges in the future? What historical, political, philosophical, and sociocultural factors will contribute to the special education of tomorrow? Will the legacy of greater inclusion in society and the public schools for individuals with disabilities continue? This handbook on special education will help you to address these questions by introducing you to the important concepts and issues in the field, while at the same time providing you with the historical, political, philosophical, and cultural factors that have and will continue to impact special education. It will also help you to learn about special education so you can collaborate with others to continue the promise of special education and shape its future.

SPENCER J. SALEND

References

Blanchett, W. J., V. Mumford, and F. Beachum. 2005. Urban school failure and disproportionality in a post-*Brown* era: Benign neglect of the constitutional rights of students of color. *Remedial and Special Education* 26:70–81.

Ferri, B. A., and D. J. Connor. 2005. In the shadow of *Brown*: Special education and overrepresentation of students of color. *Remedial and Special Education* 26:93–100.

Heward, W. L. 2006. *Exceptional children: An introduction to special education.* 8th ed. Upper Saddle River, NJ: Merrill/Prentice-Hall.

Salend, S. J. 2005. *Creating inclusive classrooms: Effective and reflective practices for all students.* 5th ed. Columbus, OH: Merrill/Prentice-Hall.

Sinclair, M. F., S. L. Christenson, and M. L. Thurlow. 2005. Promoting school completion of urban secondary youth with emotional and behavioral disabilities. *Exceptional Children* 71:465–82.

Unruh, D., and M. Bullis. 2005. Female and male juvenile offenders with disabilities: Differences in the barriers to their transition to the community. *Behavioral Disorders* 30:105–17.

Wagner, M., L. Newman, R. Cameto, N. Garza, and P. Levine. 2005. *After high school: A first look at the postschool experiences of youth with disabilities.* Menlo Park, CA: SRI International.

Wolfensberger, W. 1972. *The principle of normalization in human services.* Toronto: National Institute on Mental Retardation.

Acknowledgments

This volume was made possible by the efforts of many colleagues who saw the relevance of this project, were willing to contribute entries, and happily revised them when needed; I thank them all. I wish to recognize Marie Ellen Larcada for the conversation that gave the initial impetus for the text and for her encouragement while she was acquisitions editor for Greenwood Press. Likewise, I am grateful for the guidance and patience of Elizabeth Potenza, who was the acquisitions editor for Praeger, the imprint that published the text.

I cannot emphasize enough the contribution of my editorial assistants during the writing and editing of this text. Jennifer Foster, Dana Freed, and Beth Scanlon spent countless hours reviewing submissions and making editorial suggestions in order to make the writing consistent, clear, and accessible. Their talent and scholarship made this a solid reference text. I am also grateful that they approached the task with curiosity, efficiency, and humor. Jennifer Foster was intensively involved in all the multitude of details that we encountered when working with scores of contributors; without her effort, this handbook could not have been realized.

Finally, I wish to thank my family, Carol, Dan, Pia, and Josh, for all the ways, big and small, they contributed to the completion of this project.

Introduction

Special education is a field of contradictions. Historically rooted in the unease that disabilities evoke, special education has inherited both the charitable urge to accommodate the unfortunate among us and the opposite desire: to keep those who remind us of our human vulnerabilities safe from view. This tension between accepting and rejecting the individual with disabilities can be observed throughout the relatively short but eventful history of public special education in the United States.

This handbook addresses the need for public information about the evolving field of special education. Arguably, over the past thirty years no other area of education has been as radically transformed as the provision of services to children with disabilities. Since the mid-1970s, special education has steadily grown to reach fully 12 percent of the U.S. student population in grades K–12, and millions of additional children receive services from birth to age five. Yet, despite its promise to attenuate difficulties and provide equal access, special education has become a controversial field in many respects. Severe critiques have been fueled by the high cost and questionable effectiveness of treatments and interventions; the differential rates of placements and outcomes across localities, family income levels, and ethnicities; and other issues. These arguments and critiques, however, are not usually found in the professional literature.

The current scholarship and literature in teacher education typically highlight the legal and procedural mandates that dominate the discourse in special education, but they generally fail to explore the underlying assumptions and inconsistencies that make this area of education a controversial and unsettled enterprise. This handbook departs from that tradition in the field by presenting special education policies and practices in a more unvarnished way—exploring not only how policies and practices "should be" according to law or theory but also how they *really are* in schools and in classrooms.

Far from monolithic, special education is a constantly evolving and contested area of education. The creation of special education in the 1970s was a huge success for parents and other advocates of children with severe challenges and needs. Those children, until that time, had been excluded from public education; parents faced the enormous emotional and financial costs of educating their children in the shadows of an apathetic school system. While access to schools for children with severe needs has been recognized as righting a social wrong, an unforeseen consequence has been the exponential growth in programs for children with mild disabilities. Most of the students served by special education may not appear to be disabled beyond the demands of school; their disabilities do not incapacitate them in their life at home or in their communities. For this reason, some scholars have suggested that the special education enterprise covers for the failures of regular education (Cummins 1989; Skrtic 1995; Losen and Orfield 2002; Danforth and Taff 2004).

Special education provides a compelling alternative rationale to academic failure that short-circuits examination of "disabling" policies or pedagogy in general education classes. Rather than question why schools are failing so many children, special education policies focus attention on what might be wrong with those children. This approach places the onus of responsibility for school failure on the children, while absolving schools and staff from their own shortcomings. Once rare, now as many as 12 percent of schoolchildren are considered disabled, and their learning differences justify special treatments, which require a separate set of professionals prepared to deliver specialized services. As more children fail to meet the higher academic standards imposed by the recent federal No Child Left Behind Act, the number of children in need of testing and educational accommodations continues to grow. From this critical perspective, professionals in special education tend to serve their own interest by identifying an ever-growing number of potential clients in need of their services.

In the 1990s, displeased parents challenged the increased entrenchment of "self-contained" special education classrooms in schools. Parents and advocates of children with more severe challenges began to demand that access to services for their children be provided not only in their own community schools but also in general education classes. This movement, now known as "inclusion," challenged policies that tended to steer students with more visible disabilities to more segregated settings. Following what is now a familiar pattern in special education, the courts intervened to provide guidance. These mandates were later reflected in law. Currently, schools are implementing multiple programs under the banner of inclusion in order to satisfy parents, emerging mandates, and the increasing recognition among educators that kids with disabilities are primarily kids who would rather not be defined by their limitations.

The call for new methods and practices has led to the emerging mantra: special education is not a *place*, but a *menu of services*. Yet parents' requests for services are not always granted. Budgetary constraints are often at the core of disputes between schools and families. While families advocate for access to quality treatments and intensive services, school administrators tend to be mindful of limited fiscal and personnel resources; they typically seek to meet the requirements of the law at the lowest cost. The ensuing conflicts pit the individuals' needs against institutional priorities. Under these circumstances, knowledgeable and empowered parents can be a formidable force against reluctant administrators. Unfortunately, some parents lack the assertiveness and resources to be strong advocates for their children, and consequently their children are likely to receive fewer and less effective services. In no other field of education is the aphorism "knowledge is power" more apt than in special education. While the laws and rules of special education grant parents considerable power, most poor and immigrant families tend to acquiesce to school decisions without contest because they do not know their rights and options.

This volume is intended to help readers gain factual knowledge and conceptual understanding of special education issues and practices beyond those found in most texts and reference books. It includes alternative views and interpretations, defining concepts not simply by their intended meaning but also by the way they are implemented in schools. By expanding the discourse in special education to include the nature of contemporary issues and controversies, I hope to improve understanding and access for educators, parents, and others interested in this growing field.

References

Cummins, J. 1989. *Empowering minority students.* Sacramento: California Association of Bilingual Education.

Danforth, D., and S. D. Taff. 2004. *Crucial readings in special education.* Upper Saddle River, NJ: Pearson/Merrill/Prentice Hall.

Losen, J. D., and G. Orfield. 2002. *Racial inequity in special education.* Cambridge, MA: Harvard Education Press.

Skrtic, T. M. 1995. *Disability and democracy: Reconstructing (special) education for post-modernity.* New York: Teachers College Press.

History of Special Education

A Brief History of Intelligence Testing

The history of intelligence testing provides a lens for studying the relationship between psychology and education and for exploring how flawed understandings of human cognition led to social injustices. In the earlier part of the twentieth century, testing helped to establish psychology as a viable discipline and applied profession. The successful application of early intelligence tests to the selection and assignment of recruits during World War I was a watershed for psychology, which until then had been a rather obscure academic discipline closely tied to philosophy and the study of the occult. With a powerful tool in their hands, the founders of American psychology set out to find other meaningful applications of testing. Engaging in the ideological debates of the day, they sought to insert their empirically based testing methods into the politically charged policies of their time. Three controversial matters preoccupied the United States as an emergent world power that was rich in resources, short on traditions, and still shaping its national identity. The first was the large influx of immigrants, mostly from Eastern and Southern Europe. Second, the rise in violence and delinquency in urban centers was associated in the popular imagination with the "low intelligence and weak moral character" of various groups of immigrants and racial minorities. Finally, the newly instituted laws forbidding child labor and establishing universal and compulsory public education pitted assimilationists against nativists.

The most prominent psychologists of the day—Yerkes, Bringham, Goddard, and Terman—believed that intelligence was highly correlated with morality and was primarily an inherited trait. In a chapter of psychology's history that has been largely ignored, early American psychologists, siding with conservative forces, proposed the use of intelligence tests as a tool of social engineering. They sought to preserve the dominance of Northern European racial stock in America. To that end, some psychologists advocated restricting the access of would-be immigrants who scored below average on intelligence measures. Moreover, they promoted the use of tests to advance eugenics schemes, including the sterilization of young women with cognitive deficits, and to sort students according to native ability. Under the cover of psychometric science, psychologists wielded considerable political influence; many of their recommendations, including those listed above, were implemented at the state or national level in the 1920s and 1930s. Blatantly racist immigration quotas, based on preserving white Northern European supremacy, remained in place until 1966. The mandatory sterilization of women with cognitive deficits was in effect well into the second half of the twentieth century in many parts of the country—for example, until 1972 in Virginia.

Perhaps the most damning aspect of early psychologists' social activism was their enthusiastic endorsement of racist ideology. Under the banner of eugenic science, they justified racist policies, offering as proof the notion that "objectively measured" genetic traits were associated with specific racial groups. Their German counterparts embraced American psychologists' writings and public statements and further refined a supremacist theory of racial types. That body of flawed "scientific" research provided the Nazis with a rationale for disenfranchising, isolating, exploiting, and finally murdering individuals and entire ethnic and racial groups deemed to be inferior and parasitic.

In the United States, the use of intelligence tests eventually moved beyond immigrant competence screening, becoming widespread and most pervasive in public schools. Lewis Terman translated and adapted the Binet-Simon Test to local norms by testing a population of white middle-class children residing around Stanford University. He then promoted its use in schools. Equipped with this newly reformatted testing instrument, now known as the Stanford Binet Test, he argued that schools would be more efficient if children were tracked by ability level. He also suggested that some groups, such as blacks and Mexicans, would not profit from an academic track and should be prepared for low-level manual work. His ideas resonated in school systems that were overwhelmed with new students and were eager to apply scientific management principles to school organization. Gradually, his model of school organization, which relied on sorting children by scores on intelligence tests, gained currency in the 1920s and 1930s. Intelligence tests became commonplace and were administered in practically every public school to every pupil in the United States; this practice continued unchallenged until the 1960s. The formidable testing movement was halted only after court intervention documented that racist and segregationist school practices were justified by test use.

During the last half of the twentieth century, the reliance on intelligence tests was subjected to successful litigation brought by parents and advocacy groups; as a result, these tests have limited systemic impact today. Group administration of tests has been discontinued, and only qualified professionals are authorized to work with them. Development of contemporary intelligence tests, based on complex formulations of intelligence and more culturally conscious item selection, has led to the publication and use of more equitable and sophisticated instruments. The work of Gardner, Sternberg, Naglieri, Woodcock, and Kaufman, to name a few, has unquestionably improved the capacity of psychologists to observe and evaluate cognition and learning. Newly designed instruments and reformulated theories are more sensitive to cultural and linguistic differences, incorporate a view of learning as contextually embedded, and profit from advances in subject sampling, test norming, and psychometric analyses. Although these newer tests may still be abused or used inappropriately, their administration in schools no longer shapes education policies. In their place, measures of academic achievement developed for group administration across entire systems now exert critical influence on education policy, including evaluation of individual learners, teachers, schools, and entire school systems.

The present use of intelligence testing is largely limited to individual administration in schools for the purpose of educational planning for students evaluated for special education services. Other uses include screening of children for selective programs such as gifted and talented, and clinical and forensic applications.

Further Reading

Binet, A., and T. Simon. 1983. *The development of intelligence in children.* Reprint, Salem, NH: Ayer.

Bursztyn, A. M. 2002. The path to academic disability: Javier's school experience. In *Rethinking multicultural education: Case studies in cultural transition,* ed. C. Korn and A. M. Bursztyn, 160–83. Westport, CT: Bergin & Garvey.

Gould, S. J. 1996. *The mismeasure of man.* New York: Norton.

Kamin, L. J. 1974. *The science and politics of IQ.* Potomac, NY: Lawrence Erlbaum Associates.

Sanchez, G. I. 1951. *Concerning segregation of Spanish-speaking children in the public schools.* Inter-American Education Occasional Papers, no. 9. Austin: University of Texas Press.

Valdes, G., and R. A. Figueroa. 1994. *Bilingualism and testing: A special case of bias.* New York: Ablex.

Website

Human Intelligence (University of Indiana): http://www.indiana.edu/~intell/

ALBERTO M. BURSZTYN

Disability and Civil Rights

Although all school-age individuals in the United States are currently entitled to an education, the right of those with disabilities to receive a free and appropriate education is a relatively recent development. It was not until 1918 that all states had compulsory education laws; prior to this time, children in many places, including those with disabilities, were not required to attend school. Even after 1918, though, children with disabilities were often turned away from public schools; many were placed in special schools or institutions such as **Willowbrook State School**. Until 1973, the court system continually upheld the right of states to exclude students with disabilities from attending school. However, this situation changed after several **landmark court decisions**, which were soon followed by federal legislation specifically addressing the civil rights of individuals with disabilities.

Several important court cases were instrumental in laying the groundwork for legislation to address the civil rights issues of equal protection and due process of the law for children with disabilities. In *Brown v. Board of Education* (1954), the Supreme Court upheld the Fourteenth Amendment guarantee of equal protection under the law; this amendment also stipulates that people cannot be deprived of life, liberty, or property without due process. Simply put, a state that provides education (which is legally considered ''property'') to its children must provide an education for *every child* living in that state. Although this case pertained to race relations within the public schools, the decision has been used by individuals with disabilities to argue that they, too, deserve equal protection under the law. Two additional court decisions are noteworthy: *Pennsylvania Association for Retarded Citizens (PARC) v. Pennsylvania* (1972) established that children with disabilities must be provided a free and appropriate public education, while *Mills v. Board of Education* (1972) established due process procedures for school systems to follow.

Following these court decisions, several pieces of federal legislation have been instrumental in upholding the civil rights of individuals with disabilities. These include Section 504 of the Rehabilitation Act of 1973, Public Law 94-142, and Title II of the Americans with Disabilities Act of 1990.

Section 504 of the Rehabilitation Act protects individuals with disabilities from discrimination by any agency that receives federal assistance. Although it does not provide funding to states for education, it requires schools to create plans to accommodate students with special needs and make the environment accessible.

Public Law 94-142, also known as the **Individuals with Disabilities Education Act** (IDEA), was originally entitled the Education for All Handicapped Children Act of 1975. Reauthorizations of PL 94-142 have occurred in 1986, 1990, 1997, and 2004. Although each reauthorization has changed the specifics of the law, its basic tenets regarding civil rights remain the same:

1. All children, regardless of type or severity of disability, are eligible to receive a free and appropriate public education.

2. Nondiscriminatory evaluation and placement procedures must be followed.

3. Students should be educated in the least restrictive environment possible.

4. Due process procedures must be followed.

This law overruled common practices, previous court rulings, and other legislation that had restricted students with a variety of disabilities from access to public education and attendance of public schools. IDEA mandates that students with disabilities are to be educated in the least restrictive environment (LRE), which means that, to the fullest extent possible, they should be educated with nondisabled peers, reinforcing the right of these students to be treated like any other student within the school system. The execution of this law has reduced the number of students that are placed in institutions or separate classes for students with disabilities. IDEA also delineates the due process procedures for placement and change of placement, as well as confidentiality and the right of parents to be involved in such decisions.

The next major piece of legislation was Title II of the **Americans with Disabilities Act** (ADA) of 1990. ADA prohibits disability discrimination by public entities, including public schools, colleges, universities, and vocational schools. It also requires that public places be accessible to all individuals. ADA extended Section 504 because it mandates that reasonable accommodations be provided for individuals with disabilities in the workplace and institutions of higher learning.

These laws reinforced previous court rulings and firmly established the civil rights of individuals with disabilities regarding equal protection under the law and due process. Enforcement of these laws has protected the civil rights of individuals with disabilities and facilitated their school attendance, participation in regular education classes, and greater integration into their communities. Although efforts continue to address issues of inequity, educational opportunities for students with disabilities have greatly improved.

Further Reading

Mastropieri, M. A., and T. E. Scruggs. 2000. *The inclusive classroom: Strategies for effective instruction.* Upper Saddle River, NJ: Prentice-Hall.
Yell, M. L., D. Rogers, and E. Lodge Rodgers. 1998. The legal history of special education: What a long, strange trip it's been. *Remedial and Special Education* 19 (4): 219–29.

AMY N. SCOTT AND
MARYANN SANTOS DE BARONA

History of Autism

In the early twentieth century, German psychiatrist Emil Kraepelin classified a series of psychotic disturbances in adults as "dementia praecox," where *dementia* was defined by Kraepelin as "progressive deterioration" and *praecox* meant that the disturbance had an early onset. Later, Eugen Bleuler, a Swiss psychiatrist, gave the name "schizophrenia" to these disorders. *Schizophrenia* comes from the Greek roots *schizo-*, meaning "split," and *-phrene* meaning "mind." Bleuler's main criticism of Kraepelin's disorder was that the decline in cognitive abilities was not foreseeable and that the time of onset varied.

Around the same time, disturbances similar to those identified in adults were beginning to be seen in children as well. There were many comparisons and much debate as to whether or not adult schizophrenia and the analogous disorder in children were one and the same. Some believed the disorder reported in a small number of children was just an early form of schizophrenia, while others pointed out that, although the disorders were similar, these children were clearly not identical to adults with schizophrenia. For a time in the early 1930s, "childhood schizophrenia" became a general label for these disturbances in children.

In 1943, Austrian psychiatrist and physician Leo Kanner termed the disorder "early infantile autism" and claimed that it was different from the disturbances described by Kraepelin and Bleuler in that it had a very early onset. Kanner's research of eleven cases indicated that there were several age-related disturbances that began earlier in life than other clinical disorders (i.e., childhood schizophrenia), and he believed that these were clearly two separate disorders. Kanner's early infantile autism was characterized by deficits in communication, unusual cognitive abilities, and behavioral problems such as obsessiveness, repetitive actions, and unimaginative play. The key disturbance identified by Kanner was the child's lack of ability to relate to people and social situations during early infancy. This lack of interaction with family members and people in the lives of these children led Kanner to apply the term *autistic*, meaning "an absorption in the self." Many of Kanner's original descriptions of the disorder were also observed by other researchers and would eventually lead to the recognition of autism by the major classification systems (i.e., the *Diagnostic and Statistical Manual of Mental Disorders* and the *International Classification of Diseases: Mental Disorders*) as a distinct disorder.

A year later, Austrian pediatrician Hans Asperger published his casework on four children, identifying a similar syndrome he termed "autistic psychopathy"— renamed in the 1980s, more appropriately, **Asperger's Syndrome**—meaning "the shutting-off of relations between self and the outside world." Among these four children, Asperger noted several key features that he had observed as common characteristics of autistic psychopathy. These features included impairments in the areas of speech, nonverbal communication, social interaction, motor coordination, skills and interests, and experiences at school. More specifically, Asperger noted that these children lacked empathy, had great difficulty forming relationships with other children, and did not engage in reciprocal conversation. In addition, he found that these children had developed extensive knowledge in a specific area of interest and often referred to them as "little professors."

Over time, there has been an ongoing debate as to whether or not there is a difference between Asperger's Syndrome and autism. The main difference between children with Asperger's Syndrome and those with autism has been that a child with Asperger's Syndrome generally has intact language and cognitive abilities, whereas one with autism is generally impaired in these areas.

Throughout the 1950s and 1960s, based on a theory introduced by Bruno Bettelheim, many researchers in the medical community believed that autism was a psychological disturbance caused by mothers who were apathetic and uncaring towards their children—commonly referred to as "refrigerator mothers." Consequently, mothers of children with autism were often held responsible for causing their child's disorder. With time, this belief was challenged, and eventually the theory was disproved. In 1964, Bernard Rimland demonstrated that Bettleheim's theory was false by presenting overwhelming evidence that grounded autism as a biologically based disorder.

In the late 1970s, the first autism twin study was published by Susan Folstein and Michael Rutter. This landmark study provided evidence for a genetic link as one of the underlying causes of autism. During the next decade, research focused on gathering further evidence for a genetic component as well as clarifying and redefining the symptoms of autism. In 1980, diagnostic criteria were established for infantile autism. It was introduced as one of a group of conditions that were encompassed under the broader condition of Pervasive Developmental Disorders in the third edition of the *Diagnostic and Statistical Manual of Mental Disorders* (DSM-III), where the term *pervasive* indicated that developmental delays were seen throughout all aspects of a child's life. When the DSM-III was revised in 1987, infantile autism was renamed "autistic disorder," and sixteen new categories of diagnostic criteria were included. In 1994, the fourth edition of the *Diagnostic and Statistical Manual of Mental Disorders* (DSM-IV) further refined the diagnostic criteria, which then more closely resembled the criteria listed in the World Health Organization's tenth edition of the *International Classification of Diseases*.

During the 1990s, there were many strides made in identifying, diagnosing, and further researching issues related to autism. In 1991, the first assessment tool to identify children with autism, the Autism Diagnostic Interview, was created by Lord, Rutter, and LeCouteur. In 1994, the National Alliance for Autism Research (NAAR) was founded in the United States by parents of children with autism as the first organization dedicated to funding biomedical research of autistic disorders. In addition to increasing research interests and worldwide funding, NAAR, in conjunction with the Autism Society of America Foundation and the MIND Institute, created the Autism Tissue Program, a parent-led brain tissue donation program.

In the mid-1990s, genetic research was beginning to identify links to specific chromosomes, and in 1998, geneticists reported a link between autism and chromosomes 15q and 7q. By 2001, several researchers had completed genetic screens identifying chromosomal regions containing genes that may be associated with autism.

Over time, autism has become one of the most researched childhood disorders of which there is still no known cause or cure. Today, most researchers believe that the disorder is biologically based with both neural and genetic components. In addition, there have been a variety of other theories, both biologically and nonbiologically based, including yeast infections, food intolerance, gluten intolerance, brain injury, viral causes, immunology, vaccines, structural changes in the brain, environment, and many more (see www.autism-resources.com for more information). While researchers continue their quest to find both a cause and a cure for autism, they support and emphasize the importance of early detection and the urgency of treatment interventions.

Further Reading

Bettleheim, B. 1967. *The empty fortress: Infantile autism and the birth of the self*. New York: Free Press.

Houston, R. A., and U. Frith. 2000. *Autism in history: The case of Hugh Blair of Borgue*. Oxford, England: Blackwell.

Schreibman, L. 2005. *The science and fiction of autism*. Cambridge, MA: Harvard University Press.

Wolff, S. 2004. The history of autism. *European Child and Adolescent Psychiatry* 13:201–8.

Websites

Autism Resources: http://www.autism-resources.com/

Autism Society of America: http://www.autism-society.org/

Center for the Study of Autism: http://www.autism.org/

Cure Autism Now (CAN) Foundation: http://www.cureautismnow.org/

MIND (Mental Illness and Neuroscience Discovery) Institute: http://www.themindinstitute.org/

National Alliance for Autism Research (NAAR): http://www.naar.org/

JENNIFER FOSTER

Mental Retardation in Recent History

The recent history of mental retardation reflects a shift from ignorance and segregation to acceptance and recognition of capabilities. This gradual change continues to greatly impact multiple environments, including the education setting.

People with mental retardation once were perceived as having mental illness or as being insane. In the early part of the twentieth century, this belief evolved into the recognition that mental retardation is separate from mental illness. However, the lack of understanding that remained, combined with the belief that people with mental retardation posed a danger to both themselves and to others and therefore needed to be separated from members of the typical community, resulted in segregation in the form of *institutionalization*. It was in these highly sheltered settings, which often consisted of harsh and punitive environments, that people with mental retardation frequently were placed at birth and remained throughout their lives.

Two major events in the second half of the twentieth century facilitated the *deinstitutionalization* of people with mental retardation. The first was the return of soldiers from World War II. Medical technology had advanced to a point where soldiers with extensive and severe physical injuries, such as the loss of limbs, could survive and return to their communities. The prevalence of injured and newly disabled soldiers fostered a sense of increased concern and compassion within society. This overall greater acceptance toward physical disabilities gradually expanded into an increased sense of compassion for people with disabilities in general, including mental retardation.

The second major event was the civil rights movement. As legislation was passed stating that segregation based on race was inherently unequal, family members and advocates for people with mental retardation also began to demand equality. A series of **landmark court decisions** and legislation followed, with an emphasis on equal education and access for people with disabilities, including their **inclusion** in the same settings as their nondisabled peers. The **Americans with Disabilities Act** (ADA) of 1990 emphasized the civil rights of all people with disabilities, including equal access to employment and the community. Societal attitudes toward people with mental retardation, which included support for their independence and autonomy, resulted in the creation of programs aimed at increasing an individual's involvement in decision-making processes. These programs focused on individuals making their own life decisions, vocational development within the community, and the replacement of institutions with group homes and supervised independent living.

Changes in society's perception of people with mental retardation were also reflected within the education system. The **Individuals with Disabilities Education Act** (IDEA) initially became legislation as **Public Law 94-142**, the Education for All Handicapped Children Act, in 1975 and was renamed and amended in 1997 and 2004. This legislation stresses the provision of education along a continuum of placements, with emphasis on matching individual capabilities to the appropriate environment rather than basing educational placement solely on the diagnosis of disability. Students with disabilities are now guaranteed a free and appropriate public education (FAPE) through the age of twenty-one, with an emphasis on the provision of needed services in the least restrictive environment (LRE). This means that students with disabilities such as mental retardation are entitled to a public education in the same schools and even the same classrooms as their nondisabled peers to the extent that they can receive needed services in such inclusive situations. While the debate continues over the best placement for students with mental retardation, the inclusion movement continues to gain strength by emphasizing the provision of supports and instruction in the regular education classroom and the potential social and academic benefits from interaction with nondisabled peers.

Attitudes toward and practices involving services to those with mental retardation are continuously evolving. While an increasing number of people with mental retardation are receiving instruction in regular schools and classrooms and gaining employment in typical community environments, societal perceptions of this disability continue to shift from pity and fear to empowerment. Institutionalization is rare today, and many books and movies chronicling the successful lives of people with mental retardation are available. Within the past decade, people with mental retardation have been increasingly involved in making decisions related to their personal goals, employment, and living environment. As a result, increases in fair treatment and equality of rights have occurred, and feelings of respect have been noted in these individuals. While relationship development, community involvement, and the expansion of social networks still are known to be in need of improvement, recent societal actions continue to emphasize the importance of choice and independence in increasing the life satisfaction of people with mental retardation.

Mental retardation is currently viewed as an interaction between the individual, the person's capabilities, the environment, and available support services. This shift away from basic diagnosis toward an understanding of the impact of the environment on the development of the individual indicates an increased societal awareness of its own influence on people with mental retardation. Mental retardation increasingly is viewed not as an inherent deficit but as an indication of the need for strong support and encouragement in order for individuals to fulfill their potential. Society has begun to welcome and collaborate with individuals with mental retardation in their communities, allowing for a gradual change from punitive and avoidant attitudes into actions that foster independence and individual success.

Further Reading

American Association on Mental Retardation. 1992. *Mental retardation: Definition, classification, and systems of support*. 9th ed. Washington, DC: American Association on Mental Retardation.

Gardner, J. F., and D. T. Carran. 2005. Attainment of personal outcomes by people with developmental disabilities. *Mental Retardation* 43 (3): 157–74.

Matson, J. L., and J. A. Mulick, eds. 1991. *Handbook of mental retardation*. 2nd ed. New York: Pergamon Press.

Shapiro, J. P. 1994. *No pity: People with disabilities forging a new civil rights movement*. New York: Three Rivers Press.

Websites

American Association on Mental Retardation: http://www.aamr.org/
Americans with Disabilities Act: http://www.ada.gov/
Cognitive Disability/Mental Retardation: http://www.familyvillage.wisc.edu/lib_cdmr.htm
Individuals with Disabilities Education Improvement Act: http://www.nichcy.org/reauth/PL108-446.pdf

PAULA J. McCALL AND
MARYANN SANTOS DE BARONA

Willowbrook State School

The Willowbrook State School in Staten Island, New York, was the largest state-run institution for people with developmental disabilities in the early 1970s. Notorious for its deplorable conditions, the controversies surrounding its operation launched a public outcry that would transform the civil rights of special needs families.

In a time when the most trusted personal advisors—doctors, family members, priests, rabbis—instructed parents to institutionalize their children born with mental retardation, few questioned the advice, although most experienced profound heartbreak. Sacrificing their own emotions for the betterment of their children, families obligingly placed them in residential centers in hopes that they would receive the care and treatment their disabilities required. The high cost of residential treatment led many families to entrust their children to large, state-run facilities such as Willowbrook.

Opened in 1947 by the New York State Department of Mental Hygiene, Willowbrook State School by 1965 housed six thousand residents in a facility designed to accommodate just four thousand. Upon visiting the facility in 1965, Robert F.

Kennedy called it a "snake pit," and word of Willowbrook's unsanitary, inhumane conditions spread quickly, although action was slow to follow. Visitors to the facility found their loved ones in abysmal physical conditions: naked, caked in feces or vomit, drenched in their own urine, malnourished. Few of the children in this "school" were actually being educated. In fact, most residents were completely without any form of stimulation other than a small television set playing in the corner; some were placed in solitary confinement for up to five years at a time. The state of disarray was largely due to budget cuts that had caused the institution to downsize its staff. At Willowbrook's lowest point, there were only two or three people caring for seventy patients at a time.

The building conditions were no better. Toilets frequently backed up, overflowed onto the floor, and were left unrepaired for days on end. Mice fearlessly inhabited the wards. Furniture was so sparse that many children sat or lay on the floor for lack of chairs. Overcrowded dormitories were packed so tightly with beds that only 10 inches of space remained between frames. Close living quarters increased the spread of disease, and within six months of admission most residents experienced pneumonia, parasites, and eventually hepatitis.

As a result of such appalling conditions, there were a number of suspicious deaths from preventable causes such as choking reported at Willowbrook. Even more atrocious was a series of unethical hepatitis experiments conducted on the residents between 1963 and 1966. Like many of the state-run institutions of its time, Willowbrook was a setting that purported to improve children's lives, but instead saw their overall quality of life and health deteriorate.

In 1971 the *Staten Island Advance* ran a series of articles exposing the horrendous conditions at the school. Validated by the newspaper's findings and the public outcry that followed, the parent's association of Willowbrook was spurred into action. Two hundred and fifty members asked Governor Nelson Rockefeller for the immediate removal of the school's director and that an ombudsmen be granted access to buildings and records in an effort to protect their children. However, Willowbrook was not considered a "public school" in the legal sense, and their request was denied.

In 1972 investigative journalist Geraldo Rivera raised public awareness of the situation once more with a television series featuring Willowbrook that made the realities of the institution public through images and interviews. In August of that same year, the Richmond Society for Prevention of Cruelty to Children and the Legal Aid Society filed a class-action suit on behalf of 2,100 children living at Willowbrook. The suit demanded that New York State and the Department of Mental Hygiene take immediate steps to improve conditions at the school and to have the Department of Social Services help the children. They, too, were denied due to legal technicalities—the law stipulated that Family Court could intervene only in family matters and not in state-run facilities.

Although the lawsuits filed thus far had been unsuccessful, the efforts garnered media attention and spurred organizations such as the Association for Retarded Children (ARC) into action. In February 1972, the ARC proposed changes in legislation to afford people with metal retardation the rights they deserve, such as alternative treatments to medication; creation of a child advocacy system; the dismantling of large institutions into smaller, community-oriented "homes"; and greater parent involvement in their child's education.

The following month, an unprecedented event occurred that revolutionized the treatment of children with developmental disabilities. The New York Civil Liberties Union and the Legal Aid Society each filed a class-action suit on behalf of the five thousand residents of Willowbrook State School, calling the school an "inhumane and psychologically destructive environment" that violated a number of civil rights, including the constitutional rights to due process, privacy, and equal protection of the law. This was one of the first lawsuits to name quality treatment for persons with cognitive deficits as a civil right. The class actions pushed the state to dismantle large state-run institutions and place patients in smaller, local, community-oriented homes. They settled the suit in 1975, and Governor Hugh Carey signed the Willowbrook consent decree, which mandated the creation of noninstitutional homes and closure of large state-run facilities, as well as reforms at the school while residents remained there waiting to be placed elsewhere.

The decree is an important turning point in the history of special education. The push behind the legal action came from disenfranchised families who finally found legal footing to negotiate rights for their children, setting a precedent for parent empowerment and involvement. Its pronouncements not only set a standard for the living conditions and rights of people with developmental disabilities that triggered changes in mental health treatment across the country but also contributed to the creation of the Civil Rights of Institutionalized Persons Act, signed into federal law by President Jimmy Carter in May 1980. The Civil Rights of Institutionalized Persons Act cut a lot of the red tape that prevented initial lawsuits from being more successful, giving the "Attorney General the authority to initiate lawsuits against any public institution ... that systematically violates the rights of people confined there." In other words, state-run institutions would no longer be legally immune simply by virtue of being government run. The enactment of this law had widespread effects not only for the mental health community but also for those imprisoned or otherwise under the State's care.

It took years for Willowbrook to place all of its residents. The task was difficult to accomplish because no such "homes" existed at the time of the decree, and local communities fought the placement of this population in their neighborhoods, delaying the creation of said homes. Sadly, conditions did not improve much as the patient-to-staff ratio decreased even further at Willowbrook. However, all residents were eventually placed in much better facilities. Willowbrook State School finally closed down in 1987, and in doing so shut the door on an ugly, cruel, and dispassionate history of treatment of people with disabilities.

Further Reading

Burks, E. C. 1972. Suit is dismissed on Willowbrook. *New York Times*, August 15.

Carter, J. 1980. Civil Rights of Institutionalized Persons Act statement on signing H.R. 10 into law. Available at http://www.presidency.ucsb.edu/ws/index.php?pid=44601 (accessed September 1, 2006).

Clendinen, D. 1981. Willowbrook's goals still unmet six years after order for reforms. *New York Times*, May 25.

Dewan, S. K. 2000. Recalling a victory for the disabled. *New York Times*, May 3.

Gerston, J. 1974. Parent testifies on Willowbrook. *New York Times*, November 1.

_____. 1974. Teacher testifies on Willowbrook. *New York Times*, October 31.

Johnston, L. 1972. Ousters proposed at Willowbrook. *New York Times*, January 27.

Kaplan, M. 1972. Experts at trial decry neglect at Willowbrook. *New York Times*, December 20.

Kennedy, H. 2004. Introduction. In *A guide to Willowbrook State School resources at other institutions.* Available at http://www.library.csi.cuny.edu/archives/WillowbrookRG. htm#Intro (accessed May 7, 2006).

New York Times. 1972. Javits, in a Willowbrook tour, vows to introduce legislation. February 29.

O'Connor, J. J. 1972. TV: Willowbrook State School, "the big town's leper colony." *New York Times*, February 2.

Oelsner, L. 1972. Two suits call for eventual phase-out of Willowbrook. *New York Times*, March 18.

Phillips, M. 1965. Hospital's wards: A study in misery. *New York Times*, September 10.

ELIZABETH SCANLON

Special Education and Society

Bilingualism and Disability

Over the last several decades, there has been an increased awareness of the difficulties faced by culturally and linguistically diverse (CLD) children entering the school system. Many of these children are English-language learners (ELLs) or bilingual; they are typically recent arrivals to the United States or are raised by parents who speak little or no English. One of the major problems faced by these students is their overreferral and overrepresentation in special education.

The research literature cites various reasons for the inappropriate placement of ELLs in special education. One often-cited reason is that school personnel are unaware of the multiple variables affecting the assessment of ELLs, such as sociocultural and linguistic factors, typical second-language acquisition processes, and the limitations of many assessment instruments when assessing these children. A second reason has to do with the referral process itself. Educators often fail to recognize the impact of sociocultural and linguistic variables on learning, as well as acculturation processes affecting the social-emotional development of ELLs. A third equally important reason for confusing language and cultural differences with disabilities is the interpretation of assessment results. Potential or ongoing problems related to low levels of English proficiency, as well as normal processes of second-language acquisition, need to be differentiated from either learning difficulties or language disorders.

Learning a second language is a long and arduous process, and errors are to be expected. Because many of the behaviors that emerge as part of the second-language acquisition process are similar to those behaviors used as markers for identifying the presence of a learning disability, it is critical to understand the second-language acquisition process and how such a process influences performance in school. For instance, students who have been educated in their first language often progress more quickly in learning a new language than those who have not had a formal education.

Assessing whether an ELL has a learning disability is problematic on a number of levels. First of all, the definition of a learning disability as spelled out in the **Individuals with Disabilities Education Act** (IDEA) is complicated when applying it to ELLs. A learning disability, as defined by Turnbull, Turnbull, Shank, and Smith (2004, 104), is a

> disorder in one or more of the basic psychological processes involved in understanding or in using language, spoken or written, which disorder may manifest itself in imperfect ability to listen, think, speak, read, write, spell, or do mathematical calculations.

Exclusionary criteria include a learning problem that is primarily the result of emotional disturbance or of environmental, cultural, or economic disadvantage.

One problematic aspect of this learning disability definition with respect to ELLs is that the difficulty may include language. ELLs, by definition, are in the process of learning one or more languages, and errors are a normal process of language acquisition. For instance, when speaking in the weaker language, there may be grammatical errors that are influenced by the stronger language (e.g., the sentence structure used in English may reflect that of the speaker's first language, which is often different from standard English; this is considered a normal process of learning a second language). Another normal process is language loss, which is weakening of ability in a given language (e.g., first language) when focusing on another language. Young children who simultaneously learn two languages may initially experience some temporary speech and language delays with respect to their developmental speech milestones; however, such delays tend to disappear over time.

The learning disability definition is also problematic in that it requires the student's difficulty not be *primarily* due to environmental, cultural, or economic disadvantage. Assessment of ELLs often may not be able to determine what the primary problem is because there are so many variables at play. Furthermore, it is impossible to establish that the learning difficulty is not due to environment (e.g., poor instruction) and poverty. There is extensive research documenting the negative effects of poverty on learning, and ELLs are proportionally more likely to live under economically disadvantaged conditions. The definition also disregards the possibility of concomitance: It is entirely possible that extrinsic causes, such as poor instruction, cultural differences, and linguistic differences coexist with intrinsic causes, such as an organic brain dysfunction.

In order to differentiate between language differences and learning disabilities, a multidimensional approach is critical. Such an approach requires gathering and integrating data from multiple sources (the student; his or her parents and other family members or caretakers; service providers such as teachers, speech therapists, and others) and contexts (informal settings such as the home or playground; formal settings such as the classroom). It also requires gathering data with multiple methods (formal and informal assessment techniques; alternative assessment procedures).

In terms of assessment, it is important to compare student performance in both the first and second languages, as well as to consider the factors and processes associated with second-language acquisition. If any of the difficulties assessed seem to be related to normal second-language acquisition processes or to such related factors as education history, acculturation, or potential loss of first-language ability due to the child focusing on the development of English, then there might not be a learning disability present. However, it is possible for a child learning a second language to also experience learning difficulties.

Damico (1991) offers a descriptive model that provides markers for the identification of potential disordered processes in the first language (it should be noted that if there *is* a language-disordered process present, it exists in the first language). Such markers include the following difficulties in the first language:

1. delays in responding to questions
2. difficulties following verbal instructions
3. gaps in expressive vocabulary
4. difficulties organizing verbal responses to open-ended questions

There are also markers related to effective communicative ability (i.e., pragmatics):

1. utterances that include unusual pauses, hesitations, and repetitions
2. utterances that include revisions of what was already said
3. word-finding difficulties
4. inappropriate responses to questions
5. poor topic maintenance
6. multiple repetitions required for comprehension

While these are flags for potential disordered processes, it should be noted that weakening of ability in the first language (i.e., language loss) could be occurring due to the student focusing attention on English; if that is the case, then there might not be learning disability present after all.

Assessing ELLs for the presence of a learning disability is a complex task. However, a multidimensional approach should lead to a more accurate picture of the relationship between second-language acquisition and school performance. Furthermore, use of such an approach should result in fewer inappropriate referrals of ELLs for assessments and fewer inappropriate placements in special education.

References

Damico, J. S. 1991. Descriptive assessment of communicative ability in limited English proficient students. In *Limiting bias in the assessment of bilingual students*, ed. E. V. Hamayan and J. S. Damico. Austin, TX: Pro-Ed.

Turnbull, R., A. Turnbull, M. Shank, and S. J. Smith. 2004. *Exceptional lives: Special education in today's schools*. 4th ed. Upper Saddle River, NJ: Pearson Education.

Further Reading

Elizalde-Utnick, G. 2006. Culturally and linguistically diverse preschool children. In *Handbook of multicultural school psychology*, ed. G. B. Esquivel, E. C. Lopez, and S. Nahari, 497–525. Hillsdale, NJ: Lawrence Erlbaum Associates.

Fierro-Cobas, V., and E. Chan. 2001. Language development in bilingual children: A primer for pediatricians. *Contemporary Pediatrics* 18 (7): 79–98.

Lopez, E. C. 1997. The cognitive assessment of limited English proficient and bilingual children. In *Contemporary intellectual assessment: Theories, tests, and issues*, ed. D. P. Flanagan, J. L. Genshaft, and P. L. Harrison. New York: Guilford Press.

McLoyd, V. C. 1998. Economic disadvantage and child development. *American Psychologist* 53 (2): 185–204.

New York State Education Department. 2000. *Report on the implementation of Chapter 405 of the Laws of 1999*. Albany, NY: University of the State of New York. Available at http://unix2.nysed.gov/scandoclinks/ocm50434785.htm

Ortiz, A. A. 1997. Learning disabilities occurring concomitantly with linguistic differences. *Journal of Learning Disabilities* 30:321–32.

Rhodes, R. L., S. H. Ochoa, and S. O. Ortiz. 2005. *Assessing culturally and linguistically diverse students: A practical guide*. New York: Guilford Press.

Salend, S. J., and A. Salinas. 2003. Language differences or learning difficulties: The work of the multidisciplinary team. *Teaching Exceptional Children* 35 (4): 36–43.

Thomas, W. P., and V. P. Collier. 2002. *A national study of school effectiveness for language minority students' long-term achievement*. Berkeley: Center for Research on Education, Diversity, and Excellence, University of California. Available at http://crede.berkeley.edu/research/llaa/1.1_es.html

GRACIELA ELIZALDE-UTNICK

Digital Divide and Special Education

The term "digital divide" came into usage in the late 1990s to describe disparities in access to computers and network technologies. Initially the digital divide was conceived in terms of equipment ownership and the availability of Internet access. Studies revealed that economically disadvantaged groups and people living in rural areas and developing nations were not acquiring information and communications technologies (ICT) at the same rate as those in urban centers and industrialized countries. Troublesome as the problem was, it soon became apparent that the issue was broader than the technologies themselves. Also contributing to the digital divide were underlying material and cultural conditions such as physical infrastructure, government policy, education, and social conditioning.

Digital technologies have created opportunities and obstacles for people with disabilities. In addition to providing improved mobility, enhanced communication, and new approaches to learning, digital technologies also create their own roadblocks to accessibility and generate unforeseen problems related to use and availability. Some difficulties with digital technologies replicate broader structural and conceptual challenges facing the disabled community, while others are unique to these particular technologies.

In this context, the digital divide in special education exists on several levels: an economic divide pertaining to general educational funding disparities and to special education spending; a technological divide deriving from differential material and cultural support structures for ICT for people with disabilities; and specific issues involving hardware, software, and the vast array of media related to the Internet and other communication forms. The issue first gained broad-based attention in the United States in 1999, thanks to a white paper commissioned by the National Science Foundation and a directive from President Bill Clinton to the National Economic Council. The white paper noted that what it termed "digital barriers" affecting people with disabilities threatened the larger digital economy, adding:

> Unless the civil rights of America's 54 million people with disabilities are addressed during this period of rapid, technological development, the community will be locked out of participation on the basis of disability and the technological world will not be enriched by their diverse contributions. (Waddell 1999)

Prior to this, policy and legislation had attempted to correct the digital divide for people with disabilities through the **Individuals with Disabilities Education Act** (IDEA) and the **Americans with Disabilities Act** (ADA). Beginning in 1993, the ADA established a requirement for all telephone communications to be equipped with Telecommunication Relay Services (TRS) for those with impaired speech or hearing. Additionally, all public service announcements were required to provide closed-captioning. In 1975, **Public Law 94-142**, the Education for All Handicapped Children Act, was passed, requiring schools to allow access to all areas of education to students with learning disabilities and to encourage their participation and progress in the classroom. The Act, renamed IDEA, was amended in 1997 to mandate assistive technology devices and assistive technology services be provided to all children with learning disabilities, regardless of type or severity of disability. Assistive technology services include modifying and adapting devices for the student, coordinating the use of additional therapy methods with assistive technology devices, and supplying training and technical assistance not only to the child but also to those who are involved in the life functions of the child, such as parents and educators. Currently, the **No Child Left Behind Act**, passed in 2002, demands accountability of assistive technology, requiring testing and research to better assess what is effective in special education programming.

Despite these recent policies enacted to bridge the gap between people with disabilities and technological access, problems still persist. Consumers and service providers identify the two biggest barriers to assistive technology access to be the lack of knowledge about appropriate assistive technology and the lack of funding. Frequently, educators within the classroom do not have the technical training necessary to accommodate students in need of assistive technology. Schools are often tentative in providing assistive technology, since such devices are rarely funded by school district budgets. As a result, educators must generate funds through alternative means. Stakeholders are not fully aware of technology options, legal issues, and advocacy strategies. These stakeholders include people with disabilities, parents and mentors, government entities, paraprofessionals, policy makers and administrators, precollege and postsecondary educators, librarians, technical support staff, and employers. Studies have found that other access challenges include lack of trained professionals to evaluate assistive technology, and difficulties people with disabilities experience negotiating the bureaucracies of public programs and insurance companies.

Critics of the 1997 IDEA amendment cite the absence of specific assistive devices noted within the terms of the legislation. Presently, for the visually impaired, closed-circuit television magnification, computer screen magnification, descriptive video services, speech readers, optical character recognition, and Braille note takers are available. Devices for those students with hearing impairments include hearing aids, frequency modulated amplification systems, audio loops, infrared systems, cochlear implants, telecommunication devices, captioned television, and live speech captioning. Additionally, alternative input devices such as switches, basic adaptive keyboards, touch-sensitive screens, infrared sensors with pneumatic switches, and voice recognition are accessible for students with physical disabilities. Studies show that each of these assistive learning technologies helps students with disabilities throughout their education, improving scores by offering alternative methods to obtain academic information in the classroom.

However, recent technological innovations introduced to the classroom environment present obstacles to the student with disabilities, widening the digital divide. Increasingly used by students and educators, the transformation of the Internet from a text-based medium to a multimedia environment has created a crisis for people with visual disabilities. Text reading devices that once enabled the visually disabled to use the Internet have difficulty negotiating the graphics, imagery, and movement of new Web environments. More than 75 percent of Web material consists of images, and even when text is presented, it is difficult to translate into a verbal stream because it is formatted within images, frames, applets or animated gifs, tables, or columns. Problems with screen-reading devices also affect people with learning disabilities who sometimes need navigation assistance. In 2001, the U.S. Census reported that 56.2 percent of the disabled Internet users were blind or severely vision impaired. By October 2003, this figure had increased to 63.7 percent. Those with hearing problems have difficulties with audio streaming when captioning is missing. However, those who have hearing impairments are expanding their presence on the Internet more rapidly than those with vision impairments. From 2001 to 2003 the U.S. Census reported a substantial increase in the number of Internet users who were deaf or had a severe hearing impairment. Increasing Internet access for people with varied and multiple disabilities strengthens their digital literacy and narrows the digital divide. While more people with disabilities seek access to the Internet at home, schools need to promote technological proficiency among young people with disabilities and address the problems inherent to specific disabilities.

Today, the "digital barriers" described in the 1999 white paper have not been mended for students with disabilities. A call for equal access requires universal design among not only our computers but also the software applications they run. This concept, formally known as Universal Design for Learning (UDL), was initially introduced by the Center for Applied Special Technology (CAST). CAST recognized the demand for using technology as an educational resource within the classroom to provide various students with alternative means to engage and interact with learning material. Not only must there be a call for the expansion of necessary ICT cultural support structures, such as CAST, but adequate financial support in special education as well.

Further Reading

Kaye, H. S. 2000. *Disability and the digital divide*. Washington, DC: U.S. Department of Education.

Waddell, C. 1999. The growing digital divide in access for people with disabilities: Overcoming barriers to participation in the digital economy. White paper presented at the "Understanding the Digital Economy" conference convened by a directive from the President of the United States. May.

Websites

Americans with Disabilities Act: http://www.usdoj.gov/crt/ada/adahom1.htm

Individuals with Disabilities Education Act (IDEA) resources: http://www.ed.gov/policy/speced/guid/idea/idea2004.html

United States Census Bureau: http://www.census.gov/

JULIA NYBERG AND DAVID TREND

Disability Studies

Disability studies is an interdisciplinary field that examines the experiences of individuals with disabilities. A broad range of academic disciplines contributes to the knowledge base of disability studies, including sociology, anthropology, psychology, history, political science, law, architecture, and literature. The discipline emphasizes that research in this area should be inclusive of all varieties of physical as well as mental differences. In addition, disability studies advocates the social model of disability in opposition to the medical model of disability; the social model puts emphasis on the environmental, cultural, political, and economic factors of disability, as opposed to the medical model's reliance on impairment and limitations.

Historically, for the majority of the twentieth century, the medical model of disability was the dominant paradigm in defining how academia, as well as the public at large, viewed disability. The medical model construes disability as a physical condition within the individual. This approach emphasizes the pathology, deficits, and physical limitations of the person with a disability. Therefore, the medical model purports that problems related to disability lie within the individual in relation to the functioning of a normal, healthy person. The medical model advocates that curing, rehabilitating, or accommodating the disability should be the primary mode by which to address disability issues.

Disability studies emerged in the 1990s as an important counterpoint to the medical model. Disability studies embraced the social model of disability as its main theoretical orientation. The social model of disability stresses that social forces are the major factor by which disability should be conceptualized. It contends that disability is not inherent in the individual, but is shaped by environmental, political, and economic forces. Therefore, there is no objective concept of disability, nor dichotomous categories of disability and ability. Instead, there is a subjective continuum of disability and ability.

Many in the field of disability studies argue that individuals with disabilities have been stigmatized and marginalized throughout history. Social, political, and economic forces contribute to the assertion that individuals with disabilities have been isolated and segregated from the rest of society. Thus, environmental and attitudinal barriers, not physical or mental limitations, are viewed as the main problems that people with disabilities face.

Disability studies contends that there needs to be a focus on changing the environment, attitudes, and social and political structures that currently exist in society in order to ameliorate the negative effects these factors have on the disabling experience. For example, disability studies promotes

1. designing buildings and transportation systems that are accessible to all individuals
2. changing negative attitudes that people hold toward individuals with disabilities
3. development of assistive technologies that will qualify people with disabilities for a broader range of employment
4. reorganization of social, political, and economic structures to enable people with disabilities equal access to our society

These recommendations are in stark contrast to the medical model's approach, which emphasizes an individual's impairment and changing the physical or mental capabilities of a person.

Disability studies also stresses that individuals who possess a disability have a voice in the dialogue concerning what should be the object of study for this discipline. Much of the prior research and application of disability research has been conducted by individuals who are not members of the disabled community (e.g., medical professionals, academic professionals). People with disabilities should not just be objects of study; instead, they should have an active role in the design and implementation of disability research.

Further Reading

Albrecht, G. L. 2002. American pragmatism, sociology, and the development of disability studies. In *Disability studies today*, ed. C. Barnes, M. Oliver, and L. Barton. Malden, MA: Blackwell.

Braddock, D. L., and S. L. Parish. 2001. An institutional history of disability. In *Handbook of disability studies*, ed. G. Albrecht, K. Seelman, and M. Bury. London: Sage.

Olkin, R., and C. Pledger. 2003. Can disability studies and psychology join hands? *American Psychologist* 58 (4): 296–304.

Pfeiffer, D. 2001. The conceptualization of disability. In *Research in social science and disability*, Vol. 2, *Exploring theories and expanding methodologies: Where we are and where we need to go*, ed. S. Barnartt and B. Altman. Kidlington, Oxfordshire, England: Elsevier Science.

Titchkosky, T. 2003. *Disability, self, and society*. Toronto: University of Toronto Press.

Website

The Canadian Centre on Disability Studies: http://www.disabilitystudies.ca/

**TIMOTHY G. DOWD, AUBREY SEWELL, AND
KATHERINE L. TRUESDELL**

Funding Special Education

Prior to the existence of laws that gave children with disabilities special educational rights, these students were generally either treated like all others in a class or excluded from public education entirely. Neither practice promoted the students' educational development, leaving millions of them on society's margins unless their families could afford to provide private schooling. Since special services for students with disabilities are expensive, few were able to meet their children's needs. These added expenses—for lower student-to-teacher ratios; adaptive equipment; specially trained aides and related service providers such as speech therapists, occupational therapists, and physical therapists; additional administrative support; and more—were investments that most school districts were unwilling to make since, in the end, these students constituted a minority without the political power to ensure educational equity.

In some states and at the federal level, special education advocates were able to secure civil rights legislation for their cause so that districts were required to meet the needs of students with special needs. Special education funding thus became the classic "unfunded mandate" creating rights for students at the federal level that state and local governments are largely expected to fund. When the Elementary and Secondary Education Act (EAHCA) was enacted in 1977, Congress intended that the federal government would carry 40 percent of the cost of students' special education services. However, the federal share has never topped 20 percent of the need, and for most of the last quarter-century only between 7 and 12 percent was allocated. Thus, the special education budget has become mainly a state and local responsibility.

The reason for the nonfederal responsibility is best understood by the well-known **Individuals with Disabilities Education Act** requirement that students with disabilities are required to receive a *free* and *appropriate* public education (FAPE). In return for federal financial assistance, state education agencies enter into an agreement to meet the FAPE requirement that mandates payment of educational and related services to make it possible for the student to profit from an education. Even legal expenses to make sure districts comply with a student's special education rights are covered. Why do states enter into this fiscally disadvantageous agreement? Basically, because political forces obligate them to provide for special needs children, and the federal dollars—while less than states might like—provide needed assistance amounting to almost $10.6 billion in fiscal year 2006.

As with other public education responsibilities, states and localities are not permitted to pass along special education costs to families. Even for well-off families who might normally send their children to private school, the Supreme Court has ruled that, if no timely appropriate placement is made by the district in public school, the district is responsible for funding the child's private education. This so-called Carter funding remains a controversial aspect of special education since it allows wealthier families to place their children in a private school, pay tuition while their claim is decided by the school district or in court, and then get the money back if they win. Obviously, poorer families cannot wait months and years paying private school tuition hoping for later reimbursement.

This system has created a situation where the special education population of a district, usually about 13 percent of students, might account for 25 percent or more of the district budget. Without legal rights, these students might again face educational discrimination so that this money could be used for the nondisabled majority.

Further Reading

Florence County School District Four v. Carter, 510 U.S. 7 (1973).
Rothstein, L. 2000. *Special Education Law*. 3rd ed. New York: Longman.
Yell, M. L. 2006. *The Law and Special Education*. 2nd ed. Upper Saddle River, NJ: Pearson/Merrill/Prentice Hall.

Website

Center for Special Education Finance: http://www.csef-air.org/

DAVID C. BLOOMFIELD

Gender Issues in Special Education

The gender composition of boys and girls in special education is vastly unequal. Many more boys are referred and meet the criteria for services than girls. Approximately two-thirds of the individuals that receive services under the **Individuals with Disabilities Education Act** (IDEA) are boys, even though males and females comprise an equal proportion in the school-age population. Based on the research, it is unclear if females are underidentified, males are overidentified, or real differences exist between genders. However, two categories, mental retardation and visual impairments, have an equal number of males and females.

The causes for the discrepancy continue to be unknown, but theories exist that attempt to explain why boys are disproportionately represented in the areas of emotional disturbance, autism, and learning disabilities. Of all of the categories of disability, males comprise the highest percentage of students classified as Seriously Emotionally Disturbed (SED), one of the broadest classifications. Some theories focus on physiological and maturational differences between genders, differences in behavior predispositions, and special education identification.

Research suggests that males are more vulnerable to some genetically determined disorders and predisposed to have learning disabilities. Males are three times more likely to be diagnosed with Attention Deficit Hyperactivity Disorder (ADHD), which is believed to be a biological disorder. Males with ADHD present more disruptive behaviors in the classroom, receiving more teacher attention. Since ADHD is highly correlated with reading disabilities, most males have a better chance of being identified and placed for reading disabilities due to their disruptive behaviors. Even though the prevalence of reading disabilities is equal between males and females, girls' disabilities can often be overlooked; they generally do not receive the same attention from teachers.

Males are more likely to act out or misbehave in the classroom than females. Even when eligibility for special education services is based on academic performance, there is frequently a co-occurrence of problematic behavior. Poor achievement combined with behavioral problems leads to a referral sooner than poor achievement alone. While males are often referred for behavioral issues, female students tend to be referred primarily for academic issues.

The disproportionate number of males is also due to influences of gender bias on the referral, classification, and placement process. Bias, in this case, refers to a tendency to take a position or reach a conclusion about a person based on his or her gender. There are gender-stereotyped societal expectations for girls, resulting in teachers tolerating lower achievement in girls. Many teachers set higher standards and expectations for male students, resulting in higher referrals for male students who do not reach their elevated expectations.

The gender of the teacher plays a role; there are significant gender differences in ways teachers teach and manage their students. Teachers vary on the types of behaviors encouraged or accepted within the classroom. Research shows that male regular education teachers hold greater tolerance for rule violations, referring only students with high levels of disruptive, acting-out behaviors. Many teachers are female; it has been found that female teachers are less tolerant of male disruptive behaviors than male teachers. Therefore, male students are reprimanded and referred more often by female teachers. Even when the behaviors of boys are identical to those of girl students, all teachers respond more readily when boys misbehave.

While male problems are often associated with aggression and disruption, female-specific problem behaviors are often more internalized, leaving girls at a higher risk for **depression**. In line with school expectations, female students can hold in their emotions or display them subtly, regularly unnoticed by their teachers. Males routinely express more acting-out manifestations of their emotions, causing them to be more noticed and referred to special education by their teachers. In fact, girls referred to SED programs usually exhibit behaviors similar to boys.

Schools have the responsibility to address and eliminate gender disparities and sexual inequalities in the classroom. Most importantly, teachers need to be made aware how their own gender biases affect their teaching styles and class expectations. Teachers should be educated regarding the different ways females and males communicate through various behaviors. Closer and equal attention should be paid to each student, regardless of gender, in order to identify and provide for an individual's needs.

Further Reading

ITeachILearn.com. N.d. Gender as a factor in special education eligibility, services, and results. http://www.iteachilearn.com/uh/meisgeier/statsgov20gender.htm

McIntyre, T., and V. Tong. 1998. Where the boys are: Do cross-gender misunderstandings of language use and behavior patterns contribute to the overrepresentation of males in programs for students with emotional and behavioral disorders? *Education and Treatment of Children* 21 (3): 321–32.

Rousso, H., and M. L. Wehmeyer. 2001. *Double jeopardy: Addressing gender equity in special education.* New York: State University of New York Press.

Tschantz, J., and J. Markowitz. 2003. *Gender and special education: Current state data collection.* Alexandria, VA: National Association of State Directors of Special Education.

MICHELLE W. GREENBERG

Self-Advocacy

Self-advocacy is defined in the most basic terms as speaking up for oneself. Students who are effective self-advocates can articulate their own dreams, strengths, desires, passions, interests, and visions for the future. Self-advocacy skills can aid students in their daily lives and with planning for the future, as well as help build relationships with people throughout school and the community who can help and support them. Self-advocacy is a powerful tool for students with disabilities who are requesting needed services and support.

Self-advocacy assumes self-knowledge. In order to begin developing effective self-advocacy skills, students must realistically understand their strengths and abilities and who they are, regardless of any label or classification. Teachers and families may try to protect students with disabilities from information about their learning assessments and needs. However, this is a mistake because students with disabilities, especially teenagers, need to know what is in their **Individualized Education Program** (IEP) and why. Providing an individual with a good working knowledge of his or her personal learning style, abilities, and test results will concretely answer the question, How am I unique?

In addition to understanding oneself, effective self-advocates believe they have the right to make choices in school, life, and future goal-setting. Self-advocates are involved in all the decision-making processes that may affect their lives. They understand the connection between their involvement in the process and the outcome of their plans. A simple thing like scheduling and getting into classes can be an empowering experience. In school, an important self-advocacy goal for students is to be an active participant in their IEP meetings. Students' interests and preferences need to be considered in this meeting. Effective self-advocates can make a significant impact on their education, transition, and learning. Further, leading one's own IEP meeting can be a capstone experience for a high school student and prepares students to feel empowered to work with adults and adult service agencies from a position of strength.

Another important component of effective self-advocacy is the ability to speak to others in a variety of situations. Just knowing oneself and having the desire to be involved in decision making is not enough. Student self-advocates need practice. Even the youngest children need to be encouraged to speak up for themselves.

Instructional activities can be developed to offer opportunities for practice. Students can role-play age-appropriate situations in the classroom and later practice with teachers, family members, and regular community contacts. A common scenario of asking, for example, "What would you do if you ordered something in a restaurant but were given the wrong order?" can lead to many choices that can be discussed.

Finally, understanding that students with disabilities have specific rights under the **Individuals with Disabilities Education Act** (IDEA) and **Section 504 of the Rehabilitation Act** of 1973 is another empowering aspect for effective self-advocates. Since disability rights change after graduation from high school, students need information about their rights and what they can expect. Student advocates can be made aware of how their rights change in postsecondary educational settings and in the workplace. Preparing students to negotiate each system can be part of their transition goals.

Along with rights come responsibilities. Appropriately asking for accommodations is a skill. Students can utilize a "chain of command" by first asking their teacher for their accommodations; if they do not receive the appropriate accommodations, they should then speak to their case manager or guidance counselor. If that path proves unsuccessful as well, a letter to the school district's superintendent explaining their difficulty in receiving accommodations may ultimately be needed.

Self-advocacy teams or clubs are another way to practice self-advocacy skills as well as to gain important experience. Self-advocacy clubs may choose to start a Speakers' Bureau as a way for students to develop a comfort level in speaking to others about their experiences with having a disability and to dispel myths, help younger students, and educate the general public. The Speakers' Bureau may consider talking with a local business organization such as the Rotary Club to highlight the need for student internships. High school students may also target eighth-graders to discuss the process of transition and the IEP. Some Speakers' Bureaus have presented to other teenagers, parents, and school faculty. Speaking to the local school board of education about program needs can have surprising and dramatic results.

Effective self-advocacy skills empower students to be active participants in decision making. Self-advocates feel a responsibility for their own lives and can rise above the often lowered expectations put upon them by schools and society. Self-advocacy helps students with special needs feel heard, powerful, and independent.

Further Reading

Dybwad, G., and H. Bersani, eds. 1996. *New voices: Self-advocacy by people with disabilities.* Cambridge, MA: Brookline Books.

Field, S. 1997. *A practical guide for teaching self-determination.* New York: Council for Exceptional Children, Division on Career Development and Transition.

Furney, K. S., N. Carlson, D. Lisi, and S. Yuan. 1993. *Speak up for yourself and your future! A curriculum for building self-advocacy and self-determination skills.* Burlington: Enabling Futures Project, Department of Special Education, University of Vermont.

Presbie, D. 2003. *An educational journey from self discovery to advocacy: A handbook for students.* Hartford: Connecticut State Department of Education. Available at http://www.state.ct.us/sde/deps/special/specialedjourney03.pdf

Sands, D. J., and M. Wehmeyer. 1996. *Self-determination across the lifespan: Independence and choice for people with disabilities.* Baltimore: Brookes.

Wehmeyer, M., and D. J. Sands. 1998. *Making it happen: Student involvement in education planning, decision making, and instruction.* Baltimore: Brookes.

West, L. L., S. Corbey, A. Boyer-Stephens, B. Jones, R. J. Miller, and M. Sarkees-Wircenski. 1999. Transition and self-advocacy. Excerpted from *Integrating transition planning into the IEP process.* 2nd ed. Reston, VA: Council for Exceptional Children. Available at http://www.ldonline.org/article/7757

Websites

National Resource Center on Supporting Living and Choice Fact Sheet on Self-Advocacy: http://thechp.syr.edu/self-advocacy.pdf

The Arc's Self-Advocacy Activities: http://www.thearc.org/misc/sadescr.html

Uniquely Gifted—Especially for Kids: http://www.uniquelygifted.org/especially_for_kids.htm

TRACY AMERMAN AND JAN CARR-JONES

Social Class and Special Education

Social class divisions in American society contribute to stratification in special education services in the United States. Overrepresentation of poor children in special education classes is a widespread phenomenon. Studies have shown that a child's socioeconomic status affects where the student will go to school, his or her educational placement within the school, and the breadth and depth of services offered. With elevated social status comes a higher probability that a student will get above-average grades. Similarly, the higher the grades and test scores, the more likely an individual from any socioeconomic status is to seek out and qualify for higher education opportunities.

Socioeconomic status is among the most powerful predictors of school performance. Research suggests that the higher a family's socioeconomic status, the higher the level of their children's academic achievement. This relationship is true regardless of the measure of socioeconomic status used. For example, research on social class and education uses a variety of means to measure socioeconomic status, including the occupation of the primary wage earner, total family income, parents' education level, or a combination of measures. Throughout the research, socioeconomic status is compared to student achievement, which is measured by grades, achievement test scores, retention at grade level, course failures, truancy, suspension, dropout probability, college plans, and total amount of formal schooling. Results show that socioeconomic status predicts student achievement at least as well as academic honors, awards, elective school offices, participation in extracurricular activities, and other indications of "success" in the informal structure of the student society. Socioeconomic status and social class are so powerful that they surpass ability level and past achievement in predicting school performance.

Schools regularly use standardized achievement tests to determine a child's educational aptitude, abilities, and educational track. The measure used in the assessment is often biased, putting students in lower socioeconomic classes at a disadvantage when compared with their more affluent peers. It is important to note that lower socioeconomic status and minority group membership are closely related, particularly in urban areas of the United States, but that socioeconomic status is the major determining factor—not ethnicity.

There is a significant overlap between ethnicity and social class in the United States; however, they are not the same. Often more attention is devoted to understanding educational differences between ethnic groups than between different social classes. In special education, poor students, regardless of ethnicity, face more adversity than affluent students. Standardized test scores and scores on college aptitude exams are often depressed among socioeconomically disadvantaged minority and Caucasian students alike. The social stratification in U.S. public schools is best likened to the greater social inequality hierarchy in American society.

Stratified learning, or *tracking*, is the practice of assigning students to tracks based on three major criteria: standardized test scores, teacher grades, and recommendations or opinions about pupils. Pupil ethnicity and socioeconomic status are also related to the way "track" assignments are made in schools. Children of lower socioeconomic status are often tracked into more vocational and special education programs. As a result, this population of children is less likely to be exposed to challenging curricula, is taught less content by their teachers, and is expected to do less work, both in and out of the classroom. In fact, some researchers have found that lower socioeconomic status and ethnic minority status are directly related to track assignments, even when ability level and teacher recommendations were similar to other more affluent and ethnic-majority children.

In the United States, special education was originally designed as a model of individual instruction for students with special needs at no cost to the family. Individualized instruction was intended to meet the unique needs of a student with a disability in the classroom as well as in various other settings. Poverty-stricken schools lack appropriate resources to deal with increased numbers of children in special education classes. Unfortunately, special education in poor school districts is more understaffed and underfunded than individually designed instruction. As a result, it cannot attract a highly skilled and experienced staff, which means that the teachers assigned to work with special education students—often with minimal training and experience—are the least prepared to teach these students and consequently have lower teacher expectations, less teacher preparation, and an increased dropout rate. In addition, poverty-stricken schools face a compounding of other issues, including higher mobility rates of students and teachers, unstable parent participation, and untreated student health issues.

In more affluent schools, there are fewer students in special education, teachers are better prepared and have higher expectations for their students, and parents tend to be more involved in their child's education. Affluent parents of special education students are more effective in obtaining costly services for their children. These parents are more knowledgeable regarding the navigation of the complex educational system and are more aware of their child's rights, often due to having reached higher levels of education themselves and having the means to afford legal assistance. Parents who are socioeconomically disadvantaged often work more than one job, limiting their available time and involvement in their children's education. This predicament does not suggest that these parents are uninterested in their children's education, but rather that they are preoccupied with attending to their children's more basic hierarchical needs such as food and shelter.

Further Reading

Harry, B., C. Torguson, J. Katkavich, and M. Guerrero. 1993. Crossing social class and cultural barriers in working with families. *Teaching Exceptional Children* 26:48–51.

Persell, C. H. 1989. Social class and educational equity. In *Multicultural education: Issues and perspectives*, ed. J. A. Banks and C. A. McGee Banks, 68–86. Boston: Allyn & Bacon.

Powell-Smith, K. A., and S. A. Stollar. 2000. Families of children with disabilities. In *Children's needs II: Development, problems and alternatives*, ed. G. G. Bear, K. M. Minke, and A. Thomas, 667–80. Bethesda, MD: National Association of School Psychologists.

Sigmon, S. B. 1990. Remarks on social inequality and measured cognitive abilities in the schools. In *Critical voices on special education: Problems and progress concerning the mildly handicapped*, ed. S. B. Sigmon, 11–20. Albany: State University of New York Press.

Sleeter, C. E. 1992. Restructuring schools for multicultural education. *Journal of Teacher Education* 43 (2): 141–48.

Websites

Disability and Poverty Resources: http://www.disabilitykar.net/karreport/spring2004/resources.html

Social Class: http://www.nytimes.com/indexes/2005/05/24/national/class

SANDRA L. LÓPEZ

Social Competence and Disabilities

Children's social competence is comprised of several different abilities: the ability to behave in socially appropriate and effective ways (social skills); the ability to sense and understand the feelings and behaviors of other people (social understanding); knowing what to do when social problems occur (social problem solving); and having the confidence to overcome normal nervousness when meeting new people or joining new groups (social efficacy). Above all, social competence describes a fundamental ability to have friends, be a friend, keep friends over time, and enjoy time spent with friends. All children have this potential; however, social competence may manifest differently in children with disabilities.

Unfortunately, some disabilities can distort or even disrupt children's social competence. Children with language or cognitive delays may resemble younger children in the ways that they initiate or maintain friendships. Some elementary-age children with disabilities misread their classmates' social cues, struggle to resolve peer conflicts, and are less adept at solving social problems. Adolescents with disabilities can sometimes be drawn into peer groups that encourage disruptive or disturbing behaviors. Although some children with disabilities have exceptional social competence, on average, children with disabilities have fewer friends and less satisfying friendships than children without disabilities.

Furthermore, only some of the factors that disrupt their friendships are characteristics of the children with disabilities. In other cases, children's social isolation might be caused by the situation that they have been placed in. For example, children may become isolated when peers do not understand the differences posed by the disabilities. Differences in appearance, in the use of medical apparatuses, in language, or in abilities can prompt peers to be unresponsive to a child with disabilities. Children with disabilities are sometimes isolated if their daily schedule of activities limits the times when they can interact with peers. Alternatively, children may become isolated if their disability prevents them from joining in the routine activities of the peer group. In each of these examples, it is possible to modify the social environment to enhance the social opportunities of children with disabilities.

The social competence of children with disabilities is strengthened when adults create multiple opportunities for all children to have fun being together. For example, children have more fun playing together when their recess playground has lots of different games and when at least some of the games are simple to play. It is easier to find a friend when peers are encouraged to include everyone in their games. Friendships flourish when daily routines provide numerous times when classmates can talk with one another and do things together. These social opportunities do not always have to be considered "play." Friendships are also born when children work, solve problems, and practice new skills together, as well as play together. Consequently, friendship-building opportunities can be infused into multiple daily activities of children in schools, on playgrounds, in neighborhoods, and at home.

Some children with disabilities will also benefit from individualized interventions. Children with limitations in social cognition can practice solving common social problems with an adult or a small group of their peers. Children with deficits in social behavior can be provided with social skills instruction. Goal-setting and desensitization activities can make it possible for overanxious children to reach out to their classmates and take social risks. For example, children can set and work toward graduated goals to join their classmates' recess play—first watching the play, then approaching and speaking to a sympathetic classmate, then practicing the game with a classmate outside of recess, then asking to join the game during recess, and finally joining and playing with classmates. Alternatively, stop-and-think strategies can prevent impulsive children from inadvertently hurting or insulting their classmates.

Adults sometimes feel responsible for ensuring that children with disabilities have peer relationships that are just like those of children without disabilities, such as "best friends" or "regular friends." When children's physical or cognitive disabilities are striking, they may inevitably be cast into the role of "one needing help," and their friends without disabilities are predisposed to become "helper friends." However, the friendship type is not as important as the function that the friendship serves for the child.

Important questions for judging the adequacy of these friendships include:

- Are the children having fun being together?
- Are both children benefiting from the friendship?
- Are both children giving to as well as receiving from the friendship?

Ultimately, children's social competence is demonstrated by their ability to enter into ongoing and satisfying relationships with other people.

Further Reading

Doll, B. 1996. Children without friends: Implications for practice and policy. *School Psychology Review* 25:165–83.

Grenot-Scheyer, M., M. Fisher, and D. Staub. 2001. *At the end of the day: Lessons learned in inclusive education.* Baltimore: Brookes.

Meyer, L., S. Minondo, M. Fisher, M. Larson, S. Dunmore, J. Black, and M. D'Aquanni. 1998. Frames of friendship: Social relationships among adolescents with diverse abilities. In *Making friends: The influences of culture and development*, ed. L. Meyer, H. Park, M. Grenot-Scheyer, I. Schwartz, and B. Harry, 189–221. Baltimore: Brookes.

Meyer, L., H. Park, M. Grenot-Scheyer, I. Schwartz, and B. Harry. 1998. *Making friends: The influences of culture and development.* Baltimore: Brookes.

Odom, S., S. McConnell, and M. McEvoy. 1992. Peer-related social competence and its significance for young children with disabilities. In *Social competence of young children with disabilities*, ed. S. Odom, S. McConnell, and M. McEvoy, 3–35. Baltimore: Brookes.

Pearl, R. 2002. Students with learning disabilities and their classroom companions. In *The social dimensions of learning disabilities*, ed. B. Wong and M. Donahue, 77–91. London: Lawrence Erlbaum Associates.

BETH DOLL AND ERIN SIEMERS

Race and Special Education

Constitutional rights that were enacted by our forefathers to ensure equality in the country at large are failing to protect minority children in the classroom. When the *Plessey v. Ferguson* ruling legalized the de facto "separate but equal" doctrine sanctioning segregation between blacks and whites in 1896, it legitimized the division among races in all public facilities, including buses, restaurants, bathrooms, and schools. That decision was revoked in 1954 when a landmark civil rights case, *Brown v. Board of Education*, acknowledged that separate was never equal. However, fifty years after the ruling, minority students continue to be misclassified, segregated, and inadequately served by the public education system. As racial inequality persists, generations of minority students are consistently limited in their access to appropriate schooling, and consequently to greater opportunities in life, due to inadequate education (Harry and Anderson 1994; Losen and Orfield 2002).

Inequality exists across the board in our schools, but nowhere is it more prominently documented with facts and figures than in the demographic makeup of the special education classification. African-American students are 2.9 times more likely than white students to be classified as mentally retarded; 1.9 times more likely to be classified as emotionally disturbed; and 1.3 times more likely to be classified as having a special learning disability. African-American students with emotional and behavior disorders are less likely to receive a comprehensive academic curriculum when compared to their white counterparts (73.6 percent compared to 82.8 percent, according to the National Longitudinal Transition Study of the Special Education Students). Once identified for services, 25.9 percent of African Americans (relative to 7.02 percent for whites) are placed in restrictive environments where they are offered few opportunities to interact with non–special education peers. The African-American population as a whole is overrepresented for mental retardation in thirty-eight states, with greater risks of referral in the states of Connecticut, Mississippi, North Carolina, Nebraska, and South Carolina. Figures for Native Americans and Asian/Pacific Islanders reflect similar eligibility disparities (Parrish 2002).

Researchers in the 1970s discovered a racial imbalance in the proportion of minority children being placed in special education classrooms. Most notably, minority students were overrepresented in classrooms serving educable students with mental retardation, while gifted and talented programs were serving Caucasian children to the point of exclusivity (Mercer 1973). Subsequent reports by independent and government researchers reiterate similar disproportional demographics (Losen and Orfield 2002; Ogbu 1986; SRI International 1993; Wehmeyer and Schwartz 2001). Predominantly, minority students are overrepresented in areas where proper assessment requires skilled and in-depth interpretation, such as is the case with the classifications of mental retardation and emotional disturbance, whereas minorities are underrepresented in areas where classification is more clearly defined and assessment is straightforward, such as with deafness, hearing impairment, and visual impairment. These findings indicate that racial inequality continues to hamper the diagnosis and classification of special needs children and thus fails to serve them properly in our schools.

In 2002–2003, the U.S. Department of Education identified about six million students with disabilities. These included specific learning disorders (48 percent), speech or language impairment (19 percent), mental disturbance (10 percent), and emotional disturbance (8 percent). At the preschool level, the ratio of students served by the **Individuals with Disabilities Education Act** (IDEA) illustrates relatively equal distribution of students across racial/ethnic groups (see table). Disproportional racial identification is more clearly evident at the elementary- and secondary-school level (ages 6 through 21). It may be argued that there are smaller

Percentages of Children with Disabilities by Demographic Category, 2000–2001

	Hispanics	Whites	Blacks	Asian/ Pacific Islanders	Native Americans
Preschool children					
Specific learning disorders	6.4	2.3	3.1	3.5	3.3
Speech and language impairment	56.2	56.2	47.7	42.6	39.4
Developmental delays	19.0	27.2	32.9	29.4	48.6
Emotional disturbance	0.5	1.2	1.4	0.9	0.6
Mental retardation	5.2	4.0	5.8	5.2	1.8
Other impairments	12.7	9.1	9.1	18.4	6.3
All disabilities	100	100	100	100	100
Elementary- and secondary-school children					
Specific learning disorders	60.3	48.9	45.2	43.2	56.3
Speech and language impairment	17.3	20.8	15.1	25.2	17.1
Developmental delays	0.2	0.6	0.7	0.6	0.7
Emotional disturbance	4.5	8.0	10.7	5.3	7.5
Mental retardation	8.5	9.3	18.9	10.1	8.5
Other impairments	9.2	12.4	9.4	15.6	9.9
All disabilities	100	100	100	100	100

Source: Data Analysis System (DANS), Office of Special Education Programs, U.S. Department of Education.
Note: Other impairments include multiple disabilities, hearing impairments, visual impairments, orthopedic impairments, other health impairments, deaf-blindness, autism, and traumatic brain injury.

margins of racial difference in medically diagnosed specific learning disabilities than the more subjectively assessed mental and emotional disability categories.

In contrast, greater disparity is evident in the assignments to mental retardation and emotional categories that rely to a greater extent on referrals, checklists, and anecdotal information from teachers and administrators. Further, school psychologists determine which and how many tests to use when assessing students' eligibility for special education. In this vein, they are the front line of defense against misclassification and can avoid error by utilizing as many evaluative tools as is cost- and time-effective. The use of certain tools, such as IQ tests, have been challenged in courts of law, and in the case of California, their use on African-American children has been severely curtailed. Emerging practices in school psychology now focus of ways to increase practitioners' cultural competence.

While incidences of disability vary across states, as well as among minorities and between genders, there are substantial disparities in the number of African-American students classified as mentally retarded or emotionally disturbed. Thirty-eight states overrepresented black relative to white children in mental retardation categories. Parrish (2002) notes higher risk ratios of black students to mental retardation and emotional disturbances categories relative to specific disabilities (hearing, visual and orthopedic impairments, deaf-blindness, and traumatic brain injury) within certain Southern states—for example, Mississippi (4.31:1.07), South Carolina (4.30:1.30), Florida (3.91:1.09), and Alabama (3.89:1.11). Ogbu (1986), a noted anthropologist, attributes the overrepresentation of minority children principally to "the pattern of racial and castelike stratification and technoeconomic and sociopolitical barriers it generates" (86), and to the resultant disillusionment, survival strategies, cultural inversion, and distrust among subordinated blacks.

Differences in diagnosis also occur across gender divisions within the African-American population. African-American males have dominated special education since its inception in 1965. The *U.S. Department of Education Reports* for 1986, 1990, and 1992 indicate an overrepresentation of African-American children in the Educable Mental Retardation category. In the 1992 report, African-American males accounted for 8.23 percent of the total national school environment, and twice that number were classified in Educable Mental Retardation, Trainable Mental Retardation, and Severely Emotionally Disturbed (Harry and Anderson 1994).

Parental involvement and language barriers also play a role in misclassification of minority students. Studies have shown that Hispanic parents with limited English proficiency are often unable to make sense of the technical terms used in special education assessments and therefore cannot make an informed decision about their child's education (Artilles et al. 2002). In fact, Hispanic children are three times more likely to be labeled mentally retarded in ten of the states with the highest percentage of minority children with special education labels (Parrish 2002). Their bilingual and bicultural identity increase the likelihood of referrals to remedial education tracks.

Additional factors that influence a minority child's likelihood of being referred for special education include misdiagnosed behavior problems, racial profiling, and stereotypical beliefs held by authorities, teachers, and psychologists. Wehmeyer and Schwartz (2001) partly attribute the disproportionate representation of African-American males in special education to "cultural biases in testing, a lack of cultural competence and understanding on the part of referring teachers, and stereotypes of males from minority backgrounds" (276). While minority students account for 40 percent of the public school enrollment nationwide, minority teachers account for only 13.5 percent of public school faculty, compared with 86 percent white (and 68 percent female) teachers. A teacher's tolerance and understanding of students' cultural behavioral preferences significantly influences referrals to special education programs. These factors, which are difficult to quantify, only complicate and reinforce the overrepresentation of minority students in special education programs (Losen and Orfield 2002).

The overrepresentation of minority students in special education and their underrepresentation in gifted programs are due to biased referral, inadequate assessment, and eligibility practices. Poverty-ridden African-American, Hispanic, and male Asian students dominate the learning disability category and exhibit chronic and severe school failure. However, disparities between African Americans and Hispanics, and between genders within the African-American population, suggest the presence of factors other than social class and race. Issues of misclassification, low-quality education, and stigma fuel ongoing segregation charges. A complete renovation of existing policies and procedures for identifying and classifying minority students for special education services is necessary to reduce the substantial racial and gender disparities that continue to exist and place long-term success out of reach for America's minority students.

References

Artilles, A. J., R. Rueda, J. J. Salazar, and I. Higareda. 2002. English-language learner representation in special education in California urban school districts. In Losen and Orfield 2002, 117–36.

Education Week analysis of data from the U.S. Department of Education, Office of Special Education Programs, Data Analysis System, 2002–2003.

Harry, B., and M. G. Anderson. 1994. The disproportionate placement of African American males in special education programs: A critique of the process. *Journal of Negro Education* 63, no. 4 (Fall): 602–19.

Losen, J. L., and G. Orfield. 2002. *Racial inequity in special education*. Cambridge, MA: Harvard Education Press.

Mercer, J. R. 1973. *Labeling the mentally retarded*. Berkeley: University of California Press.

Ogbu, J. U. 1986. Castelike stratification as a risk factor for mental retardation. In Dale and McKinney 1986, 83–119.

Parrish, T. 2002. Racial disparities in identification, funding, and provision of special education. In Losen and Orfield 2002, 15–38.

SRI International. 1993. *The National Longitudinal Transition Study of Special Education Students*. Menlo Park, CA: Office of Special Education Programs, U.S. Department of Education.

Wehemeyer, M. L., and M. Schwartz. 2001. Research in gender bias in special education services. In Rousso and Wehmeyer 2002, 271–88.

Further Reading

Committee on Minority Representation in Special Education. 2002. Minority students in special and gifted education. Washington, DC: National Academy Press. Available at http://www.nap.edu/books/0309074398/html

U.S. Department of Education. 2002. To Assure the Free Appropriate Public Education of All Children with Disabilities: Twenty-fourth Annual Report to Congress on the Implementation of the Individuals with Disabilities Education Act. Washington, DC: Department of Education. Available at http://www.ed.gov/about/reports/annual/osep/2002/index.html

Website

National Center for Education Statistics: http://nces.ed.gov/pubs2001/digest/dt039.html

NAMULUNDAH FLORENCE

Law and Special Education

Americans with Disabilities Act (ADA)

Passed in 1990, the Americans with Disabilities Act (PL 101-336; 42 U.S.C. §§ 12101 et seq.) was not specifically intended to address the needs of students needing special education but rather seeks to eliminate discrimination against handicapped individuals generally, including some arguably outside of other statutes' protections, for example, people with contagious diseases and those who are associated with someone with a handicapping condition (e.g., a student with an infirm parent). In this way, the ADA more closely resembles the broad protections of **Section 504 of the Rehabilitation Act** than **Public Law 94-142**, the Education for All Handicapped Children Act (EAHCA). This is particularly important for students in private K–12 education and in higher education, where the requirements of EAHCA usually don't reach. Also, while the remedies available under EAHCA do not correct past violations, ADA claims can include demands for reasonable accommodation in the future as well as more traditional monetary damages for past harm.

Furthermore, the ADA's focus on public accommodation and employment discrimination brought important new constituencies into the fight for equal rights for all handicapped individuals. Prior to the ADA, for example, appeals for architectural barrier removal in schools—wheelchair accessibility, public transportation, and the like—were often fought on the relatively narrow grounds of Section 504 and EAHCA/**Individuals with Disabilities Education Act** compliance. With the implementation of the ADA, however, these issues also became important to workers, the elderly, and those with covered medical conditions. Through their efforts, and the work of their attorneys, new energy and horizons were extended to special education and the community of people with disabilities.

Passage of the ADA also completed the contemporary "trinity" of federal statutory law protecting the interests of students in special education: Section 504, PL 94-142 as amended, and the ADA. Each statute, while containing overlapping rights for students with disabilities, has its unique protections and case precedents. Parties need to investigate each legal quarry in order to ascertain the best strategies for successful resolution of special education disputes.

Further Reading

Crabtree, T. L., B. C. Gartin, and N. Murdick. 2001. *Special education law*. Upper Saddle River, NJ: Merrill/Prentice Hall.

Rothstein, L. 2000. *Special education law*. 3rd ed. New York: Longman.

DAVID C. BLOOMFIELD

Individuals with Disabilities Education Act (IDEA)

When **Public Law 94-142**, the Education for All Handicapped Children Act (EAHCA), was reauthorized in 1990, Congress changed its name to the Individuals with Disabilities Education Act, or IDEA. IDEA, subsequently amended in 1997 and 2004, has become the touchstone for analyzing the rights of all publicly funded special education students in the United States.

IDEA defines a student as being within its protected class if she or he needs special education or related services such as speech or occupational therapy because of mental retardation, hearing impairments (including deafness), speech or language impairments, visual impairments (including blindness), serious emotional disturbance, orthopedic impairments, autism, traumatic brain injury, other health impairments, or specific learning disabilities.

IDEA and its supporting regulations issued in 1999 maintain the primary right to a free and appropriate public education established by its predecessor, EAHCA. In addition, IDEA made major changes to important secondary rights concerning attorneys' fees, discipline, private education, and funding. These new provisions are the focus of the analysis below.

Attorneys' Fees

Attorneys' fees under IDEA were taken up by Congress through the 1986 Handicapped Children's Protection Act (HCPA) after the Supreme Court in *Smith v. Robinson* (468 U.S. 992) in 1984 ruled that such fees could not be recovered under EAHCA. The issue was revisited in the 1997 reauthorization. As a general matter, courts are permitted to award attorneys' fees to parents of children with disabilities when the parents are the prevailing party to the action, although the issue of whether parents have "prevailed" is often a matter of separate dispute between the parent's attorney and the school district, as are the particular legal work and rates involved. School districts can also be awarded attorneys' fees to be paid by the parent if the action is determined to be frivolous. The statute attempts to balance the right of parents to reasonable fees with an interest in early settlement.

The Manifestation Determination Review

A continuing frustration of general education practitioners has been IDEA's clear direction that students with disabilities not be punished for improper conduct arising from their condition, even if the student has not been formally identified as requiring special education or related services. Before a district can impose substantial disciplinary action against a student eligible for special education, IDEA's 2004 amendments require that the district conduct a manifestation determination review. The review's objective is to assess whether or not the improper conduct was precipitated by the student's disability and whether the **Individualized Education Program** (IEP), within the context of a continuing preference for the least restrictive environment, requires modification in light of the inappropriate conduct. An important change in the 2004 IDEA amendment now requires that the parent prove that the inappropriate conduct arose from the handicapping condition. Previously, the burden was on the district to prove that the behavior was *not* a manifestation of the condition. Hearings have also become easier for districts to win with the elimination of a provision that previously required consideration of whether the disability impaired the child's ability to control or understand the impact and consequences of the behavior. Parents may appeal the outcome of the manifestation determination review if they disagree with the outcome through further due-process hearings.

Private and Charter School Education

Significant issues involved in unilateral, preferential placement of students with disabilities in private and charter schools were resolved by the 1997 IDEA amendments. Students receiving private placements as a result of a district's IEP determination of a free, appropriate public education or in lieu of an appropriate district placement are entitled to full public funding. Similarly, students in charter schools, since they are public, receive free educational services according to their IEP.

According to 20 U.S.C. § 1412 (a)(10)(A)(i)(I), if a private placement is wholly based on a parent's desire for private schooling and an appropriate public setting exists, the student is still eligible for publicly funded services proportionate to what the federal share of the district's expenses would be if the child attended public school.

Funding

Two important issues face the federal government, states, and districts regarding **funding special education** under IDEA. The first is the gross amount of federal dollars allocated under the law. Consistent with the national model of education funding of the general population, the education of students with disabilities is largely a state and local responsibility. At the same time, Congress has long acknowledged a goal to fund 40 percent of the national average per pupil expenditure for students in special education because of the increased burdens of IDEA compliance. This goal has yet to be met, although the federal share has climbed in recent years to just under 20 percent and the 2004 amendment seeks to achieve "full" funding of the 40 percent federal share by 2010.

Second, the 1997 IDEA amendments sought to achieve greater equity in the allocation formula among states and districts for special education costs. This may be achieved by replacing the previous child count emphasis with census data and accounting more accurately for district needs and ability to pay. Districts were also provided with greater flexibility to share costs of assistive technology, related services, and similar expenses.

Further Reading

Crabtree, T. L., B. C. Gartin, and N. Murdick. 2001. *Special education law.* Upper Saddle River, NJ: Merrill/Prentice Hall.

Rothstein, L. 2000. *Special education law.* 3rd ed. New York: Longman.

DAVID C. BLOOMFIELD

Landmark Court Decisions

While courts around the country are constantly deciding disputes regarding special education, only a few cases are important enough to be considered "landmark decisions." These cases, usually from the U.S. Supreme Court, help to determine the outcome of other court battles. Although any listing of cases as "landmark" is subjective, the cases below, known commonly as *PARC I* and *II*, *Rowley*, *Tatro*, *Honig*, *Zobrest*, and *Carter*, provide a basis for discussion of many special education issues today. By examining these cases, school districts, parents, and advocates can begin to make informed decisions about students' rights to special education. They can also determine whether initial evaluation, placement, and funding decisions have been handled according to law.

PARC I and *II*

Pennsylvania Association for Retarded Children v. Commonwealth of Pennsylvania, 334 F.Supp. 1257 (E.D. Pa. 1971) (*PARC I*) and 343 F.Supp. 279 (E.D. Pa. 1972) (*PARC II*).

Prior to the passage of **Public Law 94-142**, the Education for All Handicapped Children Act (EAHCA), students with disabilities were regularly excluded from public education unless specifically provided for by state law. This situation began to change with *PARC I* and *II* when parents alleged that Pennsylvania had a state constitutional duty to educate *all* children. In an influential consent decree (a settlement agreement between the parties that becomes a court order), Pennsyl-vania agreed that students with disabilities had due-process and equal-protection rights to a free public education and that placement in a regular classroom (i.e., the least restrictive environment) was preferable to self-contained instructional programs.

Rowley

Board of Education of Hendrick Hudson Central School District v. Rowley, 458 U.S. 176 (1982).

The parents of Amy Rowley, a kindergarten student with a severe hearing impairment, sued the Hendrick Hudson Central School District when it provided her with an FM hearing aid. Her parents asserted that she required a sign language interpreter to maximize her educational potential in a manner similar to nondis-abled students. The Supreme Court disagreed, holding that EAHCA was not intended "to achieve strict equity services for handicapped and nonhandicapped children." Instead, the school district was permitted to provide the lesser service since that would enable Amy "to benefit" from her placement, thus satisfying the law's requirement of an "appropriate education."

Tatro

Irving Independent School District v. Tatro, 468 U.S. 883 (1984).

Under EAHCA and the **Individuals with Disabilities Education Act** (IDEA), school districts are required to provide qualified students with "related services." According to Congress, related services include "medical and counseling services, except that such medical services shall be for diagnostic and placement purposes only as may be required to assist a handicapped child to benefit from special edu-cation." *Tatro* addressed the question of whether the district was required to pro-vide regular catheterization to a student with spina bifida who could not voluntarily empty her bladder. The Supreme Court held that since (1) the student qualified for related services, (2) the related service was necessary for her to benefit from her appropriate educational placement, (3) the procedure could be conducted by a school nurse rather than a doctor, and (4) it could be done without specialized equipment, the district was required to fund the necessary care.

Honig

Honig, California Superintendent of Public Instruction v. Doe, 484 U.S. 305 (1988).

The EAHCA and IDEA require provision of public education to students what-ever their handicapping condition. Therefore, school districts are often faced with educating students whose disability causes them to be disruptive in a manner that, were they in general education, would result in long-term suspensions or transfers. Whether school districts retain such disciplinary authority over students in special education was addressed in *Honig*. The Supreme Court ruled that in cases where the inappropriate conduct is a result of the handicapping condition (such as emo-tional disturbance), districts could *not* unilaterally exclude the student for an inde-terminate amount of time. This ruling is sometimes misinterpreted to preclude *any* discipline of students in special education, but this is incorrect. *Honig* and the sub-sequent amendment of IDEA permit short-term suspensions of up to ten days and other similar measures to protect the safety of the student and others. Any suspen-sion for more than ten days would be regarded as a change of placement, requiring reconvening of the Committee on Special Education.

Zobrest

Zobrest v. Catalina Foothills School District, 509 U.S. 1 (1993).

The intersection of special education and the First Amendment's separation of church and state was addressed in *Zobrest*. The question presented to the Supreme Court was whether a hearing-impaired student attending a parochial high school was entitled to public funding for a sign language interpreter, consistent with his IEP. The Court ruled that IDEA required that the school district provide the interpreter, since it was part of a neutral government service that did not advance the religious message of the school. In addition, the placement of the public employee on religious school grounds did not present a sufficient appearance of government support of religion so as to violate the Establishment Clause.

Carter

Florence County School District Four v. Carter, 510 U.S. 7 (1993).

The continuing battle by school districts to minimize their financial obligations under IDEA was dealt a severe setback by the *Carter* decision. Here, the Supreme Court held that where a district fails to provide adequate public placement, parents are entitled to full reimbursement of tuition when they place their child in an appropriate private setting without prior district approval (often called a unilateral or one-sided placement). One consequence of the *Carter* decision has been a growing movement by wealthier families to find expensive private placements, initially pay the tuition out-of-pocket, then sue the district for "*Carter* funding," using expensive evaluators and lawyers to make the case for inappropriate public placement.

Further Reading

La Morte, M. W. 2005. *School Law: Cases and Concepts*. 8th ed. Boston: Pearson.

DAVID C. BLOOMFIELD

Legal Foundations for Inclusion

When the **Individuals with Disabilities Education Act** (IDEA) was first enacted into law in 1975, it required that the education received by students with disabilities be in the "least restricted environment" (LRE). Originally, this was understood to mean that students with disabilities should be "mainstreamed," that is, scheduled to spend a portion of each day in the general education classroom. Each reauthorization of IDEA has further strengthened the expectation for "full **inclusion**," such that students with disabilities receive their educational services in typical settings alongside students without disabilities as long as these arrangements support good educational progress (Council for Exceptional Children 1993).

More recently, the federal **No Child Left Behind Act** (NCLB) of 2001 has challenged special educators to fully include students with disabilities in the testing and accountability practices of general education classrooms. Under NCLB, school districts are permitted to establish alternative educational standards for only 1 percent of their students. All other students must participate in regular assessment of their progress toward educational standards, albeit with appropriate accommodations to ensure that the unique needs of students with disabilities are taken into account.

Current preferences for inclusion are in stark contrast to the routine segregation of people with disabilities into institutional settings that took place between 1920 and 1970 (Ward 1996). Progress toward inclusion began with Robert Irwin's programs to promote self-reliance among those with visual disabilities in the 1920s and 1930s and gradually expanded into other programs to allow persons with disabilities to lead more "productive" lives. These efforts culminated in the Architectural Barriers Act of 1968 (PL 90-480), which required all federally funded buildings to be accessible to people with disabilities. Subsequently, **Section 504 of the Rehabilitation Act** of 1973 (PL 93-112) prohibited discrimination against students with disabilities by any school receiving federal money (i.e., almost every school) and required that students be taught in a regular education classroom unless an adequate education could not be provided there. Access rights of persons with disabilities were further strengthened by the **Americans with Disabilities Act** (ADA) of 1990 (PL 101-336), which guaranteed any citizen with disabilities equal access to services and equal treatment in everyday affairs. A 1999 court decision commonly referred to as the *Olmstead* decision (*Olmstead v. L. C.*, 527 U.S. 581) then held that federal, state, and local governments must provide services to persons with disabilities in the most integrated setting appropriate.

The principal argument in favor of inclusion is that students with disabilities achieve more, behave better, and are better accepted by their classmates when they are educated in regular education classrooms (Edwards, Patrick, and Topolski 2003; Rafferty, Piscitelli, and Boettcher 2003; Renzaglia et al. 2003). Academic success is evident by the fact that students with disabilities achieve more of their **Individualized Education Program** (IEP) objectives and learn more skills when included in regular classrooms (Hunt et al. 1994). Their social gains are even more striking with evidence of increased contact with peers, meaningful friendships with nondisabled peers, and increased social awareness (Rafferty, Piscitelli, and Boettcher 2003). The quality of life of included adolescents with disabilities rises once they feel more connected to their communities (Edwards, Patrick, and Topolski 2003). Educational ethicists also note that the successful inclusion of children with disabilities protects the children's place in mainstream society and strengthens their competence to participate in that society (Bricker 2000). Consequently, the Office of Special Education Programs set a goal that 50 percent of children with disabilities be served in regular education classrooms for 80 percent of the day (U.S. Department of Education 1999).

There are two primary reasons that students with disabilities are removed from regular education settings: problem behavior (Lewis and Sugai 1999), and academic skills that are widely discrepant from other students in the class (Smith, Doll, and Gengel 2000). Two-thirds of regular teachers support the concept of inclusion (Scruggs and Mastropieri 1996), but their support diminishes rapidly if the students who are included in their classrooms demand instructional accommodations that are too large and too unfamiliar. Some special educators also worry about inclusion, because they are concerned that the unique educational needs of students with disabilities will not be met in inclusive settings, even though research shows that is untrue (McGregor and Vogelsberg 1998). Other special educators worry that students with disabilities could be stigmatized, made fun of, or bullied by their classmates if they look too different from their classmates (Rafferty, Piscitelli, and Boettcher 2003), Thus, educational inclusion is very difficult to do well, especially if it is imposed upon teachers.

References

Bricker, D. 2000. Inclusion: How the scene has changed. *Topics in Early Childhood Special Education* 20:14–19.

Council for Exceptional Children. 1993. Delivering an appropriate education. Section 3, part 1, of *CEC policy manual*. Reston, VA: Council for Exceptional Children.

Edwards, T. C., D. L. Patrick, and T. D. Topolski. 2003. Quality of life of adolescents with perceived disabilities. *Journal of Pediatric Psychology* 28:233–41.

Hunt, P., D. Staub, M. Alwell, and L. Goetz. 1994. Achievement by all students within the context of cooperative learning groups. *Journal of the Association for Persons with Severe Handicaps* 11:125–30.

Lewis, T. J., and G. Sugai. 1999. Effective behavior support: A systems approach to proactive schoolwide management. *Focus on Exceptional Children* 31:17–24.

McGregor, G., and R. T. Vogelsberg. 1998. *Inclusive schooling practices: Pedagogical and research foundations.* Pittsburgh: Allegheny University of the Health Sciences.

Rafferty, Y., V. Piscitelli, and C. Boettcher. 2003. The impact of inclusion on language development and social competence among preschoolers with disabilities. *Exceptional Children* 69:467–79.

Renzaglia, A., M. Karvonen, E. Drasgow, and C. C. Stoxen. 2003. Promoting a lifetime of inclusion. *Focus on Autism and Other Developmental Disabilities* 18:140–49.

Scruggs, T. E., and M. A. Mastropieri. 1996. Teacher perceptions of mainstreaming/inclusion, 1958–1995: A research synthesis. *Exceptional Children* 63:59–74.

Smith, A., B. Doll, and S. Gengel. 2000. *OSERS/OECD International Symposium on Inclusion and Professional Development.* Proceedings. Lincoln: Nebraska Printing Office.

U.S. Department of Education. 1999. Office of Special Education Programs. *Twenty-First Annual Report to Congress on the Implementation of the Individuals with Disabilities Act.* Washington, DC: GPO.

Ward, M. J. 1996. Coming of age in the age of self-determination: A historical and personal perspective. In *Self-determination across the life span: Independence and choice for people with disabilities,* ed. D. J. Sands and M. L. Wehmeyer, 3–16. Baltimore: Brookes.

Further Reading

Grenot-Scheyer, M., M. Fisher, and D. Staub. 2001. *At the end of the day: Lessons learned in inclusive education.* Baltimore: Brookes.

Polloway, E. A., M. H. Epstein, and W. D. Bursuck. 2003. Testing adaptations in the general education classroom: Challenges and directions. *Reading and Writing Quarterly* 19:189–92.

Sapon-Shevin, M. 1999. *Because we can change the world: A practical guide to building cooperative, inclusive classroom communities.* Boston: Allyn & Bacon.

BETH DOLL AND S. ANDREW GARBACZ

No Child Left Behind Act (NCLB)

The No Child Left Behind Act of 2001 contains the most recent amendments to the Elementary and Secondary Education Act (ESEA) of 1965. NCLB was enacted in 2002 and became the signature education statute of the George W. Bush presidency. In addition, it redefined the federal role in K–12 education. Its main objective is to ensure that all public school students in the United States—including traditionally underserved groups such as low-income students, black and Latino students, and students receiving special education—meet high academic standards by 2014. Annual tests in reading, math, and science for all students, with data separated out by grade and the specialized populations described above, is used to track progress toward this goal in meeting state standards. Districts and schools receiving federal Title I funding that fail to make "adequate yearly progress" (AYP) are required to provide parent-initiated school choice, supplementary educational services such as tutoring, and curricula validated by scientifically based research, as approved by the federal Department of Education. Each of these provisions has important consequences for students in special education.

Along with other students in grades 3–8, NCLB requires states to test students with disabilities in math, reading, and eventually science annually. The same tests are given to all students, except that a maximum of 1 percent of special-needs students—those receiving services under the **Individuals with Disabilities Education Act** (IDEA)—may be assessed by alternative means. If they achieve proficiency, it is counted by districts as making AYP. These alternate assessments differ from the grade-level tests taken by most students. They are specially designed to determine academic performance apart from students' handicapping condition or significant cognitive impairments. They measure the student's individual instructional level independent of grade-level norms. In each school, scores for special education students must show adequate yearly progress from year to year. If special education students do not make AYP according to state standards, the school may be subject to sanctions. These sanctions might initially include student eligibility for transfer to a better performing school and for free tutoring from the school district or a private provider. Low performance for three or more years results in schools' reorganization or, ultimately, closure or takeover by the state or a private management company.

Many weaknesses exist in the law. For example, while schools often fail to meet standards because they do not address the educational needs of students with disabilities, the underserved special education students are often foreclosed from taking advantage of NCLB's school choice provision because other district schools do not have classes to meet those students' needs.

Another problem is the inherent conflict between the goals of IDEA and NCLB. NCLB holds all students, schools, and districts to a common statewide definition of academic achievement and favors adoption of district-wide curricula based on scientifically based research. IDEA, on the other hand, favors an *individualized* approach to achievement and methodologies through the **Individualized Education Program** (IEP). Furthermore, the two statutes' different testing, reporting requirements, and timetables (annual testing for NCLB, biannual for IDEA) are confusing and may cause parents and districts to standardize special education instruction to meet the demands of NCLB, therefore not adhering to the individualized approach built into the IDEA.

Computation of AYP for specialized populations might have two different negative effects on referrals to special education. Since AYP is calculated based on percentages of students from different groups meeting standards, administrators may be tempted to keep students eligible for special education in general education, where their scores, if lower than the general population's, will be "hidden" within the larger denominator. On the other hand, administrators might over-refer in order to create an artificially high-performing special education cohort, thus avoiding having that separate group fall below levels of AYP and triggering school or district sanctions.

Another provision of the law, requiring what the statute calls a "highly qualified teacher" in every classroom, was one of the first mandates to be amended. It states that special education teachers do not have to be subject area specialists, as originally required. According to the U.S. Department of Education's guidance on the subject, NCLB's highly qualified teacher requirements

> apply only to teachers providing direct instruction in core academic subjects. Special educators who do not directly instruct students in core academic subjects or who provide only consultation to highly qualified teachers in adapting curricula, using behavioral supports and interventions or selecting appropriate accommodations, do not need to demonstrate subject-matter competency in those subjects. (U.S. Department of Education 2004)

Use of scientifically based research in curriculum selection for Title I schools is another NCLB provision of importance to students, parents, and special educators. The standards that meet the federal requirement have yet to be clearly determined, but a small industry is likely to arise to assess and promote materials that claim to meet the NCLB standard.

Further Reading

Freedman, Miriam K. 2004. NCLB testing requirements: What about students with disabilities? *Inquiry & Analysis* (National School Boards Association Council of School Attorneys), November: 1–4.

U.S. Department of Education. 2002. *No Child Left Behind: A desktop reference.* September.

_____. 2004. New No Child Left Behind flexibility: Highly qualified teachers. March. Available at http://www.ed.gov/nclb/methods/teachers/hqtflexibility.pdf

Websites

Education Commission of the States: http://nclb2.ecs.org/projects_centers/index.aspx
U.S. Department of Education: http://www.ed.gov/nclb/landing.jhtml

DAVID C. BLOOMFIELD

Public Law 94-142: Education for All Handicapped Children Act

Public Law 94-142 (the 142nd statute passed by the 94th Congress) is also called the Education for All Handicapped Children Act (EAHCA). It was enacted in 1975 and became effective in 1977. The law was an amendment to the Education of the Handicapped Act (EHA), passed in 1970.

PL 94-142 is basically a civil rights statute and is best understood in the context of the post–*Brown v. Board of Education* drive to secure equal rights. That Supreme Court decision described "discrete and insular" groups that are inherently in the minority and are often disadvantaged by majority rule. With the Civil Rights Act of 1964, the movement for African-American civil rights showed that it could successfully transfer its efforts from the federal courts to congressional legislation. Similarly, after the victories by the special education advocacy community in **landmark court decisions** such as *PARC I and II* and other cases in the early 1970s, these organizations, which had previously been blocked by state courts and legislatures, seized their momentum by successfully securing federal educational rights for people with disabilities through PL 94-142.

The original PL 94-142 statute and the regulations derived from it have been amended since its initial passage and is now known as the **Individuals with Disabilities Education Act** (IDEA). PL 94-142 is a historical marker; it was the first time the federal government specifically guaranteed educational rights for students with disabilities, and it provided the original legislative endorsement to many rights that exist today. Its text should not be regarded as current law, however. Some confusion may arise when the designation "PL 94-142" is used to generically identify all federally guaranteed rights of handicapped students, and this is a misuse of the term. Technically, "PL 94-142" refers only to the particular text passed by the 94th Congress.

PL 94-142 is notable for requiring that all states accepting federal special education funds provide handicapped students in public schools with a "free and appropriate public education" (FAPE) in the "least restrictive environment" (LRE), under strict regulations of the U.S. Department of Education. "Least restrictive" means that children with disabilities should receive their education in regular classrooms with as much interaction with nondisabled peers as possible. However, children may be removed from regular classrooms when education in regular classes cannot be achieved satisfactorily even with the use of services and supplementary aids.

Among these strict regulations is an important time line that requires school districts to provide students referred for special education with evaluations within thirty days and with placement within sixty days of referral. Failure of districts to meet these requirements can result in students being placed by parents in private schools without prior district approval, with the district footing the bill. Among other concepts given legislative birth by PL 94-142 are:

- Mainstreaming: Mainstreaming is the placement of a handicapped student in general education for all or part of the school day; this is the "least restrictive environment" of all. Districts may attempt to place children in the mainstream because the law requires it, and it is often cheaper to place students in regular classrooms, even with individual aides. In contrast, parents sometimes seek more segregated placements, believing their children will get more individual, professional attention than in regular classrooms. As a result, the merits of mainstreaming are most constructively debated on a case-by-case basis rather than on an ideological policy level.

- The **Individualized Education Program** (IEP): Every student identified as handicapped under PL 94-142 is required to have an IEP that establishes the educational and related services required by the student to make appropriate educational progress. The IEP is essentially a contract between the district and the parents of the handicapped student that establishes legal rights. If the contract is breached, school district funds are at risk.

- Discipline: Under PL 94-142, a handicapped student may not be excluded from instruction for an indeterminate period for behavior arising from the handicapping condition. If a student is to be suspended for more than ten days, then the IEP team should meet to determine whether the disciplinary action is a result of the handicap; if so, the IEP must be reevaluated.

- The "Stay Put" Provision: Section 415 of PL 94-142 requires that a handicapped student continue in the current educational placement while any review proceedings are taking place prior to a change in placement.

- The Unfunded Mandate Dilemma: Compliance with PL 94-142 and subsequent legislation is extremely expensive for school districts. Under constitutional law, it is understood that states and districts have a general duty to provide for the education of all public school students. However, the particular requirements of the federal legislation have placed enormous financial burdens on local and state budgets. Since these obligations are not fully reimbursed by federal funds, PL 94-142 has been continually criticized as a major unfunded mandate of the federal bureaucracy.

- The Impartial Hearing: In attempting to reconcile inevitable disputes between parents and districts over the referral, evaluation, and placement of students, PL 94-142 established the nonjudicial remedy of the "impartial hearing" for resolving these differences. At its most basic level, an example of such a dispute occurs when parents do not believe their child has a disability but the teacher disagrees. The impartial hearing, though not as procedurally complex as an appeal to the federal courts that may follow, has been an enduring source of frustration to both parties.

Further Reading

Crabtree, T. L., B. C. Gartin, and N. Murdick. 2001. *Special education law.* Upper Saddle River, NJ: Merrill/Prentice Hall.
Rothstein, L. 2000. *Special education law.* 3rd ed. New York: Longman.

Website
Wrightslaw: http://www.wrightslaw.com/

DAVID C. BLOOMFIELD

Section 504 of the Rehabilitation Act

Passed as part of the Rehabilitation Act of 1973 (PL 93-112), Section 504 prohibits discrimination against people with disabilities in programs supported by federal funds. Specifically, the law states:

> No otherwise qualified individual with a handicap ... shall solely by reason of her or his disability, be excluded from the participation in, be denied the benefits of, or be subjected to discrimination under any program or activity receiving federal financial assistance. (29 U.S.C. § 794)

Section 504 is not specifically an education-related statute; it actually grows out of a 1920 law that addressed employment and vocational rehabilitation. As a result, the definition of a person with a disability is not the same as the definition in the **Individuals with Disabilities Education Act** (IDEA) and includes "any person who (i) has a physical or mental impairment which substantially limits one or more of such person's major life activities [not just education], (ii) has a record of such an impairment, or (iii) is regarded as having such an impairment" (29 U.S.C. § 706(8)(B)). The major life activities referred to include "caring for one's self, performing manual tasks, walking, seeing, hearing, speaking, breathing, learning and working" (34 CFR § 104.3(j)(2)(ii)). Thus, even students whose disability does not necessarily put them at an educational disadvantage, such as students using wheelchairs or those discharged from special education, can qualify for Section 504. Students who qualify for section 504 do not necessarily qualify for IDEA.

The U.S. Department of Education's Office of Civil Rights (OCR), rather than individual plaintiffs, generally enforces Section 504. Once an individual complains to OCR within 180 days of the alleged adverse conduct, that agency investigates the matter and issues the appropriate order to correct the violation; financial penalties may be assessed against the violator as well if there is a finding of discrimination.

While the protected group of individuals covered by Section 504 is not as broad as those covered by the **Americans with Disabilities Act** (ADA)—Section 504 regulates only organizations receiving federal funds—the breadth of the protection (against *all* discriminatory conduct) provides sweeping rights for students with disabilities since most attend public schools in covered districts or receive federal funding for private education related to their disability. In many respects, Section 504 grants similar but less detailed rights to students with disabilities as those provided by IDEA. These include the right to a free and appropriate public education, an accommodation plan, special educational and related services, and the right to parent participation with an advocate in an impartial hearing to challenge district decisions regarding referral, evaluation, and placement.

The breadth of Section 504 and its roots in antidiscrimination has given rise to a separate body of precedent that sets it apart from IDEA litigation. For example, an important issue in these suits concerns which party bears the burden of proof. Under Section 504, the burden shifts to the defendant if the complainant can show that he or she is otherwise qualified for the benefit (an easy factual matter for students with disabilities) and that the benefit was denied. At that point, the school district or other party to the inquiry must show that the denial was for a reason *other than* the disability. This relatively low threshold makes Section 504 attractive to aggrieved parties, though its remedies may be less satisfying than those available through IDEA.

As an antidiscrimination law, Section 504 exemplifies society's aspiration that people with handicaps should have equal rights. Title IX is an example of a similar law that guarantees equal treatment—in this case, of women—in all federally supported programs, although it should be noted that neither women nor people with handicaps are accorded the full protection of the Fourteenth Amendment's Equal Protection Clause.

Section 504 is a precursor to the more detailed protections of IDEA and the ADA and is more than a historical artifact. Case law arising from Section 504 litigation continues to provide general antidiscrimination protections for individuals with handicapping conditions outside the public education and employment contexts. For example, students with handicapping conditions in a religious school that accepts federal Title I funds are protected by Section 504 even without going through the referral, evaluation, and placement procedures mandated by IDEA. By providing federal assistance for instruction in high-poverty schools, Title I has imposed annual testing and other accountability measures on all U.S. schools through the **No Child Left Behind Act**.

Further Reading

Crabtree, T. L., B. C. Gartin, and N. Murdick. 2001. *Special education law*. Upper Saddle River, NJ: Merrill/Prentice Hall.

Rothstein, L. 2000. *Special education law*. 3rd ed. New York: Longman.

DAVID C. BLOOMFIELD

Specific Disabilities

Asperger's Syndrome

Asperger's syndrome, also known as Asperger's disorder, is a pervasive developmental disorder primarily characterized by noticeable social impairment. Asperger's syndrome is named after Austrian pediatrician Hans Asperger (1906–1980), who in 1944 described a pattern of behaviors in four boys with average intellectual and language abilities, who displayed well below-average competence in social abilities. These children were described as being clumsy, socially awkward, naïve, unaware of others' feelings, and unusually absorbed in topics such as memorizing train routes in and out of Vienna. Concerned for these children, Asperger advocated providing them with an individual educational approach that would promote their individual strengths and work around their individual weaknesses.

This syndrome was not described to English-speaking countries until 1981, when Lorna Wing published a paper illustrating a pattern of behaviors similar to those first described by Hans Asperger. Wing, who bestowed the name "Asperger's syndrome," considered these behaviors to be part of an autistic spectrum characterized by the presence of restricted and repetitive behaviors and interests, as well as impairments in social and communication development. In 1994, fifty years after Hans Asperger published his paper, Asperger's syndrome was recognized formally by the American Psychiatric Association when it was included in the fourth edition of the *Diagnostic and Statistical Manual of Mental Disorders* (DSM-IV).

Asperger's syndrome is characterized by common clinical features. Individuals with Asperger's syndrome typically have an unusual preoccupation with a specific subject area (e.g., weather, dinosaurs, or computers). Their lives become centered on this area as they amass numerous facts about the subject, eager to share these facts with others. In general, these subject areas tend to change over time, such that an initial interest in dinosaurs might be later replaced with an interest in computers.

Knowledge about the prevalence of Asperger's syndrome is limited, although it has been estimated to occur at a rate of about 3.6 per 1,000 children. It is four to ten times more common in males than in females and is not specific to any race, ethnicity, or socioeconomic group. Although information about the specific cause or causes is lacking, there is evidence to suggest that genetic factors play an important role. Children with Asperger's syndrome often have a history of family members displaying "Asperger-like" characteristics.

The trademark characteristic of Asperger's syndrome is the inability to make and keep friends, which often results in social isolation. It is important to note that individuals with Asperger's syndrome *want* to make friends, but social interaction impairments significantly interfere with the ability to do so. They tend to respond inappropriately in social situations, not picking up on subtle nonverbal cues and gestures in a spontaneous manner. They tend to have difficulty putting themselves "in another person's shoes" and in understanding how their behaviors come across to others, often referred to as a "lack of empathy."

Although language development appears to develop normally for individuals with Asperger's syndrome, more subtle deficits in language also contribute to social impairment. For example, these individuals tend to have odd speech patterns such as exaggerated inflections or monotone voice. They tend to follow grammatical rules strictly and frequently interpret information literally, which often leads to the misinterpretation or misuse of jokes, idioms, and metaphors. Further, individuals with Asperger's syndrome tend not to notice the give-and-take of conversation, typically engaging in a one-sided conversation about their area of interest.

Other common features of Asperger's syndrome include motor clumsiness, inflexibility, poor organization skills, and hypersensitivity to sensory stimuli. Although academic progress may be an area of strength, school difficulties may develop because children with Asperger's syndrome tend to demonstrate a concrete learning style and have difficulty understanding abstract concepts. They tend to benefit more from a teaching approach that emphasizes structured and repeated presentations of information taught explicitly and in a parts-to-whole approach.

The clinical diagnosis of Asperger's syndrome is complex. Individuals are often diagnosed as having some type of learning or behavior disorder before an appropriate diagnosis is made. The diagnosis is best made following a comprehensive assessment by a team of professionals including psychologists, psychiatrists, pediatricians, speech-language pathologists, and occupational therapists. The comprehensive assessment should then be used to identify individual strengths and weaknesses so that the most appropriate interventions can be applied.

The school years are challenging for individuals with Asperger's syndrome. Socially, they are often misunderstood by peers and targeted by bullies. Often, some type of **Individual Education Program** (IEP) is needed. Students with Asperger's syndrome qualify to receive special education services under the broad category of "autism spectrum disorder." Disorders found in this category are primarily defined by marked impairment in social interaction. Students with Asperger's syndrome often need extra support because their social impairments interfere with learning in school.

Services for individuals with Asperger's syndrome differ, depending on the individual profile of strengths and weaknesses obtained from the comprehensive assessment. Generally, special education and related services might include occupational therapy, speech and language therapy, educational services with special education teachers, social skills training, and counseling. As a result, many different school personnel, including speech therapists, occupational therapists, special education teachers, school counselors, and school psychologists, might be involved in the education planning for these children.

Further Reading

American Psychiatric Association. 1994. *Diagnostic and statistical manual of mental disorders*. 4th ed. Washington, DC: American Psychiatric Association.

Frith, U. 2004. Emanuel Miller lecture: Confusions and controversies about Asperger syndrome. *Journal of Child Psychology and Psychiatry* 45:672–86.

Klin, A., J. McPartland, and F. R. Volkmar. 2005. Asperger's syndrome. In *Handbook of autism and pervasive developmental disorders*, ed. F. R. Volkmar, R. Paul, A. Klin, and D. Cohen, 88–125. 3rd ed. Hoboken, NJ: Wiley.

Klin, A., F. Volkmar, and S. Sparrow, eds. 2000. *Asperger syndrome*. New York: Guilford Press.

Romanowski, P., and B. Kirby. 2006. *The OASIS guide to Asperger syndrome: Advice, support, insight, and inspiration*. New York: Crown.

Website

Tony Attwood: http://www.tonyattwood.com.au/

MATTHEW R. REYNOLDS

Depression in Special Education Students

Symptoms of depression are prevalent in all populations of children and adults. There are varying degrees of depression, but essential features appear as a depressed mood, such as irritability or sadness, or the loss of interest or pleasure in most activities. An individual might experience at least four of the following additional symptoms:

- changes in appetite, weight, sleep, and/or psychomotor activity
- lower levels of energy
- feelings of worthlessness and guilt
- recurring thoughts of death or suicide
- difficulty thinking, concentrating, and/or making decisions

Research has shown a higher prevalence of depression among students in special education. It is more likely for teachers to encounter depression in students who have learning disabilities than in those without a disability. However, a learning disability does not *cause* depression, and depression does not cause a learning disability. A number of factors—including learning difficulties, lack of communication, social and academic expectations, and placement—might contribute to these findings.

Students may experience emotional, social, and academic hardships when separated from their peers. In many cases, students in need of special services are placed several times a day in a resource room or a self-contained classroom comprised of other classified students. Separating students in this way can result in feelings of inferiority and social isolation. It is important to note that students placed in gifted classes away from their peers also struggle with symptoms of depression. During adolescence as self-awareness and social pressures increase, a perceived lack of social interactions or separations from peers is likely to elevate feelings of social isolation, helplessness, and depression. Adolescents with Mild Mental Retardation are at a higher risk for developing symptoms of depression due to cognitive difficulties in processing social messages, coupled with poor social skills, often resulting in loneliness. Currently more effort is being made to form **inclusion** classes, which provide opportunities for students of various cognitive and academic levels to learn in one classroom and uphold the idea of placing a student in the least restrictive environment as required by the **Individuals with Disabilities Education Act**.

Often, students are placed into special education classes without thorough explanation as to why they are there, leading to negative feelings and behaviors regarding the situation, learning processes, and themselves. Children may not understand the causes and consequences of their learning difficulties. Prior to placement, children who are referred for an evaluation have most likely experienced frustration and repeated failure in challenging areas, resulting in poor concentration, motivation, and effort. As these learning struggles and possible academic failures continued, students' expectations for future academic successes were likely to decrease. When students believe that they are likely to fail regardless of how hard they apply themselves, they often internalize these failures and think they will fail at everything. This cognitive distortion is called *learned helplessness* and leads to the ''Why try?'' attitude. Academic failures can also generalize to other social and personal aspects of life, causing low motivation, declining sense of self-worth, self-defeating behaviors, and depressive symptoms.

It is common for students in special education with depressive disorders to also have anxiety disorders. Students with learning disabilities have been shown to experience more anxiety than their peers without disabilities. Students present symptoms of anxiety and depression in multiple ways. Externalized disorders, such as **ADHD**, Oppositional Defiant Disorder, and Conduct Disorder, are those in which children demonstrate emotional discomfort outwardly and act out. These children pose significant challenges to school systems by exhibiting disruptive, antisocial, and aggressive behaviors. Children who present depression externally tend to be referred more for special education services than children who present internalized disorders. Internalized disorders, such as Generalized Anxiety Disorder (GAD), Major Depressive Episode, and Psychosomatic Disorders, are difficult to detect.

To remedy the increasing rate of depression, parents, teachers, and counselors need to be more aware of the difficulties students face in transitioning to special education and dealing with learning disabilities. They also need to be more attentive to emotional aspects of learning and developing. Early academic interventions combined with joint efforts by both family and school can help to maintain mental health for students in special education.

Further Reading

Ingersoll, B. D., and S. Goldstein. 1995. *Lonely, sad, and angry: A parent's guide to depression in children and adolescents*. New York: Doubleday.

Newcomer, P. L., and E. Barenbaum. 1995. Depression and anxiety in children and adolescents with learning disabilities, conduct disorders, and no disabilities. *Journal of Emotional and Behavioral Disorders* 3 (1): 27–40.

Seligman, M. E. P. 1998. Science of clinical psychology: Accomplishments and future directions. In *The prediction and prevention of depression*, ed. D. K. Routh and R. J. DeReubeis, 201–14. Washington, DC: American Psychological Association.

Stark, K., D. Sommer, B. Bowen, C. Goetz, M. A. Doxey, and C. Vaughn. 1997. Depressive disorders during childhood. In *Children's needs II: Development, problems, and alternatives*, ed. G. Bear, K. Minke, and A. Thomas, 349–59. Bethesda, MD: National Association of School Psychologists.

Websites

Psycom.net: http://www.psycom.net/depression.central.children.html

Child Development Institute: http://www.childdevelopmentinfo.com/disorders/depression_in_children_and_teens.htm

MICHELLE W. GREENBERG

Emotionally and Behaviorally Disturbed: Diagnostic Concerns

In the 1960s, Eli Bower, an educational psychologist, developed a way to identify students who had difficulties learning due to severe emotional and behavioral problems. He created and refined a definition for Emotionally and Behaviorally Disturbed (EBD) children, which was later incorporated into **Public Law 94-142**. In 1997, the federal government, influenced by the **Individuals with Disabilities Education Act** (IDEA), clarified and added to Bower's definition.

EBD is classified as a condition exhibited by one or more of the following characteristics over a long period of time, adversely affecting a child's educational performance:

- an inability to learn that cannot be explained by intellectual, sensory, or health factors
- an inability to build or maintain satisfactory interpersonal relationships with peers and teachers

- inappropriate types of behavior or feelings under normal circumstances
- a general pervasive mood of unhappiness or depression
- a tendency to develop physical symptoms of fears associated with personal or school problems

The revised definition has been strongly criticized, and it remains controversial. The definition alone plays a major role in determining eligibility for special education services. Upon interpretation of the definition, there appears to be more emphasis placed on the word *emotional* than *behavioral*. As a result, the definition does not incorporate children classified as socially maladjusted or those who exhibit behaviors associated with conduct disorders. Therefore, these children are not eligible for special education services unless they have another condition or are considered Seriously Emotionally Disturbed. In addition, regardless of the behavioral or emotional characteristics these children exhibit, they cannot receive special education services unless their academic performance is adversely affected. For example, a child with EBD who is functioning on grade level is not eligible for special education services.

The National Health and Special Education Coalition is comprised of seventeen organizations that support children with EBD who are excluded from special education services. Presently, this coalition tries to lobby federal and state governments to adopt a new definition for EBD. The coalition's proposed new definition states that:

- the term *emotional or behavioral disorder* means a disability characterized by behavioral or emotional responses in school that are different from appropriate age, cultural, or ethnic norms and that adversely affect educational performance
- educational performance includes academic, social, vocational, and personal skills
- such a disability is more than a temporarily expected response to stressful events in the environment and is consistently exhibited in two different settings, at least one of which is school related
- the disability is unresponsive to direct intervention in general education

The coalition's definition also states that emotional and behavioral disorders can coexist with other disabilities. This category may include children with mental, thought, emotional, behavioral, adjustment, and anxiety disorders.

This definition of EBD is unlikely to be accepted or included in IDEA's definition because it is believed that it would lead to overidentification of children with EBD and therefore would escalate special education costs. However, research studies suggest that the new definition would result in a slightly *smaller* total number of identified students.

The debate over the definition of EBD continues to be a distraction in the special education and behavioral field. More important issues of treating and educating children with these problems remain unresolved. Students with emotional and behavioral problems continue to be underserved and underidentified in education, and those who are classified are not always helped through special education services. Because many schools districts do not have the appropriate services set up to help children with EBD function and learn, outcomes for these students are worse than for students with other kinds of problems.

Further Reading

Bower, E. M., and N. M. Lambert. 1962. *A process for in-school screening of children with emotional handicaps*. Princeton, NJ: Educational Testing Service.

Hosp, J. L., and D. J. Reschly. 2002. Predictors of restriction of placement for African American and Caucasian students. *Exceptional Children* 8:225–38.

Kauffman, J. M. 2001. *Characteristics of behavioral disorders of children and youth.* 7th ed. Columbus, OH: Merrill.

Merrel, K. W., and H. M. Walker. 2004. Deconstructing a definition: Social maladjustments versus emotional disturbance and moving the EBD field forward. *Psychology in the Schools* 41:897–911.

Townsend, B. I. 2000. The disproportionate discipline of African American learners: Reducing school suspensions and expulsions. *Exceptional Children* 66 (Spring): 381–91.

U.S. Department of Education. 1999. *Assistance to states for the education of children with disabilities and the early intervention program for infants and toddlers with disabilities: Final regulations. Federal Register* 64 (48): 12405–54; CFR parts 300 and 303.

_____. 2001. *The twenty-third annual report to Congress on the implementation of IDEA.* Washington, DC: GPO.

DANIELLE MARTINES

Fragile X Syndrome

Fragile X Syndrome is the most common inherited cause of mental retardation. Although not all children with Fragile X Syndrome have mental retardation, the vast majority of children with Fragile X Syndrome experience some type of learning difficulty. Fragile X Syndrome is caused by a mutation on the Fragile X Mental Retardation 1 (FMR1) gene. Thus, the condition is considered a congenital disorder, which means it is present from birth. Boys with Fragile X Syndrome are much more likely than girls to experience mental retardation. This is because males have only one X chromosome, while a female may randomly inactivate one of her two X chromosomes. Although the genetic basis of the disorder can be fairly complex to understand, there are different levels of the condition, based on the level of genetic anomalies: Some children may be carriers, some are in the premutation range, and others actually have the disorder. At this time, there is no known cure for Fragile X Syndrome, although behavioral interventions may help ameliorate some of the symptoms.

Although many children with Fragile X Syndrome have distinctive physical characteristics, the physical markers are often not present until adolescence. Common physical characteristics include a long face, distinctive ears, and hyperextendable finger joints. Physical anomalies are more common in boys with Fragile X Syndrome, although females with the full mutation of Fragile X Syndrome tend to demonstrate physical characteristics as well. Specific to gender, males may experience macroorchidism (enlarged testicles), while females may have menstrual problems or precocious puberty. Since young children do not usually demonstrate facial anomalies, it is important to differentiate Fragile X Syndrome from other disorders through molecular genetic testing. In the early 1990s, the majority of testing identified fragile spots on an X chromosome (hence the name Fragile X). However, more recently, DNA testing, which is more accurate, has become available. Since Fragile X Syndrome is an inherited condition, it is recommended that children of carriers of Fragile X Syndrome be tested as early as possible.

While each child with Fragile X Syndrome is unique, there are arrays of cognitive and behavioral symptoms that are commonly expressed. Children with Fragile X Syndrome may exhibit inappropriate social behavior such as withdrawal and limited eye contact. Males with the disorder exhibit about the same levels of motor activity as males with unknown causes of mental retardation; however, those with Fragile X Syndrome show significantly more restlessness, attention problems, distractibility, and impulsive tendencies.

In addition to the cognitive, social, academic, and emotional problems associated with mental retardation and/or learning problems, children with Fragile X Syndrome may be mistaken for children with autism, since they share a number of characteristics. Children with either condition often have trouble with loud noises and bright lights, engage in perseverative (repeated) play, have trouble with transitions, engage in stereotypical motor movements (i.e., hand flapping), and often have significantly decreased mental capacity. However, unlike autism, Fragile X Syndrome has a clear genetic etiology. It is also common for children with Fragile X Syndrome to have attention and hyperactivity problems.

In the classroom, children with Fragile X tend to demonstrate cognitive, academic, language, motor, and behavioral attributes that range in severity. The majority of males with Fragile X Syndrome will experience delays in language and age-inappropriate phonological distortions; females will generally exhibit fewer speech and language problems. Academically, while most males will have mental retardation, many girls, and some boys, with Fragile X Syndrome may have very specific or subtle learning difficulties, with an average IQ. Research has demonstrated children with Fragile X Syndrome perform poorly on tasks involving abstract reasoning, but better on those involving vocabulary and verbal reasoning. Thus, they are likely to perform better in reading and spelling tasks, but less well in arithmetic. Children with Fragile X Syndrome, especially boys, will learn more effectively if they are presented with all aspects of a task on many separate occasions rather than being required to build up tasks that have been broken into parts (e.g., a whole-word rather than a phonic approach to reading). It would be beneficial for teachers and parents to employ this approach in both the academic and home settings.

A questionnaire sent to teachers in special schools investigated the most common characteristics displayed by children with Fragile X Syndrome in the classroom. Results indicated that students with the disorder displayed a clear preference for practical work, especially involving physical activity, such as physical education or music. These practical activities enable the child with Fragile X to be physically active while engaged in a concrete task. It was further indicated that few of these tasks required lengthy periods of just sitting and listening. In comparison, participants noted that students with Fragile X disliked any activity involving large groups, such as lunch, assemblies, or recess.

Although children with Fragile X Syndrome demonstrate a wide array of cognitive capability and physical anomalies, they are still capable of having a positive academic experience. Behavioral interventions and medications have shown to be effective in managing maladaptive behaviors that can further stigmatize children with Fragile X Syndrome in school. As mentioned earlier, there currently is no cure for the disorder, and Fragile X Syndrome is a lifelong condition.

Further Reading

Cornish, K., V. Sudhalter, and J. Turk. 2004. Attention and language in Fragile X. *Mental Retardation and Developmental Disabilities Research Reviews* 10:11–16.

Mazzocco, M. M. M., and R. O'Connor. 1993. Fragile X Syndrome: A guide for teachers of young children. *Young Children* (November): 73–77.

Saunders, S. 2001. *Fragile X Syndrome: A guide for teachers.* London: Taylor & Francis.

_____. 1999. Teaching children with Fragile X Syndrome. *British Journal of Special Education* 26 (2): 76–79.

Symons, F. J., R. D. Clark, J. P. Roberts, and D. B. Bailey. 2001. Classroom behavior of elementary school-age boys with Fragile X Syndrome. *Journal of Special Education* 34 (4): 194–202.

York, A., N. von Fraunhofer, J. Turk, and P. Sedwick. 1999. Fragile X syndrome, Down's syndrome and autism: Awareness and knowledge amongst special educators. *Journal of Intellectual Disability Research* 43 (4): 314–24.

Websites

Fragile X Research Foundation: http://www.fraxa.org/
National Fragile X Foundation: http://www.fragilex.org/html/home.shtml

ANDREW S. DAVIS AND CHAD A. NOGGLE

Health Impairments

The term *health impairment* refers to a wide range of more than two hundred medical conditions that interfere with normal physical functioning. Due to advances in medical technology, more children are surviving previously fatal health conditions and, as a result, the numbers of children with chronic health conditions are increasing. According to the 1994 National Health Interview Survey, up to 31 percent of children have health impairments. Asthma, diabetes, epilepsy, heart disease, cerebral palsy, and cancer are the most frequently diagnosed afflictions in children. Health impairments may or may not be either visible to the casual observer, a recently acquired condition through illness or an accident, or a result of a congenital disorder that is present at birth and reflects a chronic state of impairment. Depending on specific characteristics and symptoms, health impairments can affect children in various ways. In addition to physical problems associated with particular impairments, students with health impairments may also experience psychological, academic, and social difficulties.

Psychological Problems

Children with health impairments face tremendous amounts of stress as they begin to understand their impairment and how it will impact their future. Fear, anger, and uncertainty are common reactions and can result in psychological disorders such as **depression**, low self-esteem, and anxiety. A young child's cognitive development does not allow a true understanding of how the body functions nor a valid comprehension of the condition and its physiological effects. It is not uncommon for children with health impairments such as leukemia and diabetes to experience a loss of control and helplessness as a result of disease factors. Children with leukemia do not actively participate in their treatment and are never "cured," but can be in a state of remission. Students with juvenile diabetes may feel insecure and different due to imposed dietary restrictions and the need to monitor and manage glucose levels.

Academic Problems

Children with health impairments are likely to demonstrate a decreased level of academic achievement and have a more difficult time in school. Frequent absences due to medical appointments, treatment side effects, and physical limitations may result in academic struggles. For example, children with renal conditions requiring hemodialysis may miss school up to three days a week due to medical treatments. (Hemodialysis is a medical procedure that cleanses the blood of toxins after the kidneys can no longer perform such functions; it requires several hours and is usually performed three times a week.) Children with cancer, although attending school more regularly, may experience treatment side effects from chemotherapy such as decreased concentration and comprehension that can also impact their academic experience. Other conditions, such as diabetes, can degrade academic performance through hypoglycemic episodes affecting cognitive functioning *and* frequent school absences. Moreover, many children with health conditions are not able to fully participate in their academic instruction due to fatigue and decreased energy.

Social Problems

Children with health impairments are subject to social alienation from their peers and often have difficulty developing and maintaining friendships. Because of frequent school absences, treatment side effects, and negative peer perceptions, children with medical conditions often face tremendous social obstacles.

Peer relationships require both opportunity and social skill. However, students with health impairments often have fewer opportunities to socialize with their peers as a result of time away from school. When they miss school, they also miss opportunities to establish social networks and classroom connections. Upon returning to school, students with health impairments often feel segregated from the school culture. Furthermore, without peer interaction, children fail to develop appropriate social skills, making them less appealing to other children. They may demonstrate more immature behaviors than their peers and may not be comfortable in social exchanges with classmates. In some cases, the peers of children with health impairments do not understand the condition and have misconceptions about contagion and origin, creating negative social attitudes. Young children, for example, may incorrectly believe they can ''catch'' diabetes from a classmate who has this condition. As a result, they avoid and ostracize the student with diabetes, diminishing equal social opportunities among classmates.

Educators should be aware that children with health impairments experience possible psychological, academic, and social implications in addition to obvious physical effects. Accommodations and interventions may be necessary within the school environment and classroom to create a satisfactory and positive academic experience for children with health conditions. For example, school counselors may need to help the child adjust and cope with his or her medical condition. Depending on the preferences of the child and the family, classmates may benefit from an educational discussion on the student's illness to promote a better understanding and acceptance. In addition, several classroom variables can be modified to improve the process of social interaction between students with and without disabilities. Classroom space, group composition, classroom activities, activity structure, and classroom materials are variables that can improve the process of social interaction between students with and without disabilities.

Further Reading

Gordon, P. A., D. Feldman, and J. A. Chiriboga. 2005. Helping children with disabilities develop and maintain friendships. *Journal of Teacher Education and Special Education* 28:1–9.

Tak, Y. R., and M. McCubbin. 2002. Family stress, perceived social support and coping following the diagnosis of a child's congenital heart disease. *Journal of Advanced Nursing* 39:190–99.

Thies, K. M. 1999. Identifying the educational implications of chronic illness in school children. *Journal of School Health* 69:392–97.

Weiserbs, B., and J. Gottlieb. 2000. The effect of perceived duration of physical disability on attitudes of school children toward friendship and helping. *Journal of Psychology* 134:343–46.

Yu, S. L., R. Kail, J. W. Hagen, and C. A. Wolters. 2000. Academic and social experiences of children with insulin-dependent diabetes mellitus. *Children's Health Care* 29:189–208.

JENNIFER A. CHIRIBOGA

Pediatric HIV

The first case of HIV (Human Immunodeficiency Virus) in children was not reported until 1982, which renders pediatric HIV a relatively unknown disorder in terms of long-term outcomes and research on the effects of having HIV in a school setting. Unfortunately, despite education and prevention efforts, the Joint United Nations Program on HIV/AIDS (UNAIDS) reports that there are currently 2.2 million children under 15 years of age with HIV; 640,000 children were newly diagnosed in 2004, and 510,000 children died of AIDS (Acquired Immunodeficiency Syndrome) in 2004.

HIV is the virus that causes AIDS and can be transmitted from person to person through infected body fluids. It destroys blood cells that are integral to the healthy functioning of the immune system. Physicians measure the amount of HIV in the blood, called the *viral load*, as well as the functioning of the immune system, to determine the progression of the disease. Many children will have HIV for years before the immune system is compromised to the point where AIDS develops. However, children have a shorter time between infection with HIV and the onset of AIDS, as well as a shorter life expectancy once they develop AIDS.

The most common form of transmission to children is through an HIV-positive mother, also called *vertical transmission*. Vertical transmission occurs when the disease is passed from the mother to the child during the perinatal period, which is the time before and just following birth. The three primary forms of vertical transmission are through pregnancy, labor and delivery, and breastfeeding. During pregnancy, mothers with a high viral load, infections, poor nutrition, or sexually transmitted diseases are most likely to pass the disease on to their unborn child. During labor and delivery, prolonged membrane ruptures can increase the rate of transmission, which leads some obstetricians to recommend scheduled caesarean section births. Vertical transmission can also occur through breastfeeding; risk factors include a maternal high viral load, nipple abscesses, or the child having sores in its mouth or throat. However, it is important to note that not all children born to mothers with HIV/AIDS acquire the disease. Many children born to infected mothers may test positive for HIV upon birth and then later test negative for the disease. Children and adolescents can also subsequently acquire HIV in the same way that adults can, of course, such as through unprotected sexual contact or sharing infected needles.

The influences of HIV on children are severe, not only regarding a child's health but also in terms of a child's educational and social performance. Unfortunately, HIV in children has only started to be thoroughly researched in the last ten to fifteen years, which limits the amount of information available regarding the effect of HIV on cognitive, academic, and social development. However, with advances in treatment, research regarding pediatric HIV has grown dramatically. Children with HIV seem to suffer from salient neurological impairment, which can lead to problems with cognitive functioning. Although the research in this area is not complete, many researchers agree that HIV is associated with *cortical atrophy*, which is a general shrinking, or loss, of brain tissue. Common neurological findings in children with HIV include motor difficulties, delays in meeting developmental milestones, and expressive and receptive language problems. It is also not uncommon for children with HIV to have diminished attention, concentration, and cognitive flexibility.

The social and emotional aspect of having HIV/AIDS is more difficult to measure. Children with HIV/AIDS obviously need a level of care that is greater than most other children. For example, these children are at a greater risk for contracting other diseases due to their weakened immune systems. In addition to dealing with the stigma of having HIV/AIDS, children with HIV/AIDS often have additional stressors in their lives that can cause social and emotional problems. For example, children who were infected vertically may have to deal with the loss of their mother. Furthermore, children with HIV/AIDS will have a high number of medical appointments, unpleasant medication side effects, sensory–motor difficulties, school absences, and weakness and fatigue that can interfere with normal participation in school.

It is important for educators and parents to integrate children with HIV/AIDS into as much of the curriculum as possible. It is also important to educate school personnel and peers about HIV/AIDS and to dispel common myths regarding transmission. For example, normal contact between children with HIV and other students and teachers should pose no risk for contracting the virus. Parents and educators should also be aware of laws regarding confidentiality of their child's HIV status. Children and adolescents who acquire HIV through sexual contact may pose special challenges to school personnel in regard to confidentiality and a discussion of informing sexual partners.

There is currently no cure for HIV/AIDS, although a number of medications are showing promise for extending the lifespan of infected children. The American Academy of Pediatrics has indicated that many children with vertically transmitted HIV are living until middle childhood and adolescence.

Further Reading

Armstrong, F. D., J. F. Seidel, and T. P. Swales. 1993. Pediatric HIV infection: A neuropsychological and educational challenge. *Journal of Learning Disabilities* 26:92–103.
Coleman, M., and C. Toledo. 2002. A study of the relationship between child care providers' use of HIV/AIDS information resources, knowledge of HIV/AIDS, and attitudes toward caregiving policies. *Early Childhood Education Journal* 30:67–72.
Wachsler-Felder, J. L., and C. J. Golden. 2002. Neuropsychological consequences of HIV in children: A review of current literature. *Clinical Psychology Review* 22:441–62.

Websites

HIV Infosource: http://www.hivinfosource.org/basics/children.html
Joint United Nations Program on HIV/AIDS: http://www.unaids.org/en/default.asp

ANDREW S. DAVIS AND J. JOSHUA HALL

Pediatric Seizure Disorders

It is important to distinguish between the terms *seizure* and *epilepsy*. The brain communicates, in part, through electrical discharges and reception through *neurons* (nerve cells in the brain). Although the actual mechanism is fairly complex, a seizure occurs when there is a serious disturbance of these electrical charges that interferes with the brain's normal functioning. *Epilepsy* is a term for a person who is biologically prone to, and experiences, repeated seizures.

Although electrical anomalies are not uncommon, few actually rise to the level of causing a seizure. Research has demonstrated that seizure disorders have a genetic component, meaning that a child may inherit a predisposition to seizures. Environmental and biological conditions can also trigger seizures. For example, children who are suffering from a very high fever may be prone to a seizure, called a *febrile seizure*. Neurological conditions, such as a **traumatic brain injury** or brain infection, can also lower a child's susceptibility to seizures. Many children with seizure disorders are treated with medications, usually anti-epileptic drugs (AED), which are designed to reduce, or manage, electrical activity in the brain. Unfortunately, AED can have side effects, including reduction in cognitive capability. It is extremely important for children taking AED to strictly adhere to their compliance schedule, since missed doses may actually *cause* seizures.

Seizures can be classified into two broad categories, *focal* and *generalized*, based upon their origin in the brain. Focal (partial) seizures occur, and are limited to, one area of the brain, usually the frontal or temporal lobe. Focal seizures generally fall into two categories, *simple partial* and *complex partial*. Simple partial seizures tend to affect one side of the body by producing shaking, jerking, or facial movements, and they involve no variation in consciousness. The hallmark of a complex partial seizure is a loss of consciousness. Often, children experiencing a complex partial seizure will appear uncoordinated and clumsy, make chewing or lip-smacking motions, walk in circles, or demonstrate other automatic behaviors. Children with this type of seizure generally do not remember the event.

Generalized seizures occur in both *hemispheres* (sides) of the brain and have a broader area of effect. They can be broadly classified into two primary seizure types: *tonic-clonic* (previously referred to as *grand-mal*) and *absence* (previously referred to as *petit-mal*). Children with tonic-clonic seizures will experience severe shaking, jerking, or writhing. When the seizure ends, the child will often experience unconsciousness and then fall asleep upon regaining consciousness. Children with absence seizures do not experience shaking, but briefly lose consciousness, often with no visible change in posture or motor movements. The loss of consciousness may only be a few seconds (but can last longer), and the child generally has no memory of the seizure. Absence seizures can be harder to identify, and parents and teachers may confuse this type of seizure activity with inattention or difficulty concentrating.

It is important to note that there are other types of seizures, such as *myoclonic seizures*, which are described by brief, involuntary motor movements (sometimes called jerks). Although space limitations preclude a full discussion (the reader is directed toward the resources below), three will be briefly discussed. *Infantile Spasms*, sometimes referred to as West's Syndrome, is an early-onset seizure disorder. Children with this disorder experience seizures that result in repeating spasms that usually cause the child to fold her body together, relax, and then repeat the sequence. Although some children respond well to treatment, in others, Infantile Spasms is a marker for development of a more serious seizure disorder. *Lennox-Gastaut Syndrome* is a treatment-resistant form of seizure disorder that often arises in children who have had Infantile Spasms. The type of seizures may vary, although many children will experience *atonic* seizures, in which the child drops to the floor. Children with Lennox-Gastaut Syndrome often experience a decrease in intellectual development. *Benign Rolandic Epilepsy* is a seizure disorder that has a very good prognosis; most children outgrow it during puberty. The seizures for children with Benign Rolandic Epilepsy are partial seizures and may involve different types of seizure activity. This type of seizure generally occurs at night. Children with this disorder may experience seizures consisting of unilateral paresthesias and facial movements. Speech arrest often accompanies this type of seizure.

The type of educational intervention a child receives will often depend on the type of seizure, as well as the etiology of the seizure. Staff education may be the most important intervention when working with children with seizure disorder. For example, absence seizures are often misattributed to daydreaming or lack of concentration. In addition to staff education, peer education is also important. For example, seizures may make students very uncomfortable, which may cause them to react aggressively or cruelly to a child with a seizure disorder. Special education services or a **Section 504** Behavior Plan may be appropriate for some students with a seizure disorder, especially in cases where a school nurse needs to administer medication. School personnel should be well versed in the nature of a child's specific seizure disorder and should have a ready plan that can be enacted if the child experiences a seizure in school. This plan should be developed in consultation with the child, the child's family, the child's physicians, special education staff, and school administration.

Further Reading

Freeman, J. M., E. P. G. Vining, and D. J. Pillas. 2002. *Seizures and epilepsy in childhood: A guide*. Baltimore: Johns Hopkins University Press.

Williams, J., and G. B. Sharp. 2000. Epilepsy. In *Pediatric neuropsychology: Research, theory, and practice*, ed. K. O. Yeats, M. D. Ris, and H. G. Taylor, 47–73. New York: Guilford Press.

Websites

Epilepsy Foundation: http://www.epilepsyfoundation.org/
Epilepsy.com: http://www.epilepsy.com/

ANDREW S. DAVIS AND JAMES M. TRINKLE II

Speech and Language Disorders

The emergence of speech and language in children represents the attainment of a significant developmental milestone. Disruptions in the typical course of development may result from a range of neurophysiological, structural, cognitive, social-emotional, and environmental factors. Interferences in normal development may occur congenitally prior to the onset of speech and language, or disorders may result from impaired ability due to acquired conditions.

Speech and language disorders, also referred to as communication disorders, have different categories. These include articulation and phonology, fluency, voice, swallowing, and language learning. These disorders may appear as primary conditions or may be secondary to other diagnostic entities, such as cerebral palsy, cleft palate, hearing impairment, and autistic spectrum disorders.

Articulation and Phonology

Articulation and phonological disorders involve the child's production and/or organization of the speech sound system of language. The child may substitute or omit specific sound segments, known as *phonemes*, or may have difficulty using rules for producing and sequencing syllable structures within words, resulting in the persistence of immature speech patterns. For example, children may reduce the number of syllables in words such as *banana* to "nana" or transpose sounds within words as in "ephelant" for *elephant*.

Neurologically based disorders such as dyspraxia, dysarthria, or oral-motor dysfunction may impede the precise motor planning (plan for volitional movement) and/or execution necessary for speech sound production. Structural anomalies such as cleft lip and palate, dental malocclusion (misalignment of the teeth), and ankylosis of the frenum (tongue-tied) may affect placement and movement of the oral structures for speech sound production. These disorders will have variable influence on overall intelligibility of speech, depending on severity.

Fluency

Fluency disorders involve disturbances in the flow and rate of speech production, associated with prolongation, interjection, hesitation, and repetition of sounds, syllables, and words. Many children exhibit episodes of disfluency during speech and language development. However, when tension and fragmentation or blocking accompany disruption in the flow of speech, it is likely to be referred to as *stuttering*. The persistence of stuttering from the preschool to school-age and adolescent periods often leads to embarrassment and avoidance of speaking interactions, impacting both academic and social functioning. Various theories have been presented to account for the onset and progression of stuttering, including those based on neuromotor immaturity, disruptions in the auditory feedback loop (the way the child hears himself), anxiety reactions (the emotional reactions of the child to his perceived difficulty), and conditioned behavior (the child's learned response related to speech blocks).

When speech fluency is marked by excessively rapid rate, seemingly inadvertent omission of words or merging of syllables and words, and overall disorganization of spoken output, the disorder is referred to as *cluttering*. Whereas children who stutter are likely to be self-conscious about speaking, those who clutter generally seem to be unaware of their speaking difficulty. While stuttering and cluttering both impact the flow and intelligibility of speech, treatment of these problems will vary considerably.

Voice

Voice disorders involve disturbances in respiration, phonation, and/or resonance, which may affect volume, pitch, quality, and variability of vocal output. They may result from primary neurophysiological conditions such as cerebral palsy or vocal cord paralysis, structural anomalies such as cleft palate or enlarged tonsils and adenoids, or hearing impairment. However, they are most often related to hyperfunctional (excessive) use of the vocal mechanism associated with habitual patterns of vocal misuse observed in children. Persistent misuse of the voice can lead to vocal cord nodules or polyps, resulting in chronic hoarseness and strained vocal quality. Other conditions observed in children include hyper- (excessive) or hypo- (insufficient) nasal resonance, pitch monotony, and inadequate vocal projection, all of which may impact on overall speech intelligibility.

Swallowing

Swallowing disorders, also known as *dysphagia*, may be caused by neurological conditions such as cerebral palsy, gastrointestinal disturbances associated with premature birth, or structural anomalies such as cleft lip or palate. They may include excessive drooling, gagging and coughing during feeding, or difficulty coordinating breathing during eating and drinking. Children with swallowing disorders are at risk for poor nutrition, aspiration, and persistent upper respiratory infection. The process of swallowing is directly related to the anatomical structures within the oral cavity and throat (pharynx) involved in voice and speech production, resulting in significant overlap between speech and swallowing disorders.

Language

Children with language disorders are observed to have varying degrees of difficulty with semantic (vocabulary), syntactic-morphological (grammatical), and pragmatic (social and interactive) aspects of communication that affect comprehension (receptive language) and/or production (expressive language). Additionally, they often exhibit weaknesses in auditory processing (selective attention to and interpretation of auditorally presented input), metalinguistic skills (ability to analyze and reflect on language), and verbal working memory (ability to process, store, reorganize, and retrieve verbal input).

Language disorders are attributed to neurological disturbances that impact the efficient transmission of information to and from specific cortical regions in the brain. They place children at significant risk for academic performance in that they impinge on decoding for reading, spoken and written text comprehension, classroom interactions, and problem-solving across subject areas.

While the range of speech and language disorders is considerable, it is essential that they be clearly distinguished from issues affecting **bilingual special education**. Children for whom English is not the native language—both those who are simultaneous bilingual-language learners (acquiring two languages before the age of 3) and those who are sequential bilingual-language learners (acquiring a second language after the establishment of the first)—must be assessed in *both* languages to determine the presence of a disorder.

Evaluation of the child by a speech-language pathologist will consist of standardized and informal measures and may lead to referral to a neurologist, otolaryngologist, psychologist, orthodontist, or audiologist. The resulting treatment plan will involve close collaboration with the classroom teacher and parent and should result in a more favorable educational outcome for the youngster.

Further Reading

Bernthal, J. E., and N. W. Bankson. 2003. *Articulation and phonological disorders*. Boston: Allyn & Bacon.
Bloodstein, O. 1995. *A handbook on stuttering*. San Diego: Singular.
Boone, D. R., S. C. McFarlane, and S. L. Von Berg. 2004. *The voice and voice therapy*. Boston: Allyn & Bacon.
Hegde, M. N. 2001. *Introduction to communication disorders*. Austin, TX: Pro-ed.
Nelson, N. W. 1998. *Childhood language disorders in context: Infancy through adolescence*. Boston: Allyn & Bacon.

Website

American Speech-Language-Hearing Association: http://www.asha.org/

GAIL B. GURLAND

Tourette's Syndrome

Tourette's Syndrome is a brain-based tic disorder named for Georges Gilles de la Tourette, the French neurologist who first described its features. Tourette's Syndrome constitutes a unique set of symptoms that differentiate it from other vocal and motor tic disorders. According to the American Psychiatric Association' *Diagnostic and Statistical Manual of Mental Disorders* (*DSM*-IV), for a child to be diagnosed with Tourette's Syndrome the following three criteria must be met:

1. There must be multiple motor tics and at least one vocal tic present that occur several times a day or intermittently for a period longer than one year.
2. Tic-free periods last less than three consecutive months.
3. The onset must be before age 18.

Many children demonstrate short-lived vocal or motor tics (or a combination of vocal and motor tics) that do not meet these criteria; these children are not considered to have Tourette's Syndrome. Additionally, tics may be caused as the result of medication, illicit substances, or another neurological condition, all of which preclude a diagnosis of Tourette's Syndrome. Children with Tourette's Syndrome usually experience their first tics in the early grades of elementary school, although the age of onset varies. The first tics are usually motor tics that start with the head or face area and gradually progress downward into the lower extremities as the child ages. Generally, motor tics precede vocal tics. For some children, the disorder will remit during later adolescence, although many children will continue to experience Tourette's Syndrome into adulthood.

Tics are involuntary, repetitive, stereotypical motor movements or vocalized utterances. Motor tics may manifest as facial grimacing, eye blinking, neck flicking, shoulder shrugging, grooming (e.g., hair grooming), or lower extremity movements. Vocal tics may include grunting, throat clearing, clicking sounds, *echolalia* (repetition of sounds, words, or phrases), yelping, and other vocalizations. Despite evidence presented in the media, *coprolalia* (uttering or yelling obscenities) appears in only a small percentage of children with Tourette's Syndrome.

One of the most important features of which educators should be aware is that the tics are involuntary and can not be easily controlled. In many cases, trying to stop the tics will result in anxious feelings that tend to exacerbate the tics. Although research is still evolving, there appears to be a clear genetic and neurological basis for Tourette's Syndrome. Similarly, Tourette's Syndrome has been closely linked with an anxiety disorder, Obsessive Compulsive Disorder (OCD), and many children with Tourette's Syndrome will demonstrate signs and symptoms of OCD. Children with OCD feel compelled to perform specific actions to relieve built-up anxiety, and children with Tourette's Syndrome often report their tics relieve a similar constrained anxiety. Interestingly, many tics will abate when the child is asleep, causing some treatments to be focused on relaxation therapies. Other current treatment modalities focus on behavioral interventions and medication.

In addition to OCD symptoms, it is not uncommon for children with Tourette's Syndrome to demonstrate signs and symptoms of Attention-Deficit/Hyperactivity Disorder (**ADHD**) and learning disabilities (LD). This may be due to a neurological similarity to ADHD and LD, or it may be related to environmental factors. The most likely explanation is a combination of neurological impairment and environmental stressors that result in attention and learning problems in children with Tourette's Syndrome.

In school, children will be best served by educators addressing individual signs of the disorder, as each child with Tourette's Syndrome will express a unique set of problems. However, some general guidelines should focus on reducing stress, helping the child to cope with the stigma associated with tics, educating classmates and school personnel, and addressing specific learning problems on an **Individualized Education Program** (IEP).

Further Reading

Haerle, T. 1992. *Children with Tourette's Syndrome: A parent's guide* (Special Needs Collection). Bethesda, MD: Woodbine House.

Heyman, I. 2004. *Tics and Tourette's Syndrome: A handbook for parents and professionals*. London: Jessica Kingsley.

Websites

Tourettes-Disorder.com: http://www.tourettes-disorder.com/
Tourette Syndrome Association: http://www.tsa-usa.org/

ANDREW S. DAVIS AND TIFFANY J. NEAL

Traumatic Brain Injury

A traumatic brain injury (TBI) occurs when the brain is wounded due to some kind of external blow to an individual's head. A TBI may result from a car accident, physical abuse, sports injuries, or other events that involve the potential for physical harm to the brain. More than a million learners suffer a TBI each year, and as many as four out of every hundred people experience one in their lifetime (Semrud-Clikeman 2001). In fact, more TBIs occur each year than are reported, since adults are often unaware when a child has suffered a TBI. These injuries occur more frequently for children and adolescents than adults, and males are more likely than females to sustain a TBI.

The effects of a learner's TBI can range in severity from extremely mild to extensive. While some injuries are barely noticeable, others may dramatically change an individual's life, including the ability to speak or walk. Following a TBI, a previously bright and popular student may struggle learning new material, have difficulty paying attention, and display behavior problems. The difficulties experienced by the individual will vary based on the areas of the brain that were impacted, the amount of damage, the age when the accident occurred, and the type of treatment and support received. The duration and depth of a coma resulting from a TBI and the amount of time it takes to recover continuous memory following injury are the two best predictors of injury severity. Especially problematic is the fact that the effects of a TBI may not be immediately apparent, but may appear months or even years later, as the child or adolescent develops (e.g., executive functions). Unlike an adult, the brain of a learner is still developing. Therefore, the impact of a TBI will be different for each individual and may change over time as the child grows.

A TBI may be the result of either a closed-head or open-head injury. In a closed-head injury, there is internal damage to the brain with no visible effects on the surface of the skull. Open-head injuries typically result when an object—a bullet, for example—penetrates the skull. Damage to the brain caused by infections, tumors, metabolic disorders, or anoxic injuries are different from a TBI and may be referred to as an acquired brain injury (ABI) since there was no external force that caused the injury. Regardless of definitional disputes, children with an ABI or a TBI often qualify for educational services under the "traumatic brain injury" or "health-impaired" special education categories.

Considering the wide range of effects a TBI can cause, it is important that a student receive a neuropsychological assessment of current functioning. A variety of abilities should be evaluated, including perceptual and motor skills, intellectual functioning, academic achievement, information processing, language, communication, personality, and behavior. If the student has been hospitalized, education professionals should work with the family and medical staff to prepare the child for the transition back to school.

After a multidisciplinary team has evaluated the learner, appropriate interventions must be developed if the student is to succeed. Such interventions should include controlling or modifying the *structure, organization*, and *strategies* (see D'Amato and Rothlisberg 1996) that the child receives. A TBI often leads to confusion and a low tolerance for change. Therefore, it is important for the student to have clear structure (e.g., rules), so he or she can focus on learning. Consistency at home and school is also critical. For high school students, developing a community college or work release program can help them prepare for the transition to the college or work world. It is important for the teacher to establish a routine for the student and to have understandable expectations for *all* behavior. An individual with a TBI may be overwhelmed and unable to concentrate in a noisy classroom, and therefore study carrels, headphones, and special learning areas may be needed. Since a student with TBI may tire easily, the length of the school day or number of breaks may need to be adjusted.

Organization is important for a student who has sustained a TBI because these students often have decreased planning abilities. As a result, classroom expectations often need to be adjusted. For example, the teacher might allow the student to tape-record material to compensate for poor note-taking skills. Assignments might need to be broken down into smaller sections. Teaching everyday life-organization skills, such as how to greet others, use a telephone, and balance a checkbook can also enhance the life of a student with a TBI.

Problem-solving strategies will help students with TBIs learn more efficiently. In addition, positive relationships with peers and adults aid educational and social skills. A structured social skills group can help students with TBIs practice conversation skills, select topics to talk about, and understand appropriate nonverbal communication. Learners with TBIs pose one of education's greatest challenges, given the wide variety of possible problems they exhibit and the variability displayed each day.

Further Reading

D'Amato, R. C., and B. A Rothlisberg. 1996. How education should respond to students with traumatic brain injury. *Journal of Learning Disabilities* 29:670–83.
Semrud-Clikeman, M. 2001. *Traumatic brain injury in children and adolescents: Assessment and intervention*. New York: Guilford.

Websites

Brain Injury Association of America: http://www.biausa.org/
BrainInjury.com: http://www.braininjury.com/
National Resource Center for Traumatic Brain Injury: http://www.neuro.pmr.vcu.edu/

JONATHAN TITLEY AND
RIK CARL D'AMATO

Teaching Methods and Interventions

Adeli Suit

The Adeli Suit was originally developed by the Russian space program as a way to combat the adverse effects of prolonged weightlessness. Doctors at the Euromed Center in Poland adapted this suit for the use of people with cerebral palsy. Since then, there has been an increasing interest in this intensive rehabilitation program among parents of children with cerebral palsy. Many parents and their children have traveled from the United States to Poland for the therapy, and they report amazing results from this approach. There are currently several centers in the United States using variants of the Adeli Suit.

Use of the Adeli Suit involves fitting the body with a suit composed of elastic bands stretched between metal supports that hold the limbs in proper alignment. The bands, which are placed between a series of rings around various parts of the body, provide controlled resistance for exercising various groups of muscles. According to its proponents, the Adeli Suit helps children with cerebral palsy gain better control over their muscles by restricting movement of the muscles and strengthens muscles by providing controlled resistance to muscle movement.

At the Euromed Center in Poland, Adeli Suit treatments are administered for thirty minutes to two hours a day, five to six days a week for four weeks. It is important to note that use of the Adeli Suit is only one component of the overall approach; it is generally combined with more traditional therapy approaches. Unfortunately, obtaining treatment in Poland is very costly for families from the United States. Current costs are approximately $4,000 for twenty-eight days of treatment, not including travel expenses. However, in 1999 the Euro-Peds Center opened at the North Oakland Medical Center in Michigan. This center offers the Adeli Suit to local children as well as to visitors from other parts of the country. For those who live in the area, treatment takes place in two-hour sessions three times a week. Use of the Adeli Suit is offered in addition to the usual regimen of treatments at an additional cost. For families who can't afford the therapy, there is a program called "Adopt a EuroKid" to help them finance the therapy. According to the Euro-Peds Center, insurance is accepted, provided the individual's insurance policy offers coverage for physical therapy and the person receiving the therapy lives in Michigan.

As previously mentioned, Adeli Suit therapy is a treatment approach used in combination with more traditional physical therapy methods such as soft tissue massage, stretching, and therapeutic exercising. However, because of the specialized equipment and training involved in the use of the Adeli Suit, it cannot be offered at the school the child attends and, in most cases, the treatment is not even available in the state where the child lives. As a result, use of the Adeli Suit is separate from the services a child receives from their school through their **Individualized Education Program**. More than likely, the child and her or his family will have to travel to another state or country to receive the treatment, which can disrupt the child's schooling.

Adeli Suit therapy was developed by the Euromed Center as a treatment for neurobiological impairments resulting in movement disorders, tonal issues, and strength deficits. Specifically, it treats muscle weakness and lack of coordination in

A young girl with cerebral palsy uses the Adeli Suit.

children with cerebral palsy. Many parents of children with cerebral palsy claim extraordinary benefits to their child after treatments at the Euromed Center in Poland. The Euromed Center has claimed that 67 percent of the people they treat, regardless of the severity of their cerebral palsy, achieved significant results. The Adeli Suit does not have any known negative side effects. The Euro-Peds Center is currently reviewing possible research partners for a long-term study on the effectiveness of it as a form of physical therapy; however, the center's adaptation of the Adeli Suit is only one component of the therapy used there. Researchers at the Gait and Motion Analysis Laboratory and Wayne State University's College of Pharmacy and Allied Health Professions are currently assessing the effects of use of the Adeli Suit on adults with motor disabilities, but results of their research are not yet available.

There are three other prototypes of the Adeli Suit currently available in the United States: the Therasuit, the Bungie Suit, and the NeuroSuit. Overall, all the suits are similar in their concept and purpose. However, there are some differences in materials, construction, and size. In addition, the NeuroSuit is also available in an aquatic version that allows the individual to experience weight-bearing effects within a minimal gravity environment. Regardless of the differences, all suits provide rehabilitative effects in the areas of muscle control and movement patterns and give cerebral palsy patients hope for the future.

Further Reading

Bar-Haim, S., N. Harries, M. Belokopytov, A. Frank, L. Copeliovitch, J. Kaplanski, and E. Lahat. 2006. Comparison of efficacy of Adeli suit and neurodevelopmental treatments in children with cerebral palsy. *Developmental Medicine and Child Neurology* 48:325–30.

Emmons, M. 1998. A step of faith. *Detroit Free Press*, January 30.

KidPower. 2001. Patrick and the Adeli Suit. http://www.kid-power.org/adelitherapy. html

Mehl-Madrona, L. 2001. The Adeli Suit for cerebral palsy. Available through Healing Arts Online, http://healing-arts.org/children/

Websites

Euromed Center: http://www.euromed.pl/
Euro-Peds Center: http://www.europeds.org/
Rehabilitation Institute of Michigan: http://www.rimrehab.org/
United Cerebral Palsy Association: http://www.ucpa.org/

CHRISTINE E. PAWELSKI AND JENNIFER FOSTER

ADHD and Psychopharmacology

Attention-Deficit/Hyperactivity Disorder (ADHD) is a neurodevelopmental disorder usually first diagnosed in childhood. The disorder is characterized by atypical difficulty sustaining attention, poor impulse control, and/or excessive activity. According to the most recent edition of the American Psychiatric Association's *Diagnostic and Statistical Manual of Mental Disorders* (DSM IV-TR), there are three distinct subtypes of ADHD. A diagnosis of Predominately Hyperactive/Impulsive Type indicates that the child has excessive difficulty with hyperactivity and impulsive behavior, but may have few or no problems attending to stimuli. Conversely, the Primarily Inattentive Type of ADHD denotes that the child may be easily distracted, may have a hard time completing tasks, and generally has difficulty sustaining an adequate attention span; however, motor activity and impulse control are within normal limits. Lastly, a diagnosis of Combined Type (exhibiting clinically significant levels of both problems) is possible.

Attention-Deficit/Hyperactivity Disorder is one of the most common afflictions affecting school-age children. A 2003 estimate indicated that 3–5 percent of children have ADHD. The structure of the classroom places demands on children they may not have at home, which often causes ADHD behaviors to be first noticed in school, rendering educators an essential part of the ADHD diagnostic and treatment process. At school, a child diagnosed with ADHD may present with both academic and behavioral difficulties. Children with hyperactivity and impulsivity will likely have difficulty sitting still at their desk and may prematurely blurt out answers to questions, talk excessively, and be seemingly unable to wait their turn. At home, parents may notice that their child appears always "on the go" or is unable to remain quiet in social settings that require such appropriate behavior. Children demonstrating symptoms of inattention will have difficulty paying attention to their teacher (and may often appear as if they are "daydreaming") and may skip from one activity to another, have difficulty completing homework or seatwork, and make frequent careless mistakes. Parents are likely to notice similar behavior and may find that their children have difficulty following directions.

Since the 1960s, both pharmacological (medication) and behavioral/psychosocial (therapy) treatment modalities have been examined. When compared to therapeutic treatment alone, stimulant medication or a combination of the two is generally better at reducing ADHD symptomology. However, other types of medication are emerging. Parents and educators play an integral role in not only the diagnostic process of ADHD, but also the intervention. For example, parents and educators need to assist in monitoring pre and post medication behaviors and performances to evaluate the effectiveness of treatments. Thus, these important individuals should have a basic knowledge of the medications used to treat ADHD so as to best assist children in managing the treatment of the disorder.

The most common psychotropic drugs used to treat the symptoms associated with ADHD are psychostimulant medications. Some general positive effects seen as a result of stimulant use are improvements in short-term memory and attention, and decreased hyperactivity. However, it is important to note that the specific effects of a stimulant drug will vary according to both the individual child and his or her environment. Recent research has suggested that stimulants may not improve academic performance directly as much as it does social and behavioral problems. However, a recent study indicated a negative relationship between ADHD behavioral symptomology and school performance. Therefore, while stimulants may not directly improve academic performance, it is reasonable to assume that if a child's ADHD-related difficulties are alleviated, it will be easier for that child to achieve academically. Additionally, when parents and teachers are helping children manage their medicinal or therapeutic interventions, those with ADHD demonstrate improved academic performance.

Some general side effects of the stimulant class of medication are decreased appetite (sometimes leading to anorexia), insomnia, stomachaches, headaches, and irritability. There may also be growth difficulties, tic development, and raised blood pressure. Some individuals who have taken very high doses of psychostimulants have exhibited compulsive behaviors or movement disorders, and, although rare, hallucinogenic responses. Additionally, more studies need to be concluded before the long-term effects of medicinal use (particularly psychostimulants) are known. Due to the limited available data, long-term use of stimulant medication is controversial. For example, it is unclear whether some evidenced growth delays are due to long-term stimulant use or to the disorder itself. However, there is no evidence that the long-term use of a carefully controlled regimen of stimulants is harmful. There is also a risk for substance abuse, as stimulants are a documented recreational and diet control drug. In fact, one concern raised about long-term stimulant use is the possibility that it will lead to substance abuse later in life. Parents and educators should ensure that other students do not have unrestricted access to the medication. Most stimulant side effects desist when the medication is stopped. However, if there is a sudden cessation in dosage, rebound effects may also occur, with increased hyperactivity, talkativeness, irritability, and insomnia.

The most common stimulant drug is methylphenidate, the generic name for the brand medication Ritalin. Ritalin has been shown to improve a broad range of behavioral, emotional, and academic difficulties. It has also helped with antisocial and aggressive behavior, and children taking Ritalin have demonstrated improved relationships with adults and peers. A time-release version is available, which reduces the number of times children need to take the medication. General side effects of Ritalin include headaches, stomachaches, decreased appetite, insomnia, and dizziness. Additionally, due to possible side effects, caution should be taken before prescribing Ritalin to children with tic disorders, children who are anxious, or children with psychotic disorders. Although Ritalin is the most well-known stimulant medication, there are other stimulant medications for ADHD, such as dextroamphetamine (Dexedrine). Although Dexedrine may be as beneficial as Ritalin, it is not prescribed as frequently, most likely because of the higher risk of side effects. Dexedrine has similar side effects and cautions as Ritalin, although insomnia, decreased appetite, irritability, anxiousness, and nightmares may cause greater difficulty. If the child has a tic disorder, hypertension, glaucoma, or cardiovascular difficulties, Dexedrine should be prescribed with caution.

Another drug in the stimulant class prescribed for the treatment of ADHD symptoms is pemoline (brand name Cylert). One advantage of Cylert is once-a-day dosing. Additionally, Cylert has the least substance-abuse possibilities. Despite these advantages, Cylert is not as frequently prescribed due to possibly dangerous side effects. The major risk is fatal liver failure, although this is a rare complication and, if the liver failure is found early, it can be treated and reversed. Because of this risk, Cylert should not be used with children with liver problems and is often considered a last resort even in healthy children. If Cylert is prescribed, liver function should be monitored.

When children do not respond to stimulants, antidepressants are often prescribed. Antidepressants increase the number of neurotransmitters (chemical messengers in the brain) available to the child's brain by blocking the reuptake (absorption) of neurotransmitters. Tricyclic antidepressants are the ones most often used when antidepressants are selected to treat ADHD symptoms. An advantage of tricyclics compared to stimulants is the relatively longer half-life (and therefore, longer-acting effects). As well as being longer acting, there is less potential for abuse with tricyclic antidepressants. However, it may take several weeks before effects of the medication are seen. While tricyclics may be effective for improving behavioral problems, they tend to be less effective than stimulants in improved concentration and ability to attend to stimuli. Common tricyclics used to treat ADHD are Norpramin (Desipramine), Tofranil (Imipramine), and Elavil (Amitriptyline). Another type of antidepressant sometimes used for the treatment of ADHD symptoms is selective serotonin reuptake inhibitors (SSRIs). Common SSRIs used to treat ADHD are Sertraline (Zoloft) and Venlaflaxine (Effexor). Some side effects of tricyclics and SSRIs include lowered blood pressure, dry mouth, upset stomach, constipation, dry eyes, dizziness, and drowsiness. The U.S. Food and Drug Administration has recently called for warnings of increased suicidal thoughts and behaviors for children taking antidepressants, although many large empirical studies have minimized the connection between suicidal ideation and antidepressants.

A new nonstimulant medication with the brand name of Strattera is gaining in popularity. Strattera is a norepinephrine reuptake inhibitor, which works to keep more norepinephrine available to receptors in the brain. Norepinephrine is a neurotransmitter implicated in the body's reaction to stress. Strattera does not have as many long-term studies as some of the other medications available, but it shows promise in reducing behavioral and social problems associated with ADHD, with limited side effects.

The use of psychotropic medications alone will generally not ameliorate a child's problem behaviors. Medication does not alter environmental factors that may contribute to sustaining the problem behaviors. As previously mentioned, some controversy surrounds the long-term use of drug therapy for the treatment of ADHD. However, a review of the literature indicates that the long-term use of a carefully controlled regimen of stimulants is not harmful. Regardless, a family may also wish to try nonmedicinal therapy before medication is introduced. Parent training in managing difficult behavior and direct counseling for the child are two possibilities. Other considerations, such as symptom severity and cost of treatments compared to the family's ability to pay, can influence what type of intervention is right for the child. Additionally, if regimens cannot be put in place to monitor the child's dosage, or if the household includes a substance abuser, medication may not be the best alternative. In sum, it is important to note that ADHD is a multifaceted disorder, and parents and educators should seek consultation with medical and psychological professionals to assist in determining the best course of treatment.

Further Reading

Barkley, R. A. 2001. *Taking charge of ADHD: The complete, authoritative guide for parents.* Rev. ed. New York: Guilford.

Barry, T. D., R. D. Lyman, and L. G. Klinger. 2002. Academic underachievement and attention-deficit/hyperactivity disorder. *Journal of School Psychology* 40 (3): 259–83.

Hall, A. S., and A. G. Gushee. 2002. Medication intervention for ADHD youth: A primer for school and mental health counselors. *Journal of Mental Health Counseling* 24 (2): 140–53.

Kollins, S. H., R. A. Barkley, and G. J. DuPaul. 2001. Use and management of medications for children diagnosed with attention deficit hyperactivity disorder (ADHD). *Focus on Exceptional Children* 33 (5): 1–24.

Snider, V. E., T. Busch, and L. Arrowood. 2003. Teacher knowledge of stimulant medication and ADHD. *Remedial and Special Education* 24 (1): 47–57.

Websites

National Institute of Mental Health: http://www.nimh.nih.gov/publicat/adhd.cfm
ADHDnews.com: http://www.adhdnews.com/

KATHLEEN M. MARKER AND ANDREW S. DAVIS

Assessing and Responding to Early Signs of EBD

The main objective in assessing and responding to early signs of **Emotionally and Behaviorally Disturbed** (EBD) is to prevent problem behaviors from becoming severe. There is a greater likelihood of achieving successful outcomes if behaviors have not yet set or fully developed. Early response and intervention can prevent students identified with emotional or behavioral problems before the age of six from exhibiting problem behaviors for the next three to six years. Assessing and responding to early signs of EBD pertains not only to younger children, as it can also be made applicable to the identification of emotional or behavioral difficulties in early and late adolescence. Early intervention detects emerging emotional and behavioral problems in older and more developed children and institutes treatment before disorders become unmanageable. Oftentimes, emotional and behavioral problems do not manifest until late childhood or adolescence. For example, some children gradually develop emotional or behavioral problems in response to a continuous, trying situation in their lives. If parents and professionals are aware of warning signs (e.g., social withdrawal, uncontrollable anger, low school interest, and poor academic performance, etc.) and do not ignore them, treatment can potentially alter behaviors before they become deeply ingrained and negatively impact the child's overall environment.

Nationwide, one in ten children has mental health needs, but unfortunately, less than 20 percent of these individuals receive the necessary care. Frequently, many emotional or behavioral problems go unrecognized due to a number of contributing factors in the assessment procedures, including inadequate physician training and time to perform developmental evaluations, minimum reimbursements from health plans, and overconcern for labeling young children. This lack of identification further decreases the likelihood of a child receiving any type of prevention services or early intervention. Instead, many children are given treatment in the middle to late elementary school years, even though parents and educators often have noticed symptoms much earlier. Most students are not even identified until they exhibit severely challenging behaviors, making the intervention process all the more challenging. Additionally, there is a continuous decline in academic performance and learning while an untreated child struggles with an emotional or behavioral problem. Despite the current legislation such as the **No Child Left Behind Act**; the Good Start, the Grow Smart initiatives; and trends toward early intervention and the promotion of social and emotional development, many children still go unnoticed and unassisted.

Young children can be systematically screened for at-risk behaviors for EBD; examples of such behaviors are extreme aggression, frequent emotional outbursts, consistent sadness, and disengagement from others. Even though a number of assessment tools exist for early identification and response, early screenings are not used regularly. The Early Screening Project is an example of a systemwide preschool early identification process involving three steps. First, a teacher identifies which students in his or her class exhibit internalized (**depression**, anxiety, etc.) or externalized (hyperactivity, aggression, etc.) behaviors. Second, the teacher rates adaptive and maladaptive behaviors, aggression, and social interaction to identify children who exhibit these types of behaviors in the clinically significant range or more often than their peers. Last, parents complete a questionnaire and another qualified professional observes the noted children. Many schools do not use early screening procedures due to minimal teacher participation and the need for more teacher training in this area. Schools typically wait until kindergarten or later to identify and refer a child.

Often educators, parents, and other professionals do not intentionally ignore symptoms but simply are unclear whether certain behaviors qualify as a problem.

Normal childhood behaviors can overlap with unusual behaviors, frequently leaving parents and educators attributing maladaptive behaviors to delays in social or emotional maturation. Also, they do not want to overreact and believe a "typical" child is "disturbed," especially an agitated adolescent whenever he or she acts overly irrational. Since identifying and labeling consistent inappropriate behaviors is not an exact science; it causes trepidation in both parents and professionals to initiate the first step in the process.

Early identification of an EBD child requires a tremendous amount of effort from parents, which is not an easy task considering the series of difficulties embedded in the identification process at any age. Many parents do not want to believe that their child has an emotional or behavioral problem that needs treatment, often insisting that the child will "grow out of it." Parents may experience feelings of anger or guilt, not wanting to admit that their family dynamics or actions could possibly reinforce negative behaviors and painful emotions in their child. Treatment in these cases must include the family as well.

The initial evaluation of a young child should assess communication and relational skills, types of play, and self-regulating behaviors. It is important to remember that young children do show a range of behaviors. Interviews with the family can provide information regarding other external factors that could be contributing to the emotional or behavioral problem, such as a physical, health-related condition; problems in school; changes in the family; or drug and alcohol experimentation in an adolescent. Accurate descriptions, including duration, frequency, and intensity of the inappropriate behaviors, help to assess if the behavior is developmentally appropriate or unusual. However, parents may have an especially difficult time describing the behavior objectively. A **Functional Behavioral Assessment** should be conducted in settings where the child exhibits the behaviors in order to learn what function the behavior serves.

Many professionals resist labeling young children with an emotional or behavioral problem for fear of stigmatization, but children need a classification in order to receive an intervention. Fortunately, since the **Individuals with Disabilities Education Act** (IDEA) amendments of 1997 and the IDEA Improvement Act of 2004, children with social, emotional, or behavioral difficulties can be classified with developmental delays under criteria in the Part B Disabilities Categories, instead of receiving an emotional disturbance classification. A child can qualify as developmentally delayed between the ages of three and nine. Variations exist, however, among state policies regarding age range, eligibility criteria, terminology, and restrictions on the use of developmental delay as a classification. An **Individualized Education Program** will provide a child with more descriptive goals and objectives to address her or his specific emotional, social, or behavioral needs.

An ideal and effective early intervention program needs to be consistent and must exist across multiple settings over a lengthy period of time. The intervention should not primarily focus on the child's behavior, but instead should incorporate parents, teachers, and peers, with the understanding that each interaction in the child's life affects his or her behavior and development. Parents should receive training to provide positive behavior support, while children are taught to use more adaptive, pro-social behaviors both inside and outside the classroom. If an early intervention program takes into account the multiple internal and external factors contributing to the problem behaviors, there are more chances for success. Additionally, consistent implementation can build stability, consistency, and predictability so the child feels supported over time, possibly resulting in positive relationships with others, increased academic achievement, and improved social, behavioral, and communication skills.

Further Reading

Baltodano, H., R. Gable, J. Hendrickson, P. Hester, and S. Tonelson. 2003. Early intervention with children at risk of emotional/behavioral disorders: A critical examination of research methodology and practices. *Education and Treatment of Children* 26:362–81.

Danaher, J. 2005. Eligibility policies and practices for young children under part B of IDEA. Chapel Hill: University of North Carolina, FPG Child Development Institute, National Early Childhood Technical Assistance Center. Available at http://www.nectac.org/~pdfs/pubs/nnotes15.pdf

Forness, S. 2003. Parting reflection on education of children with emotional or behavioral disorders. *Education and Treatment of Children* 26:320–24.

Forness, S., M. Hale, K. Kavale, K. Lambros, E. Nielson, and L. Serna. 2003. A model for early detection and primary prevention of emotional or behavioral disorders. *Education and Treatment of Children* 23:325–45.

Halfon, N., M. Regalado, and K. T. McLearn. 2003. Building a bridge from birth to school: Improving developmental and behavioral health services for young children. The Commonwealth Fund, May. http://www.cmwf.org/publications/publications_show.htm?doc_id=221307

Kaufman, J., T. Landrum, and M. Tankersley. 2003. What is special about special education for students with emotional or behavioral disorders? *Journal of Special Education* 37 (3): 148–57.

PACER Center. 1996. Does my child have an emotional or behavioral disorder? http://www.pacer.org/text/ebd/ebdart.htm.

———. 2003. Parents search for new ways to handle behaviors. *Early Childhood Connection* (Summer). Available at http://www.pacer.org/parent/childhood/ec_summer2003.htm

DANA FREED

Assistive Technology

Assistive technology allows students with a wide range of disabilities encompassing both cognitive and physical impairments to participate entirely and independently in a variety of school-related and leisure activities. Assistive technology encompasses an assortment of devices, from low-tech items such as pencil grips, splints, paper stabilizers, and calculators to more high-tech items like computers, voice synthesizers, and Braille readers. Supportive tools and equipment such as adaptive spoons, wheelchairs, and computer systems for environmental control also fall under the heading of assistive technology devices.

According to the **Individuals with Disabilities Education Act** (IDEA) of 1997, an assistive technology device is defined as "any item, piece of equipment, or product system, whether acquired commercially off the shelf, modified, or customized, that is used to increase, maintain, or improve functional capabilities of a child with a disability." With the reauthorization of IDEA in 2004, the definition was narrowed to exclude surgically implanted medical devices or the replacement of such devices. Another important definition included in IDEA is the term *assistive technology service*, which is defined as "any service that directly assists a child with a disability in the selection, acquisition, or use of an assistive technology device." These services may include, but are not limited to, an evaluation of an individual's technological needs; purchasing devices; selecting, fitting, and maintaining devices; and providing training or technical assistance.

The first law addressing the need for and mandating use of assistive technology was the Technology-Related Assistance for Individuals with Disabilities Act of 1988 (PL 100-407). Known as the Tech Act, it provided federal funds for states to develop training and delivery systems for assistive technology devices and services. The Act was reauthorized in 1998 as the Assistive Technology Act (ATA, PL 105-394) to continue funding efforts and expand federal support for assistive technology use. Under the new law, all states would be eligible to receive ten years of federal funding for their assistive technology program.

The benefits of providing assistive technology devices to students with disabilities are vast. Children with multiple disabilities can be given mastery and control over their environment. For the first time in their lives, these children may be able to engage in play activities and gain independence in their daily living activities. The greatest advantage of assistive technology devices in the lives of students has been the facilitation of independence. Through the use of technological devices, students gain the ability to make their own choices. In addition, students report an increase in positive social interactions, self-esteem, and motivation.

It is important to note that while the use of assistive technology devices has been beneficial for many students, access to and availability of the devices is not always certain. Barriers to the use of assistive technology devices in school settings include staff training and attitudes, assessment, planning and funding issues, equipment issues, and time constraints.

Staff training and attitude issues such as a lack of training and support services, inadequate follow-up support, and little or no on-site assistance all negatively impact the proper use of devices. As a result, students wind up not using equipment as intended and fail to reap the full benefits of the devices.

Problems with proper assessment of a student's assistive technology needs can lead to the student's inability to use the equipment, ultimately leading to abandonment of the device. In addition, factors such as equipment storage, integration with equipment already in use, and environmental modifications can also be a source of frustration and eventual abandonment.

Planning the ways in which students will use their assistive technology devices to meet the goals stated in their **Individualized Education Programs** (IEPs) has also created problems. Unfortunately, there has been a lack of planning to give students the opportunity to use their assistive devices on a regular basis within the classroom. A large part of this problem may have to do with the fact that the use of such devices is often minimally defined within a student's IEP.

Funding and equipment issues play a major role in poor implementation of assistive technology devices. Social class frequently determines the availability of assistive technology devices. Students in affluent school districts may have the funding to provide assistive technology devices as early interventions and to continue the provision of those services throughout a student's educational experience. In contrast, students who attend school in many of the nation's urban districts in poverty-stricken neighborhoods are not afforded the same accommodations due to lack of funding. In general, the cost of many of these devices is beyond what a school district's budget allows for spending, creating a social injustice and an inequity in education. In addition, when purchasing assistive devices, the cost of maintaining and repairing the equipment is rarely considered, leading to budget problems. Furthermore, accessing equipment is not always easy and is considered a major barrier to assistive technology use.

Time constraints are often considered a factor in all the aforementioned barriers, as an enormous amount of time can be spent researching, locating, purchasing, programming, and installing a device and training teachers. There is also time spent transporting equipment and troubleshooting problems.

Due to these many barriers, teachers as well as students often abandon use of the devices altogether. However, the benefit of the device for any student tends to outweigh any initial difficulties, so as often as possible preventive and collaborative measures should be put into place to decrease the possibility of device abandonment.

To combat issues related to staff training and support, research recommends a multidimensional approach where individuals within a school system, such as occupational therapists, have advanced knowledge and skills for successful implementation. In this manner, "knowledge" refers to knowledge of disabilities, hardware and software, adaptive devices, systems for obtaining equipment, design and construction, individual accommodations, and an awareness of the setting in which the device will be used. A few ways to gain this knowledge have been recommended. First, graduate and postgraduate training should include formal coursework to prepare occupational therapists and special educators prior to entering the field. Second, teachers generally prefer more direct and organized training on assistive technology use, so instructional units as well as workshops and group training sessions should be offered to teachers. Finally, having on-site consultants or regular visits by technology consultants has been viewed by teachers as beneficial.

In relation to assessment and implementation, it has been recommended that more effective assessment methods guided by the student's goals and future needs be used when determining student needs and selecting equipment. It has also been suggested that educational teams conduct research and gather data over long periods of time, including direct observations of equipment in use, in order to make informed decisions when choosing which devices would be most beneficial. Within this process, educational teams collaborate with the students and their families to ensure that all opinions and concerns are heard. In addition, within the IEP, the use of assistive technology should be tied to both short- and long-term goals. In this capacity, all members of the educational team will be well aware of how a given device will help the students achieve their goals. Another area that is often overlooked is an assessment of the classroom environment and teacher time and resources, which are crucial to the use of assistive technology.

One way to ensure that training, support, assessment, and implementation within the school setting is successful would be to develop an assistive technology plan to ensure that all individuals involved understand their specific roles and responsibilities. A team-based assessment approach is recommended, where collaboration among all members is necessary. Through this method, the educational team is guided by a technology consultant who delegates team roles and responsibilities, guides the assessment and goal setting, and gathers student and family input. Ultimately, the educational team works together to develop a detailed technology plan to best serve the students' needs. In addition, an expert with sufficient knowledge of certain devices should be employed to help with choosing and purchasing equipment, providing training, and troubleshooting any problems that may arise. In doing so, assistive technology devices can be smoothly incorporated into a student's current educational program, allowing the student ample time to train and practice with the equipment before full inclusion into his or her routine.

Further Reading

Copley, J., and J. Ziviani. 2004. Barriers to the use of assistive technology for children with multiple disabilities. *Occupational Therapy International* 11 (4): 229–43.

Day, S. L., and B. J. Edwards. 1996. Assistive technology for postsecondary students with learning disabilities. *Journal of Learning Disabilities* 29 (5): 486–503.

Forgrave, K. F. 2002. Assistive technology: Empowering students with learning disabilities. *Assistive Technology* 75 (3): 122–26.

Paraette, H. P., and M. J. Brotherson. 2004. Family-centered and culturally responsive assistive technology decision making. *Infants and Young Children* 17 (4): 355–67.

Websites

Center for Family, School, and Community: http://www2.edc.org/fsc/
Center for Implementing Technology in Education: http://www.citeducation.org/

Family Center on Technology and Disability: http://www.fctd.info/
NIMAS Development and Technical Assistance Centers: http://nimas.cast.org/

JENNIFER FOSTER

Behavior Management

Behavior management is an aspect of school and classroom management that deals with reducing or eliminating problem behaviors and/or introducing or increasing desirable behaviors. Because classroom instruction can be compromised by behavioral deficits and excesses, behavior management is often critical for creating a positive learning environment for all students. Approaches to behavior management may be considered either *proactive* or *reactive*. A proactive behavior management strategy is preventative; it is introduced with the intent to head off behaviors before they arise or reach problematic levels. A reactive strategy is implemented after a behavioral problem has been identified.

Although behavior management is often done informally, formal assessment of behavior is a recommended starting point in the process. The **functional behavior assessment** is a common assessment method that consists of interviews, behavioral rating scales, an Antecedent-Behavior-Consequence (A-B-C) assessment, and direct measurement of behavior. An A-B-C assessment is an observation aimed at identifying antecedents and consequences of behavior. Results of an A-B-C assessment may be used to generate hypotheses about the function a particular behavior serves for a student and to implicate environmental factors that can be removed or added to promote pro-social behaviors. Direct measurement of a student's behavior may confirm or disconfirm whether the behavior occurs at inappropriate levels. The method of measuring behavior depends upon the characteristics of the problem behavior. Measurement might be used to indicate how often a behavior occurs (*event* or *interval recording*), how long a behavior persists (*duration recording*), or how long it takes a student to start doing something after being prompted (*latency recording*).

If the behavior assessment shows the target behavior(s) to be problematic, the next step is intervention. This process is often conceived as a tiered model, wherein the least intrusive intervention is attempted first. If unsuccessful, then another, perhaps more intrusive, intervention can be implemented. The benefits of a formal behavior management plan include greater confidence that an intervention was effective and was causally related to the change in behavior, as well as providing documentation for parents and school personnel.

Manipulating a student's environment is often less intrusive than other behavior management techniques. Examples of environmental management are positioning desks in strategic ways, posting rules, setting schedules, varying the pace of instruction, and monitoring transition periods. In this manner, the behavior of a target student, as well as an entire class, can be positively influenced. Consideration of a student's cultural background can be very important when administering behavioral consequences, because responses may vary significantly among students from different cultures.

Some common reinforcement procedures are *positive reinforcement, contracting, modeling*, and *token economies*. These procedures are used to establish and increase desired behaviors. Positive reinforcement is the presentation of a rewarding stimulus, such as praise, free time, stickers, or food, contingent on a specific behavior. Contracting involves drafting an agreement with a student to perform a teacher-preferred behavior in order to get a student-selected reward. Modeling enlists a teacher or peer to demonstrate behavior that students then learn through imitation and observation. Lastly, a token economy may be set up to manage behaviors for an entire group. Student behaviors are rewarded immediately with points or coupons, which may later be converted into tangible rewards.

Concerns exist about the long-term effectiveness and residual effects on students of punishment procedures (sometimes called *aversives*). Many traditional forms of school discipline are considered aversive, including spanking, suspensions, and scolding. Critics of these methods cite a number of problematic features and outcomes. First, those who administer punishment must often use increasingly severe levels to suppress behavior over time. This cycle can adversely affect both the student and the disciplinarian and may lead to abuses. Second, punishment alone does not teach desired replacement behaviors; thus, it is a consequence that does nothing to inform students how they should behave. Lastly, what appears to be punishment may in fact reinforce behavior. This is evident with students who act out in order to leave class, which itself may be the aversive.

Given the potential for these shortcomings, certain punishment procedures are viewed more favorably than others. **Time-out** and *response cost* have been used extensively in classrooms. Time-out (from reinforcement) is the removal of a reinforcing environment, perhaps placing a student in an isolated location. Response cost may be used as a component of a token economy, where previously obtained points or tokens are taken from the student for misbehavior.

As an alternative to methods of punishment, *differential reinforcement* may be used. Differential reinforcement rewards the occurrence of socially desirable behaviors or more appropriate levels of behavior in place of problem behaviors (or levels of behavior) that have previously occurred. As an example, actively reinforcing a student for on-task behavior may serve to curtail a problem with off-task behavior because the two behaviors are incompatible with one another. *Extinction* may be paired with differential reinforcement as a means of ignoring reoccurrences of a problem behavior. Extinction is the withholding of an expected reinforcer and resembles punishment in that the target behavior becomes less frequent over time. However, extinction is not suitable for behaviors that are harmful to a student or others (e.g., self-injurious behavior or biting) or if the behavior is not sustained by attention from the teacher or other students.

The final and ongoing step in managing behavior is evaluating an intervention and modifying the plan as needed. If an intervention was effective, then eventually reinforcement can be phased out when the target behavior persists in the absence of reinforcement. If, however, data indicate that the intervention is not working satisfactorily, then a new intervention may be needed.

Further Reading

Alberto, P. A., and A. C. Troutman. 2003. *Applied behavior analysis for teachers.* 6th ed. Upper Saddle River, NJ: Pearson Prentice Hall.

Walker, J. E., and T. M. Shea. 1999. *Behavior management: A practical approach for educators.* 7th ed. Upper Saddle River, NJ: Prentice Hall.

Wielkiewicz, R. M. 1995. *Behavior management in the schools: Principles and procedures.* 2nd ed. Boston: Allyn & Bacon.

Websites

Dr. Mac's Amazing Behavior Management Advice Site: http://www.behavioradvisor. com/

J. PATRICK JONES AND ANDREW S. DAVIS

Collaborative Consultation

Collaborative consultation is a problem-solving process used by educators to assist students who are experiencing academic, behavioral, or social problems. It is a structured procedure in which a consultant, usually a school psychologist or special educator, collaborates with a consultee. Within the school setting, a teacher generally takes on the role of the consultee. The premise for this collaborative relationship is to improve the functioning of a student, who is referred to as the client. The consultant and consultee both collect pertinent information related to a student's problem and then combine their diverse expertise to generate creative solutions to help the student become a more successful learner.

Although the primary goal of collaborative consultation is to promote student learning and mental health, the consultant and consultee also benefit from this process. During the analysis of a student's difficulties and the implementation of solutions, the consultant and the consultee acquire knowledge and skills that they can use to manage similar situations in the future. A secondary goal of collaborative consultation is to improve the consultee's ability to prevent or respond more appropriately to similar problems with other students in the future.

The public tends to think of consultants as experts in their field. For example, a business owner may hire a financial consultant to manage the profits of a business. In this example, the consultant uses his or her expertise to make recommendations that the business owner can follow to become more successful. In schools, this type of expert consultation has limitations. In order to achieve the secondary goal of collaborative consultation—improving the knowledge and skills of consultees so that independently they can prevent and better manage similar situations in the future—consultees need to become active decision makers during consultation. From the combination of consultant and consultee perspectives and expertise, better solutions are generated for students. Further, it is important for the integrity of the process that consultees engage voluntarily and understand that they may freely accept or reject any intervention that results from the process. Throughout the collaboration, the consultant and consultee work together and as a result, the consultee becomes more confident in her or his own ability to generate useful solutions to problems. This empowerment in turn fosters a sense of ownership on the part of the consultee and increases the likelihood of successfully implementing interventions.

Participants involved in consultation move through a series of stages. They begin by jointly defining a student's academic, behavioral, or social problem. Subsequently, the consultant and consultee work together to obtain information that will help them understand the problem and plan an effective intervention. Generally, the consultee is responsible for implementing any solutions that arise from the consultation process, since it is the teacher who spends the most time and has already developed a meaningful relationship with the student. Once the teacher implements the plan, the consultant's job is to support the intervention. Ongoing evaluation of interventions is essential to determine if the intervention is successful or if it requires modification.

Another important feature of successful collaborative consultation is the added involvement of parents. Interventions applied both in the home and the classroom will likely be more effective than interventions applied in just one setting.

The collaborative consultation process in its simplest form looks like this. A math teacher asks the consultant for assistance with a student who creates chaos in his third-period algebra class. The student constantly calls out inappropriate remarks and completes little work. The consultant and teacher meet initially to discuss the problem. The two collect as much information as possible related to the student and the problem by observing the student in various settings, interviewing the student as well as those familiar with the student and the problem, and reviewing school records. Then the problem or problems are defined and a plan is decided upon, implemented, and evaluated. The process of collaborative consultation is complex and requires the consultant to use well-honed communication and interpersonal skills.

Although the consultant–consultee dyad is the most common form of collaborative consultation, other models are often practiced in schools. For example, multiple consultants can form a team designed to work with either an individual teacher or a team of teachers. Teams of consultants are generally made up of school psychologists, special educators, and administrators. A team of consultees could be, for example, all fifth-grade teachers or all teachers involved in a new reading program. In addition, there may be numerous students targeted by the consultation. Collaborators may identify a problem experienced by many students within a school and work toward developing a program that has a positive impact on the majority of them. For example, when collaborators identify several middle school students having difficulty completing homework, an after-school homework club might be organized to provide students with an opportunity to use the school gym after receiving assistance with their homework.

Consultation approaches succeed both for individual students and in solving school-wide problems because participants in the problem-solving process bring together varied expertise, knowledge, skills, and attitudes that, when combined, enable the collaborators to assist students more effectively than any of them could if managing the problems alone. Within the structure of collaborative consultation, students receive immediate attention, and classroom teachers receive immediate support. School staff increase communication with each other and build relationships with families. Importantly, resolving problems at the general education classroom level reduces the number of referrals to special education.

Further Reading

Allen, S. J., and J. L. Graden. 2002. Best practices in collaborative problem solving for intervention design. In *Best practices in school psychology IV*, ed. A. Thomas and J. Grimes, 564–82. Washington, DC: National Association of School Psychologists.

Brown, D., W. B. Pryzwansky, and A. C. Schulte. 2006. *Psychological consultation and collaboration: Introduction to theory and practice.* Boston: Pearson.

Dettmer, P., L. P. Thurston, and N. Dyck. 2002. *Consultation, collaboration, and teamwork for students with special needs.* Boston: Allyn & Bacon.

Kampwirth, T. J. 2003. *Collaborative consultation in the schools: Effective practices for students with learning and behavior problems.* Upper Saddle River, NJ: Merrill/Prentice Hall.

Pugach, M. C., and L. J. Johnson. 2001. *Collaborative practitioners, collaborative schools.* Denver: Love.

FLORENCE RUBINSON

Conductive Education

Conductive Education (CE), also called the Petö Method after its founder Andràs Petö, M.D. (1893–1967), is a rehabilitative-pedagogical program for individuals with motor (physical movement) disorders. The foundation of CE can be traced to its origin in Budapest, Hungary, in the late 1940s at the Institute for Movement Therapy, later renamed Petö Institute. The original institute was a residential program for children with "incurable motor disorders," and its primary goal was to increase the mobility and independence in these children so that they might transition back into community school programs.

Dr. Petö, working with his colleagues, began seeing increased physical gains in these children when they became engaged in small-group, highly structured activities involving a variety of repetitive tasks (eventually called *task series*). This sequence of motor learning was systematically implemented throughout the day and integrated into every phase of a child's life. In addition, rhythm and language were critical features of the approach, often through song and rhymes that supported the consistent pacing and intensity of the work (later referred to as *rhythmic intent*).

While the movement activities of the Petö Method are facilitated by a trained *conductor* (the coined name for the professional who leads and guides the learner using this particular pedagogical style), the ultimate coordination and initiation of complex movements is developed by the individual through her or his own experience. Thus, the underlying premise of the CE approach is the development of self-sufficiency and personal achievement. CE refers to this outcome as the development of "orthofunctioning," the ability of an individual to internally organize and coordinate functions through a planned set of activities that supports positive and independent movement.

Although originally conceived for children with motor problems, the CE approach has also been used with adults having a variety of central nervous system disorders who are capable of learning. This includes primarily individuals with cerebral palsy and multiple sclerosis, as well as those with **traumatic brain injury** and strokes. Adults with Parkinson's disease have also been participants in CE activities in programs around the world.

The full implementation of a CE program involves a series of instructional periods with preestablished sets of activities called "task series" (e.g., a lying program, a sitting and standing program, and so forth) that are designed to increase independent motor functioning. These motor learning activities utilize wooden plinths (tables) with slats and straight-backed chairs which have become synonymous with the Hungarian CE tradition.

Although the wooden, nonsupportive furniture assists in focusing a child on developing internal and self-designed strategies for movement, current CE advocates minimize the focus on the unique furniture. Rather, supporters of CE stress the integrative rehabilitative techniques this holistic system provides that address functional and socialization concepts resulting in active and self-motivated learners.

Unlike a typical special or general education classroom that focuses on academic work, generally in a sitting position, the routines of a conductive education environment are focused on a physically intensive movement program carried out in a supportive group setting. The group facilitator (conductor) leads the children each day through a set series of planned activities emphasizing various types of movement, using repetition, rhythm, and play. Using the simple wooden furniture and equipment, each child completes a daily series of specific physical tasks that represents a small component of functional movement: reaching, grasping, rolling, pulling, pushing, standing, walking, and so on. To the degree possible, these tasks are introduced in an educational context (e.g., number counting, letter and word recognition), and mastery is achieved through a combination of physical repetition, while requiring the children to repeat the components of the movement within a rhythmic beat or song. For example, "I lift my hand up in the air: one-two-three-four" or "We are standing tall; we are standing tall; one-two-three-four, we are standing tall." Simple melodies, often based on Hungarian folk tunes, are sung as part of an overall exercise and movement program.

Whereas academics are stressed in the traditional educational classroom, movement and learning how to initiate that movement become the keystone for children

A Conductive Education classroom in Hungary.

with motor disorders participating in CE programs. The CE method bases its approach on the belief that through the development of greater physical fluidity and self-initiated motor planning, children can achieve enhanced cognitive processing, independence, and self-confidence. Although this educational method is easier to implement in programs with children of younger ages, given less academic requirements, the CE approach has been utilized with children of all ages.

In addition, unlike more traditional special education programs that involve adding specialists in physical, occupational, and speech therapy to provide "treatments" for children—oftentimes in isolated nonclassroom settings—conductors with training in a combination of education, psychology, and physiotherapy lead the Petö Method classrooms. This eliminates the need for separate, individualized sessions with other specialists and reinforces its more holistic approach to service delivery. CE also capitalizes on group process, encouraging children to participate in one another's success by cheering each other on, allowing for modeling, and development of socialization skills.

The Petö Method has become an internationally and scientifically accepted method of education, especially in Europe, although its neurobiological basis has yet to be fully validated. Until the early 1960s, CE remained almost unknown to the West, with the only limited information available coming as a result of presentations at professional conferences such as the National Society for Crippled Children and Adults and the International Society for Rehabilitation of the Disabled.

U.S. federal research monies were provided in 1969 to a team in Eau Claire, Wisconsin, to study the impact of CE on a small group of children with cerebral palsy, including a control group. The researchers found that CE engendered significantly superior functioning, especially in the areas of self-care and communication. Dr. Laird Heal completed this study in 1972, additionally describing the positive results of CE practices on 866 Hungarian children treated in programs in Hungary between 1950 and 1965. It was the publication of this work that prompted physicians to explore the methods involved.

The International College of Pediatrics held its annual meeting in Hungary in 1985, allowing U.S. members to visit the Petö Institute, many for the first time.

The table or plinth used by conductors.

Shortly thereafter, in 1986, the first CE instruction was offered in the United States by a Petö Institute–certified conductor. By 1992, Dr. Frieda Spivak, director of the Hospital Clinic Center at Kingsbrook Jewish Medical Center in Brooklyn, was leading the way in the formation of the Inter-American Conductive Education Association (IACEA), an information resource on CE largely run by parents and affiliated professionals. The Ontario March of Dimes brought CE to Canada, and in 1995, the first year-round program in North America was established in Picton, Ontario. The IACEA reports that between twenty-five and fifty conductive education programs are in existence in North America in any one year, including summer programs organized by parents.

The practice of CE continues to be challenged, however, especially in the United States, because of its lack of controlled research and its utilization of professionals (i.e., conductors) who do not possess the traditional teacher certification and licensing required for **Individualized Education Program** (IEP) options. However, parents are succeeding in adding CE to their child's IEP in a number of states (e.g., Minnesota, Illinois, and California). This strong parent advocacy has resulted in the establishment of the first U.S. conductor-teacher bachelor's degree program, at Aquinas College in Grand Rapids, Michigan; it graduated its first set of teacher-conductors in spring 2005. The National Institute of Conductive Education in Birmingham, England, already offers a CE training program with the University of Wolverhampton, and teacher-conductors are being trained by Tsad Kadima in Israel and ASPACE (Association of Cerebral Paralysis) in Spain.

The CE approach supports a model of self-contained, homogenous grouping of students, as opposed to inclusive practices. It also encourages a child to adapt to the environment rather than supporting a philosophy that incorporates technology to adapt the surroundings for the child. Both of these programmatic facts contribute to the ongoing challenges facing this promising, yet controversial, alternative practice for children and adults with motor disorders.

Further Reading

Bochner, S., et al. 1999. How effective are programs based on conductive education: A report of two studies. *Journal of Intellectual and Developmental Disabilities* 24 (3): 227–42.

Hári, M. 2001. The history of conductive education. In *Conductive Education: Occasional Papers*, suppl. 2. Hungary: International Petö Institute.

Heal, L. 1972. *Evaluating an integrated approach to the management of cerebral palsy: An analysis of the evaluation and follow-up from the Institute for Movement Therapy in Budapest, Hungary.* Vol. 4. Eau Claire: University of Wisconsin.

Schor, B. J. 2001. Conductive education, a holistic approach to educating motor disabled children. In *Conductive Education: Occasional Papers*, no. 7: 75–88. Hungary: International Petö Institute.

Sutton, A. 1992. Conductive education: A complex question for psychology. *Educational and Child Psychology* 9 (1): 48–56.

————. 2000. Conductive education: Developing a relevant system. *British Journal of Therapy and Rehabilitation* 7 (3): 130–33.

Websites

Petö Institute: http://www.peto.hu/

Foundation for Conductive Education: http://www.conductive-education.org.uk/

CHRISTINE E. PAWELSKI

Deaf Instruction

The educational needs of hearing-impaired and deaf children involve a range of different strategies and approaches that are based on treating all areas of development affected by hearing loss. According to the **Individuals with Disabilities Education Act** of 1990, the federal definition of the word *deaf* is a hearing loss that adversely affects educational performance and is so severe that the child is impaired in processing linguistic (communication) information through hearing, with or without amplification (hearing aids). The definition of *hearing impairment* is a hearing loss, which may be permanent or fluctuating, that adversely affects a child's educational performance but also allows the child to acquire and access some degree of communication with or without amplification. Students with hearing loss may be significantly impacted in the ability to acquire and use communication systems effectively.

There are four major types of hearing loss. The first is called a *conductive loss*. This type of hearing loss involves disease or obstructions in the outer or middle ear, which impede sound waves from being conducted, or carried, to the inner ear. The second type of loss is *sensorineural loss*, which occurs with damage to the inner ear or the auditory nerve and results in an impediment of the sound waves or message being sent to the brain. The third type is referred to as a *mixed loss*. This type of hearing loss refers to a combination of conductive and sensorineural problems in both the outer and middle ear. *Central auditory processing disorder* is the fourth type of loss. It is present when the child's neural system involved in understanding spoken language is distorted or impaired even though there is no specific physical damage to the ear itself. Children with a central auditory processing disorder may have normal hearing as measured by an audiometer (the device used to test hearing levels), but often have difficulty understanding what they hear.

Hearing impairment or deafness does not directly impair intellectual abilities in the child. However, when compared to same-age peers with normal hearing, the average hearing-impaired student experiences an increased gap in vocabulary growth, concept formation, and complex sentence construction and comprehension over time. Hearing-impaired children can learn to talk, understand speech, and learn language by relying on cues in their environment. Furthermore, if their academic difficulties are identified, they should benefit from inclusion in the regular classroom with special services or modifications made to meet their educational needs. Some services may include speech, language, and auditory training from a speech and language professional. Other services—such as providing sign language interpreters, notetakers, captioned visual aids, or amplification devices, including hearing aids and classroom amplifiers—can also be used in the classroom and in the child's environment. Students can be observed in terms of their ability to understand speech, the ability to progress in school, and the extent to which their abilities are affected by hearing loss.

Families also need to consider the different types of educational approaches for the hearing-impaired and deaf child. An *oral deaf education* approach involves intensive language, speech, and auditory training using residual hearing and amplification devices to be used with the child in order to maximize the child's receptive and expressive communication skills. Speech and language professionals work with the child and the family in the home environment, vocational setting, and the public or private schools or centers. This approach allows the child to have early (preferably before school age) language and auditory intervention that may provide better communication skills needed for school success with **inclusion** in the regular classroom.

An alternative educational program uses a *total communication* approach. This approach uses a variety of methods, including sign language, lip reading, written language, cued speech (special hand gestures and positions cueing the speech sounds), auditory training, speech, pictures, or any method that works for the child in the educational and home setting. Although speech, auditory training, and sign language are encouraged, the emphasis of oral and auditory skills alone is not the main focus. The total communication approach may be used in the regular classroom setting with an interpreter, in a resource room or self-contained classroom for hearing-impaired students, or in a residential or day program at a school for the deaf. It promotes expressive communication skills in any form and works well with children who experience difficulty acquiring oral communication.

The ability to communicate with others and understand the world is crucial to an individual's future psychological and academic success. In addition, the development of self, which is believed to be the foundation for the development of strong self-esteem and self-concept, has both a language and social-emotional component. Further, early identification of hearing loss has been found to be related not only to the language development of children who are deaf or hard of hearing but also to the social-emotional development of these children. Thus, it is important for the child and family to obtain early identification of the hearing loss and to begin language training programs as early as possible. Since the educational needs for hearing-impaired and deaf children may vary with each child, parents are encouraged to actively seek available programs for their hearing-impaired or deaf child in their area and determine which choice is best for the family and child.

Further Reading

Easterbrooks, S., and S. Baker. 2002. Language learning in children who are deaf and hard of hearing. Boston: Allyn & Bacon.

French, M. 1999. Starting with assessment: A developmental approach to deaf children's literacy. Washington, DC: Gallaudet University Pre-College National Mission Programs.

Leslie, L., and J. Caldwell. 2001. *Qualitative reading inventory 3*. New York: Longman.

Marschark, M., and P. E. Spencer. 2003. *Oxford handbook of deaf studies, language, and education*. New York: Oxford University Press.

Pressley, M., and V. Woloshyn, eds. 1995. *Cognitive strategy instruction that really improves children's academic performance*. Cambridge: Brookline Books.

Schirmer, B. R. 2000. Language and literacy development in children who are deaf. Needham Heights, MA: Allyn & Bacon.

TERRY L. REESE AND ANDREW S. DAVIS

Differentiated Instruction

Differentiated instruction is the thoughtful process of considering the learning styles, abilities, challenges, technological needs, diverse backgrounds, and interests of students when planning multidisciplinary units, individual lessons, and field trips. This process assumes that teachers know their students and consider this knowledge as they tailor their lessons, materials, and teaching methods. Teachers who differentiate their instruction are cognizant of the diversity of their students and strive to ensure that each student is able to be a participating member of the classroom community through participation in rich, challenging, and accessible curricula.

Driven by the movement to include students with disabilities in general education curricula, differentiated instruction is based on the premise that all students can be academically challenged with thoughtful preparation on the part of the teacher. This process assumes that teachers align their teaching method, materials, content, and technology simultaneously with their planning of lessons. Differentiated instruction differs greatly from the processes of modifying or adapting curricula, in which a lesson is developed to address the mythical "average student" and the diverse needs of students with special needs are considered afterward. Differentiated instruction supports the **inclusion** of all students, as teachers consider differences in student ability and learning styles to be attributes of diversity rather than identified characteristics used to sort and segregate students.

The process of differentiating instruction for students requires teachers to have a breadth of knowledge about diversity and the willingness to seek resources and admit when they do not know what to do. While many teacher training programs review theories of multiple intelligences—implications of dialect, religious, ethnic, racial, socioeconomic, and ability differences in the classroom—less time is spent on how to consider this diversity in the day-to-day planning of lessons. Using a reflective decision-making model, collaborating with colleagues and parents, and seeking outside resources to further knowledge on specific topics will support classroom teachers in the process of planning to meet the needs of all of their students.

One example of a reflective decision-making model offers a step-by-step process that poses reflective questions and considerations for the teacher when planning lessons. Considerations are made for instructional arrangement, lesson format, style of teaching, lesson goals, classroom environment, materials, modes of participation, support for students, and alternate activities. This model frames a way for teachers to organize their thinking and planning, providing one way to start the differentiating process.

Teachers who differentiate their instruction take the following factors into consideration:

- content (what to teach)
- process (how to teach)
- product (how to assess student learning and performance)
- affect (how students connect their thinking with feelings)
- learning environment (how to design the classroom environment and what instructional approaches to use)

A framework for designing differentiated classrooms can be composed of:

- creating a climate (i.e., safe, nurturing, inclusive, multicultural, challenging, collaborative)

- knowing the learner (i.e., learning styles, strengths/talents, needs)
- assessing the learner (i.e., prior knowledge)
- curricular and standards (i.e., content standards, course objectives)
- instructional approaches (i.e., role play, graphic organizer, use of media, use of **assistive technology**, compare and contrast, grouping, modeling)
- assessing the learning and performance (i.e., quiz, presentation, rubrics for evaluating finished assignments and projects)

Teachers should not think that they are solely responsible for differentiating their instruction. Individual schools and school systems have myriad resources for teachers to access. The most immediate resource is colleagues with varying expertise within the same school building. Collaborating with occupational, physical, and speech therapists, as well as special educators, music and art teachers, teachers of the gifted and talented, school counselors, and other professionals, allows multiple perspectives and experience to be shared when planning lessons. This collaboration process educates everyone involved through shared expertise and enriches the teacher's ability to differentiate instruction, benefiting all of the students in the classroom.

Many school systems provide in-service training or professional development opportunities. This is an opportunity for the school system to support teachers in developing differentiation skills by providing training that focuses on specific skills identified by teachers. For example, many students require the use of assistive technology in order to participate in curricula. These devices are complex, yet teachers are given little training in their use. Identifying outside (of the school system) resources, such as a local university with assistive technology proficiency, can provide instruction for teachers and the technology specialist who work in the school. Training in this manner encourages a continuous collaboration between the teacher and school technology specialist and supports differentiated instruction.

Teachers should also include parents in the collaboration process. In doing so, parents will feel that their knowledge of their child is respected and valued by school personnel. For example, a parent may know which type of visual organizers is most effective in helping their child arrange information and therefore that allows the child to comprehend what was read. Parents contribute long-term knowledge of strategies that support their child's learning and can inform the process of differentiating instruction.

Differentiating instruction does not mean simply modifying or adapting a preexisting curriculum. Rather, it is the planning of instruction while at the time considering students' myriad learning styles, ethnicity, religion, race, socioeconomic status, ability, language, and so on. Teachers, who shape their instruction methods, materials, and environments to reflect the diversity of their students through the differentiating process convey an acceptance of diversity and a desire to value and include all students in rich curricula and the classroom community.

Further Reading

The Process: A Decision-Making Model for Differentiating Instruction
Udvari-Solner, A. 1996. Examining teacher thinking: Constructing a process to design curricular adaptations. *Remedial and Special Education* 17:245–54.

Differentiating Instruction
Biklen, D. P., P. Kluth, and D. M. Straut, eds. 2003a. *Access to academics for all students.* Mahwah, NJ: Lawrence Erlbaum Associates.
Campbell, L., B. Campbell, and D. Dickinson. 1996a. *Teaching and learning through multiple intelligences.* Needham Heights, MA: Simon & Schuster.

Kliewer, C., and D. Landis. 1999. Individualizing literacy instruction for young children with moderate to severe disabilities. *Exceptional Children* 66 (1): 85–100.

Differentiating Instruction via Technology
Erickson, K., and D. Koppenhaver. 1995. Developing a literacy program for children with severe disabilities. *Reading Teacher* 48 (8): 676–84.
Madsen, K. 2003. Providing access to arts education: An illustration through music. In Biklen, Kluth, and Straut 2003a, 155–65.

Differentiating Assessment
Kearns, J., H. Kleinert, and S. Kennedy. 1999. We need not exclude anyone. *Educational Leadership* (March): 33–38.
Kluth, P., and D. M. Straut. 2003. Towards standards for diverse learners: Examining assumptions. In Biklen, Kluth, and Straut 2003a, 33–48.
McColskey, W., and N. McMunn. 2000. Strategies for dealing with high-stakes state tests. *Phi Delta Kappan* (October): 115–20.

Authentic Assessment
Tillotson, J. W., and P. Kluth. 2003. Auto mechanics in the physics lab: Science education for all. In Biklen, Kluth, and Straut 2003a, 133–54.

Collaboration and Co-Teaching
Cook, L., and M. Friend. 1995. Co-teaching: Guidelines for creating effective practices. *Focus on Exceptional Children* 28 (3): 1–16.
Giangreco, M. 1997. Helping or hovering? Effects of instructional assistant proximity on students with disabilities. *Exceptional Children* 64 (1): 7–18.
Kluth, P., D. P. Biklen, and D. M. Straut. 2003b. Academics, access, and action. In Biklen, Kluth, and Straut 2003a, 185–95.
Sapon-Shevin, M., and P. Kluth. 2003. In the pool, on the stage, and at the concert: Access to academics beyond classroom walls. In Biklen, Kluth, and Straut 2003a, 167–83.

Working with Families toward Differentiated Instruction
Knight, T. 2003. Academic access and the family. In Biklen, Kluth, and Straut 2003a, 49–68.

PATRICIA ENGLISH-SAND AND CHUN ZHANG

Direct Instruction

Direct instruction (DI) is a model of effective instruction developed by Siegfried Englemann in the 1960s. It is different from many educational approaches in that the focus is on learning (rather than teaching) via "direct" instruction. In this model, teachers focus on the single task of learning. DI can be distinguished from other models of explicit instruction by its focus on curriculum design and effective instructional delivery. The guiding principles of DI include the idea that every child can learn if carefully taught and that all teachers can be successful when given effective programs containing effective instructional delivery techniques. These principles maintain that teachers are ultimately responsible for their students' learning and that students are not to be blamed for their failure to learn.

The 2004 legislation extending the **Individuals with Disabilities Education Act** (IDEA) required schools and teachers to provide specially designed, research-based programs for students with disabilities. These programs are to provide the type of instruction that will best meet the needs of students and their specific disabilities. IDEA also includes an increased focus on using instructional programs that have been scientifically validated through rigorous scientific experimentation. The use of scientifically based, research-based, and evidence-based interventions with students who have disabilities promotes treatment power and ensures that students will receive the best possible services for their given disabilities. Direct instruction programs are considered scientifically based and have been validated through research and scientific experimentation.

The main goal of DI is to increase student learning by carefully controlling the elements of curriculum design and instructional delivery. In other words, teachers use DI to focus on effective instruction so they can provide more learning in less time. In order to achieve the main goal of DI, many programs possess three major components: program design, organization of instruction, and teacher–student interactions. *Program design* relates to teaching concepts that give the big picture (the main ideas), using clear communication and instructional formats, teaching skills sequentially, and allowing multiple lessons and opportunities over time to solidify new knowledge. The *organization of instruction* centers on increasing success opportunities by providing more instructional time, using flexible skill groupings among students, and conducting continuous evaluation of instructional practice between teachers and students. The component of *teacher–student interactions* includes facilitating active student participation, having teachers encourage students to verbally respond together through the use of cues, and getting teachers to promote active student engagement, that is, time on task. DI encourages teachers to instruct until a level of mastery is achieved, to sequence instruction to minimize errors, and to enhance motivation through the provision of high levels of student success.

There are a variety of programs that utilize DI—in reading, mathematics, writing, spelling, language, and other content areas such as science or history. A typical DI lesson in any of these areas will include unambiguous and carefully planned instruction provided by the teacher. Within a DI program, transitions between activities should be short, and the teacher will often model appropriate learning strategies and provide continual opportunities for students to practice their skills over time. The focus of DI should be on structured student learning based on precise student data. Thus, teachers should focus on educational planning, classroom management, instructional delivery, and student evaluation. For meaningful learning to take place, the educational environment must have clear classroom rules, and he or she must utilize appropriate classroom management techniques. Teachers should actively monitor learning and continuously provide feedback in an effort to teach for understanding. In DI, teachers should display explicit expectations, offer sufficient time to learn, and create a classroom environment that is academic and task oriented.

Direct instruction is supported by a vast body of research, more so than any other commercially available instructional program. As a result, DI is widely used and can be employed for many types of students, including gifted and talented or those with diverse language backgrounds. Additionally, DI is often used with special education or at-risk students, due to the many positive academic gains that have been reported. This scientifically based approach appears promising as the educational enterprise strives to reach all students.

Further Reading

Adams, G. L., and S. Engelmann. 1996. *Research on direct instruction: Twenty-five years beyond DISTAR*. Seattle: Educational Achievement Systems.

D'Amato, R. C., E. Fletcher-Janzen, and C. R. Reynolds, eds. 2005. *The handbook of school neuropsychology*. New York: Wiley.

Marchand-Martella, N. E., R. C. Martella, and K. Ausdemore. 2005. An overview of direct instruction. Seattle: New Horizons for Learning. http://www.newhorizons.org/spneeds/inclusion/teaching/marchand%20martella%20ausdemore.htm.

Reynolds, C. R., and T. B. Gutkin, eds. 1999. *The handbook of school psychology*. 3rd ed. New York: Wiley.

Shaywitz, S. E. 2003. *Overcoming dyslexia: A new and complete science-based program for reading-based problems at any level*. New York: Knopf.

Wolfgang, C. H. 2005. *Solving discipline and classroom management problems: Methods and models for today's teachers*. 6th ed. New York: Wiley.

Websites

Association for Direct Instruction: http://www.adihome.org/phpshop/members.php

JeffLindsay.com: http://www.jefflindsay.com/EducData.shtml

National Institute for Direct Instruction: http://www.nifdi.org/

Vocational and Educational Services for Individuals with Disabilities (VESID), Individuals with Disabilities Education Improvement Act 2004: http://www.vesid.nysed.gov/specialed/idea/home.html

HOWARD B. WAKKINEN AND RIK CARL D'AMATO

Emerging Treatments and Interventions

Since the enactment in the United States of **Public Law 94-142**, the Education for All Handicapped Children Act—later reauthorized in 1990 as the **Individuals with Disabilities Education Act** (IDEA)—special education services have been regulated by law. Legislation, supplemented by court mandates, establishes policies, procedures, and educational supports for children with disabilities and their families. Although these services are meant to meet the needs of children with disabilities and their families, for some parents the options offered by schools and government agencies seem limited or limiting. An undercurrent of discontent among parents and advocates fuels an ongoing quest for different approaches and treatments that may enhance the independence and quality of life for their children with disabilities.

Special education practices, many of them not recognized by established authorities in education and health, bring a measure of hope to parents; they, in turn, challenge established systems, conventional academic training, and treatments. This client-driven challenge to the professions is similar to what in medical circles is known as "alternative and/or complementary" treatment options. These emerging treatments and interventions may incorporate new knowledge or may merely offer a repackaged set of approaches. In some instances, the treatments have a long history of acceptance in other countries. Usually these alternative practices have limited empirical evidence on their side, not necessarily because they hold little value but rather because they represent paradigms of treatment that do not fit easily into conventional research. For parents with children with disabilities, the pursuit and promotion of these interventions often reflect a wish for greater intensity of treatment without necessarily abandoning conventional approaches. One parent explained it this way: "I think that what exists is not bad ... it's just not enough."

The emerging treatments and interventions being explored at this time around the world fall into many categories and can be found across disability groups. In Western societies, there is a growing momentum in the search for new treatments, reflecting dissatisfaction with biomedical science. Modern medicine's narrow definition of what constitutes health and healing, the emphasis on clinical trials, and the focus on somatic-based disease are being challenged by individuals who see a strong connection between states of mind and health and those who believe in spiritual dimensions of health. Therefore, the support for new treatments in special education often falls into alternative medicine or complementary activities that refocus attention on the individual's experiences, their inner resources. In these approaches, there is less concern for outside validation because success is measured on an individual basis. The focus on unique individual experiences renders comparisons across individuals a low priority. Holistic approaches to treatment require the patient or student to take a more active role in its implementation; success hinges on engagement and commitment to treatment by the child and his or her parents.

Many of the emerging treatments and interventions, although lacking empirical validation on specific populations of children, continue to attract families who have experienced little success with conventional treatments but have not given up hope for finding more effective approaches. The perceived quality of an intervention, therefore, is based on personal experiences instead of validated results—i.e., whether a group of "similar" individuals undergoing the treatment has achieved similar measurable results. Lack of empirical validation, however, does not imply that the methods are not effective; they may simply not have been studied by conventional empirical research, or the treatment may not be easily adapted for conventional study.

Since special education is mandated in some form in many countries, along with supportive services and systems of due process, pressure from individuals and families is forcing insurance companies and medical and educational institutions to reexamine their offerings, policies, and professional licensing standards. In the United States and other industrialized countries, there is mounting pressure to include alternative and complementary treatments as legitimate approaches, not merely as controlled experiments or pilots—regardless of the quality of research data available.

What are these emerging practices and interventions? And whom do they serve? It is impossible to accurately list all of them, because new strategies and approaches are constantly gaining recognition and adherents. They range from the therapeutic effects of swimming with dolphins to the use of magnets that may "direct the body's energy flow." Some of these treatments have emerged as a result of expanded research in biosciences, including a more in-depth understanding of human behavior and the recognition of brain plasticity that allows for a greater capacity to change or adapt given appropriate conditions. Both of these developments have opened doors to the consideration of numerous types of creative approaches or procedures.

Internet communication has also greatly added to the emergence of many treatments that can now be shared, implemented, discussed, and improved upon in ways over which the scientific community has no control. The laboratory is being replaced by uncontrolled field experiments. Therefore, more than ever before, emerging practices in special education are being influenced by developments in diverse societies and cultures (e.g., in Eastern Europe, Asia, or Latin America). Adapting and adopting treatments developed in other countries presents not only linguistic challenges in understanding the theories and traditions upon which practices are based but also difficulties in establishing who the qualified professionals are that can deliver the appropriate "treatments." Credentialing and professional preparation remain a unique challenge across disciplines (medicine, physiotherapy, rehabilitation, education), and it is exacerbated across languages, cultures, and continents.

Despite the lack of scientific endorsement and approval by the U.S. Food and Drug Administration, individuals—especially parents—continue to seek alternative treatments and are willing to explore how these approaches and techniques may suit their children with disabilities. In 2002, Christine Pawelski surveyed a special education school serving students with severe physical disabilities and health impairments. She found that 20 percent of the parents had pursued or were interested in pursuing an array of emerging treatments and interventions they had heard about from various sources (e.g., other parents, internet chat rooms, or private organization newsletters). In addition, the majority (62%) felt that if an approach seemed successful for *some* children and was offered to parents as an *alternative* treatment or therapy, then schools should include it as part of the *traditional* program—even if it didn't work for *all* children. An additional 36 percent of parents felt that these alternatives should be made available after school or on weekends within a school environment; if necessary, the parents said they would be willing to pay for them. All of the activities being suggested had a limited research base, were not officially listed as an **Individualized Education Program**-related service support, and would not be delivered by a traditionally credentialed professional. Most were largely promoted through "parent or individual testimonials" and were being viewed as "doing no harm," but could possibly be more effective than standard methods.

Most emerging practices advocated currently are less dependent on drug treatments or diets. They tend to involve efforts to support "natural" remedies, including the manipulation of the body to improve "flow"; are usually directed at involving the whole person (mind and body) in the treatment; and, regardless of the intervention, are usually intensive, requiring consistent movements or regimens over time. The better known and well regarded emerging educational interventions include **Conductive Education** and therapies such as the **Adeli Suit** or Hyperbaric Oxygen Treatment (HBOT). Other treatments that have a sizable following include Cranial Sacral Therapy, Reiki, the Kozijavkin Method, MEDEK, and Feldenkrais. Some of these treatments are elaborations of forms of massage therapy, attempting to retrain or reeducate the central nervous system (CNS) into new patterns of functioning. Many of these approaches share notions of improving muscle tone, control, and coordination through various types of intensive exercises and routines.

Cranial Sacral Therapy is involved in trying to improve the "flow" of the cerebrospinal fluid, with an underlying belief that when this flow is interrupted, it can cause pain all over the body. Good flow of the cerebrospinal fluid is thought to help nourish cells and remove toxins from the body. Restoring the natural flow of cerebrospinal fluid alleviates the symptoms of many disorders, for example, CNS disorders, autism, learning disabilities, and chronic back pain. Therapists apply gentle pressure to stimulate this flow.

Practitioners of *Reiki* also seek to "restore internal harmony to the body," which will then release physical and emotional "blockages" in the body that can cause it not to function optimally. Although coming from different parts of the world and requiring different types of practitioners and handling, both Cranial Sacral Therapy and Reiki seek to achieve the same ends. Individuals with cerebral palsy, or even learning disabilities, report being more relaxed and better able to make eye contact and stay focused; they can often be more verbal following these types of treatments. The implied theory in these approaches is that the flow and ultimate functioning of the entire body has been "opened" and thus is able to allow for improved performance.

The *Kozijavkin Method* (also known as the Intensive Neurophysiological Rehabilitations System), which originated in Ukraine and was developed by Volodymyr Kozijavkin, M.D., and *MEDEK*, developed in Venezuela by Chilean physical therapist Ramon Cuevos, are both extreme forms of physiotherapy. They support attempts to retrain the brain through various intensive types of exercises and muscle strengthening—in the Kozijavkin Method's case, along with added types of activities. They both provide more aggressive approaches to stimulating functioning than standard physiotherapy regimens and seek to improve the gross motor skills, especially of young children with various physical disabilities or neurological problems.

Israel's *Feldenkrais* approach also attempts to reeducate the CNS into new patterns of functioning through a series of sensorimotor balancing activities and manipulations. The desired outcome is to reestablish proper neuromotor patterns and balance in the body. The Kozijavkin Method and MEDEK both involve something being "done" to the individual, whereas the Feldenkrais approach attempts to facilitate greater involvement of the individual in executing the treatment.

A number of emerging treatments and interventions are gaining adherents in the United States, though most lack official sanction and few have access to public or insurance funding. An unknown, but certainly growing, number of children and adults with disabilities or health disorders participate in these alternative treatments in the shadow of the official special education system. Lack of standardization of treatments and the paucity of research contribute to the confusion over why some approaches and not others seem to be effective for some children. The complex nature of the interactions among treatments and the lack of quality control over professional training present difficult dilemmas for the education and health establishments. One of the greatest challenges continues to be who should fund these treatments that are not on the approved list. Unfortunately, unless special education moves to a more individualized outcome approach to treatment, promising emerging treatments and interventions may never reach all the individuals that could benefit from participation in these practices.

Further Reading

Buchanan, P. A., and B. D. Ulrich. 2001. The Feldenkrais method: A dynamic approach to changing motor behavior. *Research Quarterly for Exercise and Sport* 72 (4): 315–23.

Micozzi, M. S., ed. 2001. Fundamentals of complementary and alternative medicine. New York: Churchill Livingstone.

Osborne, A. G. 1996. *Legal issues in special education.* Boston: Allyn & Bacon.

Pawelski, C. E. 2002. The role of conductive education and other complementary practices within mandated U.S. educational services: Is it possible? In *Recent Advances in Conductive Education*, ed. A. Sutton, 90–101. Birmingham, England: Foundation for Conductive Education.

Rosenbaum, P. 2003. Controversial treatment of spasticity: Exploring alternative therapies for motor function in children with cerebral palsy. *Journal of Child Neurology* 18 (1): S89–S94.

CHRISTINE E. PAWELSKI

Facilitated Communication

Facilitated communication (FC) is an alternative communication technique that purports to enable individuals with severe language difficulties to express themselves. One of the many methods of augmentative and alternative communication (AAC), FC's distinct characteristic is its requirement of a facilitator who supports the individual's arm, wrist, hand, or finger in either typing on a keyboard or typewriter or pointing to letters on a letter board. FC has been used with individuals with autism, mental retardation, **traumatic brain injury**, Rett's Syndrome, **Fragile X Syndrome**, pervasive developmental disorder, schizophrenia, and cerebral palsy. The common feature for each of these populations is that, although they are unable to speak, they may have the ability to read and write.

During the 1970s, Australian teacher Rosemary Crossley developed facilitated communication while working to assist people with cerebral palsy to communicate. Syracuse University professor Douglas Biklen brought the technique to the United States in 1989 and popularized its use with individuals with disabilities, specifically autism. In 1992, Dr. Biklen founded the Facilitated Communication Institute (FCI) at Syracuse University. Although FC received considerable attention as an AAC for nonverbal persons demonstrating near-normal levels of expressive communication, questions have been raised regarding whether it reflects statements from the individual or the facilitator. The controversy has not been resolved empirically.

Traditional FC training requires varying levels of physical, communicative, and emotional support. *Physical support* refers to the backward pressure and resistance given by the facilitator to assist the communicator in planning and executing movements. *Communicative support* refers to the goal of independent communication *without* physical support; therefore, physical prompting is faded as quickly as possible. *Emotional support* refers to the encouragement, patience, and maintenance of high expectations provided to the communicator by the facilitator.

Proponents of FC have identified several advantages of this technique. First, FC is easy to establish, because it incorporates assistance and capitalizes on existing skills such as the ability to read and write. Second, physical contact and one-on-one attention may provide a powerful schedule for reinforcement. Third, since FC uses existing functionally equivalent relations (e.g., written words with spoken words or objects) and FC is written English, the listener does not need any special training.

In addition to concerns that facilitators unduly influence the content of the responses, concerns also have been expressed that the use of FC often excludes the implementation of other, perhaps more effective or appropriate interventions. Additionally, allegations of abuse or mistreatment have also arisen.

The disadvantages of FC include the learner's inability to communicate in the natural environment without access to a keyboard and facilitator. Since problems have been noted generalizing to other facilitators and/or parents, there is continued dependence on a trained facilitator, often at a high cost. Another disadvantage is that FC requires that the learner be literate and have the ability to read and write. Typing words involves a complex skill that requires the learner to scan and discriminate among textual stimuli, to spell and type, and to be able to emit a complex chain of behaviors. Finally, there is an extremely slow response time compared to speech or sign, and it is possible to easily lose the listener's attention.

In the 1990s, based on a review of the available empirical information, the American Speech-Language-Hearing Association (ASHA), the American Psychological Association (APA), and the American Association on Mental Retardation (AAMR) all agreed that facilitated communication was ineffective as a scientifically valid technique for individuals. In 1993, the ASHA concluded that FC may have negative consequences if it prevents the use of effective and appropriate treatment, replaces other forms of communication, or leads to false or unsubstantiated allegations of abuse or mistreatment. In 1994, the APA adopted the position that FC was a controversial and unproven communicative procedure with no scientifically demonstrated support for its efficacy. Also in 1994, the AAMR concluded that information obtained via FC should not be used to confirm or deny allegations of abuse or to make diagnostic or treatment decisions.

Despite the controversy, FC continues to be a system used in schools and other settings. Although there is evidence both for and against its use, most research is limited by a lack of scientific rigor. It appears that questions related to the effectiveness of this technique will not be settled until rigorous empirical research is conducted and clear procedures for use are developed.

Further Reading

American Academy of Child and Adolescent Psychiatry. 1994. Policy statement on facilitated communication. *AACAP Newsletter* (February).

American Association on Mental Retardation. 1994. AAMR Board approves policy on facilitated communication. *AAMR News and Notes* 7 (1): 1.

American Psychological Association. 1994. Resolution on facilitated communication. http://www.apa.org/about/division/cpmscientific.html#6.

American Speech-Language-Hearing Association. 1995. Position statement: Facilitated communication. *ASHA* 37 (March): 22.

Jacobson, J. W., J. A. Mulick, and A. A. Schwartz. 1995. A history of facilitated communication. *American Psychologist* 50:750–65.

Sundberg, M. L. 1993. Selecting a response form for nonverbal persons: Facilitated communication, pointing systems, or sign language? *Analysis of Verbal Behavior* 11:99–116.

Websites

Autism Resources: http://www.autism-resources.com/nonfictiontopics/fc.html

Facilitated Communication Institute: http://soeweb.syr.edu/thefci/

LAKISHA LEWIS AND MARYANN SANTOS DE BARONA

Facilities Available for Students with EBD

Students classified as Emotionally and Behaviorally Disturbed (EBD) exhibit maladaptive behaviors that can cause difficulties in learning for them or their peers in the classroom. Oftentimes, various in-school prevention and intervention procedures are unsuccessful at addressing the problem behaviors. In these cases, students may need more treatment, structure, and support than is available in less restrictive settings, such as regular public school, home, and in the community. Children classified as EBD have a higher rate of placement in separate settings than children with other disabilities. Multiple facilities and treatment settings with varied levels of support are available for students within the mental health service system, including emergency and crisis services, traditional clinical hospital inpatient or outpatient services, residential treatment facilities (RTFs), day-treatment programs, and outpatient settings such as community health centers. Services in these facilities vary from traditional to less traditional models. The level of care depends on the child's current functioning, a review of needs and behaviors that occurred within the year, or the degree of reoccurring risk and harm to the child or others involved in the child's life.

Certain behaviors exhibited by a child with EBD can warrant treatment outside a public school or home. Some examples include fire-setting, suicide attempts, sexual offenses, physical aggressions, homicide threats, and severe symptomatic expressions of various mental illnesses such as **depression**, schizophrenia, or bipolar disorder. In these particular cases, a physician or mental health professional conducts a crisis evaluation to determine if a child is in need of hospitalization for psychiatric services or if a community-based crisis intervention (case management, therapeutic foster care, etc.) will adequately meet the child's needs. If the crisis is severe enough and meets admission criteria, then the child needs *acute stabilization*, immediate hospital care to stabilize him or her; general hospitals mostly provide acute psychiatric care. Acute care consists of a medical evaluation, close observation and supervision in a secured setting, general hospital treatment (e.g., medication), and an inpatient diagnostic evaluation to identify treatment needs. The physician treating the child can refer her or him for extended psychiatric services; a child can only be referred to extended psychiatric services (inpatient or residential settings) from the physicians involved with the acute care.

Extended psychiatric services immediately follow acute hospitalization and provide the most intensive and costly treatment of all available long-term facilities.

The child's length of stay should exceed forty-five days, with a six-month limit; however, the length of stay varies according to the child, family, facility, and state. In many cases, if a child cannot return to his or her family or is not ready to attend an alternative setting, then the child attends a residential treatment facility (RTF). However, shortages of beds in many RTFs do not allow for the influx of children from inpatient care, leaving children in psychiatric care for an unknown extended period of time, or until "a bed opens up."

Children referred to extended psychiatric care need twenty-four-hour care, including food, lodging, medical care, and schooling in addition to their treatment plans. These settings are usually "locked down" facilities, meaning that children are unable to move about freely; staff members are given keys to enter or vacate specific areas. The physical limitations of the setting provide a high degree of structure and make this the most restrictive setting. This type of inpatient care is known as a last resort and is reserved for extreme situations after all other attempts have been made to stabilize the child's emotional and behavioral state.

In an inpatient program, the care should address the needs of the child as well as the family with a mix of integrated services. Each individual is given a treatment plan to meet his or her needs and specific problems. A treatment plan can include medication, various therapies (e.g., individual, family, and group), a behavioral plan, life skills training, specialized diets, and an education in accordance with his or her **Individualized Education Program** (IEP). Additionally, a discharge plan provides specific goals, services, and a time line to meet the goals as soon as a child enters the facility. The overall environment should attempt to provide a milieu therapy, which is a structured and therapeutic environment where rules and routines are predictable and appropriate behaviors are consistently reinforced. The success of a program and therapeutic environment is contingent on the quality of direct care that the children receive. Direct care is the multiple care providers that interact directly with the children, families, and their support systems. Unfortunately, the individuals directly involved with the child's care may not always be consistent, and consistency is the most important part of treatment for a child with EBD.

Most twenty-four-hour facilities include a school area where children are given opportunities to learn and socialize. Within the schools are teachers, therapy aides, a school psychologist, and a principal. These students most likely have IEP created by the public school they attended; the IEP dictates what each child needs in order to maximize her or his learning by specifying the necessary accommodations. However, a main difference between a school in a mental health facility and a regular school is that the emphasis is on mental health and ensuring that students are stable. Learning is not the top priority. In fact, instead of coordinating a curriculum in line with state and local standards, many facilities base curricula on a child's IEP, which does not have adequate curriculum information—only academic goals, objectives, and accommodations. This is a problem when elementary- or high school–age children transition back to public school or a less restrictive environment; they are often unprepared. Also, teacher qualifications can differ (according to state) from public school standards and qualifications. Transitioning back to more traditional school settings is often unsuccessful; students usually go to alternative schools, return to juvenile corrections, or drop out, depending on their ages.

Most of the children placed in extended psychiatric care have EBD classifications with major skill deficits, are victims of abuse or neglect, and have family problems. In addition, many of the children are "system kids," meaning they have been in and out of the system most of their lives. This pattern will continue if states and communities do not have sufficient resources to provide continuous and intensive care outside of inpatient facilities.

Further Reading

Crouch, W. 1998. The therapeutic milieu and treatment of emotionally disturbed children: Clinical application. *Clinical Child Psychology and Psychiatry* 3 (1): 115–29.

Georgia. Department of Human Resources. 2003. Levels of care indicator manual. Available at http://www.gahsc.org/nm/pp/2003/locindicatormanual20031104.doc

Pacer Center. 2003. Residential programs for children with emotional and behavioral disorders: Things for parents to consider. http://www.pacer.org/parent/php/PHP-c85.pdf

Pottick, K. J., et al. Answers to key policy questions. *Latest findings in children's mental health* 2 (1): 2. Available at http://www.aecf.org/publications/data/issue_brief3.pdf

Wyoming. Department of Family Services. 1998. Psychiatric care (for children). In *Family Services Manual*, vol. 7, chap. 2, sec. D. Available at http://dfsweb.state.wy.us/childprotection/cpmanual.html

DANA FREED

Functional Behavioral Assessment

Functional Behavioral Assessment (FBA) is a method for understanding and identifying the primary cause and function of a student's behavior in relationship to the environment in which it occurs. It also acts as a tool for gathering information regarding factors that motivate and sustain a particular behavior. The objective of an FBA is to develop individually tailored interventions that address specific problem behaviors. FBAs should be written in clear and simple language so they are accessible to all individuals in a child's life.

In 1997, amendments were made to the **Individual with Disabilities Education Act** to provide more protection for students with disabilities from school-based disciplinary tactics that do not take the child's individual needs into account. In fact, procedures involved in these amendments encourage schools to provide positive behavior supports prior to or in place of punishment. Currently, local education agencies are mandated to conduct FBAs and to develop Behavioral Intervention Plans (BIPs) for students with disabilities whose challenging behaviors result in out-of-school suspensions greater than ten consecutive days or who are assigned a new placement; the FBA must be conducted within ten school days of the initial removal from school. Functional Behavioral Assessments are also included in comprehensive evaluations and triennial reevaluations for students with behavior problems, **Section 504** accommodation plans, and prereferral intervention processes. FBAs are also used to help determine eligibility for special education services for students who exhibit behaviors that infringe on their classroom learning or the learning of their peers.

A series of steps needs to be executed to effectively conduct an FBA. Ideally an FBA should be implemented by a group of people—a general education teacher, a special education teacher, parents, a school psychologist, an administrator, and possibly the child—rather than by one individual; within the group, one qualified person who understands the concept of an FBA should assign roles and lead the others through the process. However, most often, a school psychologist conducts the process with only the teacher.

A large part of an FBA is identifying the student's behavior that is most problematic and challenging. The best way to learn which behavior should be targeted is to interview the referring teacher and find out all of the problem behaviors exhibited by the student. An FBA should tackle one behavior at a time, usually beginning with the most challenging one. In order to fully understand the function of the behavior, the interviewer should also inquire about the physical environments, instructional expectations, and behavioral expectations that exist when the behavior occurs. The target behavior needs to be described in a way that is easily understood, objective, and observable. For example, a behavior cannot be described as "disruptive"; instead, the description should specify what it is about the behavior that is disruptive, such as "hits peers" or "calls out while the teacher is talking." The behavior should be specific, as opposed to a behavioral concept, which can lead teachers to negatively label children and say, "This student is always disruptive." By focusing on specific behaviors, teachers or others involved with the child can learn to separate the behavior from the child.

After identifying and describing the target behavior, it is important to review files and previous interventions already attempted with the student. All people involved with the child should be interviewed to obtain as much information as possible. Physical settings, class schedules, curricula, and the teacher's style should be observed and evaluated to see if they influence the child's behavior. Finally, the child should be directly observed to decipher the function or need of the behavior and to collect data on the frequency, intensity, duration, antecedents, and consequences of the target behavior. Functions or reasons of a behavior usually involve avoidance of a task or situation, control over people or events, and/or attention from adults or peers.

Following the previously noted steps, the individual conducting the FBA will develop a hypothesis—a brief summary sentence that describes the external factors contributing to the existence and frequency of the problem behavior. The hypothesis will clearly state why the behavior occurs and will become the basis for formulating a BIP intended to change or lessen the maladaptive behavior and replace it with a more appropriate and positive behavior. The BIP is an attempt to manipulate the antecedents that sustain the behavior, make modifications to the existing curriculum or instructional implementation, alter physical settings in which the behavior occurs, and teach replacement behaviors. The intervention must be easy to do and age-appropriate, and individuals implementing the plan should be knowledgeable and comfortable with it. Once the BIP is in effect, the intervention should be evaluated to determine its effectiveness and then altered, if necessary.

The ultimate goal of an FBA is to modify the problem behavior of a child with disabilities to improve academic successes. However, another important outcome of an FBA is to educate the teacher on understanding causes and functions of problem behaviors in children. If teachers are able to internalize the underlying concepts of an FBA, they can understand the various functions behaviors serve and respond effectively and independently.

Further Reading

Center for Effective Collaboration and Practice. 2001. *Functional behavioral assessment.* Retrieved on May 15, 2006. http://cecp.air.org/fba/

Conroy, M., C. Liaupsin, J. McIntyrem, M. Nelson, L. Payne, and T. Scott. 2005. An examination of the relation between functional behavioral assessment and selected intervention strategies with school based teams. *Journal of Positive Behavior Interventions* 7:205–15.

Cox, C., P. Hilvitz, M. McConnell, and D. Thomas. 2001. *Functional behavioral assessment: A systematic process for assessment and intervention in general and special education classrooms.* Denver: Love.

Lehigh University. Center for Promoting Research to Practice. N.d. Summary of functional behavior assessment to help decrease problem behavior. http://www.lehigh.edu/projectreach/research/funct-behavior-asses.htm

Van Acker, R., and R. Gable. 2005. Are we on the right course? Lessons learned about current FBA/BIP practices in schools. *Journal of Behavioral Education* 14:35–56.

DANA FREED

Peer-Assisted Learning

Learning is a social endeavor. Friends help each other learn, shape each other's enjoyment of school, and encourage each other to stay in school and do well there (Doll 1996). When learning with friends, students can ask each other for help, learn new information or skills from each other, and help each other through difficult work. Alternatively, students who are disliked by peers often learn in isolation, without the assistance and encouragement of friends. Too often, children with disabilities are among those isolated students, and so miss out on the benefits of having friends that help them learn.

Peer-assisted learning (PAL) is an instructional strategy that promotes classroom friendships at the same time that it strengthens students' academic achievement. Similar to cooperative learning, some PAL students act as tutors for other students in their classes, helping classmates acquire both knowledge and skills (Topping 2002; Topping and Ehly 1998). To do this, PAL uses carefully planned activities that involve students in frequent verbal discussions with each other and prompts tutoring students to give learning students immediate and useful feedback about their performance.

In some PAL classrooms, certain students are assigned to be tutors while others are assigned to learn from the tutors. Other classrooms use reciprocal peer tutoring, a special form of PAL in which classmates switch back and forth between being tutors and learners. PAL strategies were originally designed to improve reading skills for elementary students. Since then, PAL has been extended to different subjects (e.g., math, thinking, writing, spelling, and science) as well as to students in preschool and secondary school classrooms and students with academic and behavioral difficulties.

PAL tutors model the correct way to perform an unfamiliar task, explain the steps for completing a problem, praise correct responses, and explain how to fix incorrect responses (Fuchs, Fuchs, and Burish 2000; Topping 2002). Using PAL procedures, pairs of classmates read aloud to each other and complete comprehension activities. For example, in Partner Reading, each student reads aloud for five minutes, with the better reader going first. During Paragraph Shrinking, the pair stops reading at the end of each paragraph and describes the main idea. They ask each other questions such as "What was the paragraph mainly about?" and "What was the most important thing we learned?" In Prediction Relay, the learner predicts what will come next in the passage and then reads on to confirm or disconfirm the predictions. In all three activities, when learners make errors, tutors help them to identify the error and direct the learners to repeat the correct word, reread the sentence correctly, skim the paragraph, or think of a better prediction.

PAL is based on the theories of Jean Piaget, Lev Vygotsky, and Barbara Rogoff, all of whom believed that learning occurs best through interactions with peers (Topping and Ehly 1998; Rohrbeck et al. 2003). Piaget believed that different children understand problems in different ways and, when they talk together, each of them is prompted to examine their own understanding, elaborate their thinking, and justify their conclusions. Vygotsky added that conversations with a more experienced peer are most effective, because the peer's instruction and guidance is only slightly more advanced than that of the learner and so is within the range of skills that the learner is ready to master. Rogoff emphasized that peers use the same language and have had similar problems, and so they model effective learning strategies for each other.

The benefits of PAL strategies are well documented (Fuchs, Fuchs, and Burish 2000; Topping and Ehly 1998). They have been shown to improve reading fluency and reading comprehension for elementary and high school students; to improve early reading and prereading skills of first-grade students; to improve math skills of elementary students with and without learning disabilities; and to increase the phonics skills of kindergarten students with behavior disabilities. Just as important,

PAL activities improved the relationships between students with learning disabilities and their classmates (Fuchs et al. 2002).

Despite the many benefits of PAL strategies, some disadvantages have been described (Maheady 1998). Teachers must spend extra time systematically training students to be PAL tutors, and they must keep checking to make sure that the tutors are using good tutoring practices. It also takes time for teachers to adapt curricular objectives and materials to fit a peer-teaching format. In some cases, the pace of student learning may be slower than if the teacher simply provided instruction in traditional ways. It takes a special effort to design PAL activities so that more experienced students have enough opportunities to learn more challenging content. Finally, students' sometimes elect not to participate in PAL because they find it too difficult to do or too aversive to learn from classmates.

References

Doll, B. 1996. Children without friends: Implications for practice and policy. *School Psychology Review* 25:165–83.

Fuchs, D., L. S. Fuchs, and P. Burish. 2000. Peer-assisted learning strategies: An evidence-based practice to promote reading achievement. *Learning Disabilities Research and Practice* 15 (2): 85–91.

Fuchs, D., L. S. Fuchs, P. G. Mathes, and E. A. Martinez. 2002. Preliminary evidence on the social standing of students with learning disabilities in PALS and no-PALS classrooms. *Learning Disabilities Research and Practice* 17 (4): 205–15.

Maheady, L. 1998. Advantages and disadvantages of peer-assisted learning strategies. In *Peer-assisted learning*, ed. K. J. Topping and S. W. Ehly, 45–65. Mahwah, NJ: Lawrence Erlbaum Associates.

Rohrbeck, C. A., M. D. Ginsburg-Block, J. W. Fantuzzo, and T. R. Miller. 2003. Peer-assisted learning interventions with elementary school students: A meta-analytic review. *Journal of Educational Psychology* 95 (2): 240–57.

Topping, K. 2002. Peer and parent assisted learning. In *Advances in psychology research*, vol. 13, ed. S. P. Shohov, 109–28. Hauppauge, NY: Nova Science.

Topping, K., and S. Ehly, eds. 1998. *Peer-assisted learning*. Mahwah, NJ: Lawrence Erlbaum Associates.

Further Reading

Fuchs, D., L. S. Fuchs, A. Tompson, E. Sevenson, L. Yen, S. L. Otaiba, N. Yang, K. N. McMaster, K. Prentice, S. Kaxdan, and L. Saenz. 2001. Peer-assisted learning strategies in reading: Extension for kindergarten, first grade, and high school. *Remedial and Special Education* 22 (1): 15–21.

Topping, K. J., and S. W Ehly. 2001. Peer assisted learning: A framework for consultation. *Journal of Educational and Psychological Consultation* 12 (2): 113–32.

Website

Vanderbilt Kennedy Center for Research on Human Development: http://kc.vanderbilt.edu/kennedy/pals/

BETH DOLL AND M. KELLY HAACK

Response to Intervention

Response to intervention (RTI) is a systematic and data-based decision-making process for identifying, preventing, and resolving students' academic or behavioral challenges. RTI is both an individualized and a comprehensive student-centered assessment and intervention model that uses a problem-solving approach to identify and address students' learning and behavioral difficulties.

The new **Individuals with Disabilities Education Act** (IDEA) of 2004 (PL 108-446) has dramatically changed the use of the IQ–achievement discrepancy formula in the identification of Specific Learning Disabilities. The local educational agencies (LEAs) are not required to use a severe discrepancy between achievement and intellectual ability; instead, RTI can be considered as an alternative. The LEAs may thus use a process to determine if a child responds adequately to scientific, research-based intervention for the identification of children with Specific Learning Disabilities.

In 2003, the National Association for School Psychology (NASP) recommended that the ability–achievement discrepancy requirement be replaced with a multitiered model based on two criteria: significantly low underachievement and insufficient response to intervention. Tier 1 is the provision of high-quality, research-based instruction for all students within the general education setting. Tier 2 support includes intensive interventions targeted toward students who are not progressing at a rate comparable with their grades and settings. Before evaluation for special education by a multidisciplinary team is considered, the first two tiers of supports within the general education classroom would be required. Only students who continue to demonstrate low achievement with insufficient response to research-based interventions at the Tier 2 level would then be referred for a multidisciplinary team evaluation (Tier 3) to determine their need for special education services.

In the Tier 1 process, high-quality instruction needs to be provided to all students in the general education classroom, while in the Tier 2 process, individualized intervention is provided to some students who exhibit difficulties despite the high-quality instruction. During the Tier 2 phase, the rate and extent of RTI are documented for monitoring student performance. If students continue to struggle significantly despite high-quality instruction and intensive individualized interventions and their RTI is minimal, they will be referred to a multidisciplinary team for further evaluation to determine eligibility for special education (Tier 3). The criteria for determining eligibility for special education should include the following:

- large performance gaps from peer or grade levels in one or more relevant domains of achievement using peer comparisons and benchmarks toward **high-stakes testing**
- low rate of learning or low rate of RTI compared to peers despite high-quality interventions
- exclusion of factors (e.g., English as a second language) that affect students' learning
- documented adverse impact of events or situations (poor health, divorce of parents, etc.) on educational performance
- documented need for specially designed instruction (e.g., documentation of rate of response to individually designed and consistently implemented intensive intervention)

This problem-solving model is useful in both eligibility determination and special education intervention design, ensuring a close integration of assessment and intervention.

Eligibility for special education services should be considered only when there is a determination that the learning difficulties are a result of a disability rather than limited exposure to curriculum; linguistic or cultural differences; or problems that are primarily the result of visual, hearing, or motor disabilities, mental retardation, emotional disturbance, or environmental, cultural, or economic disadvantages. Only when these exclusionary factors are ruled out as the primary causes of the learning difficulties and the students remain unresponsive to interventions that are validated and consistently implemented should the students be considered to have a disability.

Although this RTI model was initially proposed specifically for identifying and intervening for students with Specific Learning Disabilities, researchers and practitioners have been trying to apply such a model with children with other disabilities (e.g., emotional and behavioral disorders, or language impairments). The multiple tiers of academic and behavioral interventions are designed to prevent problems through effective instruction to all children, early identification and intervention for children who exhibit emerging problems, determination of eligibility for services, and determination of the need for special education for those who do not respond to intensive interventions adequately. Clearly the emphasis of these efforts is on early identification, prevention, and intervention.

A problem-solving model such as RTI is often controversial. The implementation of such a model requires school-wide intervention that has the potential to benefit all students and to reduce the possibility of excessive referrals and placements of students in special education. Compared with other options and the current special education system, this problem-solving model requires the most change from current practices and the most comprehensive education reform at state education agencies and LEAs, which will require efforts from the entire education community.

Further Reading

Bradley, R., and L. Danielson. 2004. The Office of Special Education Program's LD initiative: A context for inquiry and consensus. *Learning Disability Quarterly* 27 (4): 186–88.

Deshler, D. D., D. F. Mellard, J. M. Tollefson, and S. E. Byrd. 2005. Research topics in responsiveness to intervention: Introduction to the special series. *Journal of Learning Disabilities* 38 (6): 483–84.

Fuchs, D., and L. S. Fuchs. 2006. Introduction to response to intervention: What, why, and how valid is it? *Reading Research Quarterly* 41 (1): 92–99.

Gersten, R., and J. A. Edomono. 2006. RIT (response to intervention): Rethinking special education for students with reading difficulties (yet again). *Reading Research Quarterly* 41 (1): 99–108.

Mastropieri, M. A., and T. E. Scruggs. 2005. Feasibility and consequences of response to intervention: Examination of the issues and scientific evidence as a model for the identification of individuals with learning disabilities. *Journal of Learning Disabilities* 38 (6): 525–31.

National Association of School Psychologists. 2003. NASP recommendations: LD eligibility and identification for IDEA reauthorization. *Communique* 31 (8): 1–6.

Reschly, D. J. 2005. Learning disabilities identification: Primary intervention, secondary intervention, and then what? *Journal of Learning Disabilities* 38 (6): 510–15.

Websites

Council for Exceptional Children: http://www.cec.sped.org/
National Association of School Psychologists: http://www.nasponline.org/
National Research Center on Learning Disabilities: http://www.nrcld.org/html/research/rti/concepts.html

CHUN ZHANG

Self-Contained Classrooms

General education is based on the assumption that children in regular education classroom settings working with regular education teachers learn approximately a year of material with instruction minimally modified to meet the needs of an average child. Thus, the majority of children in the educational enterprise receive regular education services as they progress from grade to grade. This is not typically the case in special education programs.

Special education services fall along what is often called a *cascade* (or *continuum*) *of services* model. Where a child falls on the continuum is dependent on the needs of the individual child in special education. At one end of the continuum, they may spend an entire day in a special education classroom, requiring the provision of needs-based services; at the other end of the continuum, the child in special education may spend the entire day in a regular education classroom, with individualization provided by the regular education teacher (after consulting with a special education teacher).

Self-contained classrooms are utilized in special education when a student with a disability is *not* able to benefit from instruction in the regular education classroom. Self-contained special education classes enroll approximately fifteen or fewer students at one time with particular characteristics or needs. Generally, the teacher has been trained as a special educator and provides all or most of the instruction. In a self-contained classroom, the curriculum can be created to meet the distinctive needs of students and can accommodate traditional subject matter, such as reading, arithmetic, science, health, and other school subjects. The curriculum can also be organized psychologically or behaviorally, so individual students can learn to control and modify their own behavior. Additional classroom activities often focus on developing a framework for solving life problems, such as interactions with family, using leisure time, managing money, and understanding health and safety issues. In the main, the curriculum should be organized around the development and practice of basic life skill behaviors.

The role of the teacher in a self-contained classroom revolves around being responsive to a number of student concerns. The teacher must have a good grasp of each student's ability level as it varies across areas such that lessons correlate to students' knowledge and skills, enabling them to make relevant associations. The teacher must structure the learning situation, reduce distractions, and present material clearly and sequentially, utilizing positive reinforcement throughout. When the student makes an incorrect response, the teacher should encourage the student and reevaluate whether he or she has overestimated the student's ability or behavior, parts of the lesson were confusing, or the student is not ready to engage in that particular learning situation and needs more preparation.

In severe cases, self-contained classrooms may be located at a Residential Treatment Center (RTC) and these children may spend evenings in the RTC as well as their school days. Children are frequently placed in a residential setting when they are a danger to themselves or others. Children that do well in a RTC may be reassigned to a self-contained day-treatment program run by a public school and, if needed, may spend their nights in a group home or with parents or legal guardians. Often such self-contained day-treatment programs are located not within the public schools, but in the community at large.

Students who have profited from day-treatment programs may be moved to self-contained classrooms located within their local public schools. Not all school buildings offer self-contained classrooms, but a few elementary schools may share a self-contained program located in one of the schools. Students assigned to self-contained classes usually spend most or all of the school day separated from their nondisabled peers. Such students interact with children without disabilities only at certain times, such as during lunch, recess, or perhaps art and music.

In cases where children do not require full-time placement in a separate classroom, students are in the regular classrooms for the majority of the school day but go to a special education resource room for specialized instruction for part of each school day. Resource room instruction is provided either individually or in small groups. Students needing less individualized educational support receive a prescribed program under the direction of the regular classroom teacher, along with supplementary instruction and related services within the regular classroom. A special educator and/or a paraeducator provides these supplemental instruction and services.

Children requiring a minimal level of educational support services receive a prescribed program under the direction of the regular education teacher. Special educators support the regular education teacher by providing ongoing consultation on how to most effectively help students achieve in the classroom. Finally, students with the least severe disabilities receive a prescribed program under the direction of the regular education teacher. The greatest number of children with disabilities are served at this end of the continuum.

Special education law requires placement of students with disabilities in the least restrictive environment. That is, these students should be separated as little as possible from their nondisabled classmates and from home, family, and community. It has been pointed out, however, that greater restriction of the physical environment does not necessarily mean greater restriction of psychological freedom or human potential. In fact, it is conceivable that some students could be *more* restricted in the long run in a regular class where they are rejected by others and fail to learn necessary skills than in a separate class where they can learn and be happy. Such students may benefit from the services offered through the use of a self-contained classroom.

Some special educators believe that the continuum of services should be dismantled and all students with disabilities placed in regular classrooms. Such individuals support the notion of *full* **inclusion**. Advocates of full inclusion contend that the continuum-of-services model promotes restrictive environments and infringes on children's rights. Many special educators support the responsible inclusion of students with disabilities in regular classrooms and the development and evaluation of new models for working more cooperatively with general educators to serve all students. Most special educators, however, are not in favor of dismantling the continuum of services.

The Council for Exceptional Children, the major professional organization in special education, supports inclusion as a *meaningful goal* to be pursued by schools but contends that the continuum-of-services and program options must be maintained and that **Individualized Education Program** planning teams must make placement decisions based on the student's individual educational needs. To appropriately serve all students, a full range of special education services are required, ranging from an RTC at one end of the continuum to a regular education classroom at the other end. Self-contained classrooms are a critical part of any comprehensive special education service model.

There appears to be no substitute for case-by-case determination by a comprehensive multidisciplinary team, which should determine the best placement of each student with a disability. Based on current research, intensive evidence-based instruction is required for students with disabilities if they are to learn. Data must be presented about learning and behavior in an effort to demonstrate that services in less-restrictive environments have not succeeded in meeting student needs. Intensive educational and psychological services will, at times, need to be delivered in separate special education settings, such as resource rooms or self-contained classrooms.

Further Reading

Culatta, R. A., J. R. Tompkins, and M. G. Werts. 2003. *Fundamentals of special education.* 2nd ed. Columbus, OH: Merrill/Prentice Hall.

Hallahan, D. P., and J. M. Kauffman. 2003. *Exceptional learners: Introduction to special education.* 9th ed. Boston: Allyn & Bacon.

Heward, W. L. 2003. *Exceptional children: An introduction to special education.* 7th ed. Columbus, OH: Merrill/Prentice Hall.

Skalski, A. K. 2000. *Guidebook for determining the eligibility of students with significant identifiable emotional disability.* Denver: Colorado Department of Education, Special Education Services Unit. Available at http://www.cde.state.co.us/cdesped/download/pdf/sied.pdf

Websites

Council for Exceptional Children: http://www.cec.sped.org/

National Institute of Mental Health: http://www.nimh.nih.gov/

U.S. Department of Education, Office of Special Education and Rehabilitative Services: http://www.ed.gov/about/offices/list/osers/index.html?src=mr

AMANDA H. STOECKEL AND RIK CARL D'AMATO

Student-Centered Planning

Person- or student-centered planning is about focusing on the individual when planning for his or her future. In doing so, the individual's interests, strengths, passions, and dreams become vital to the process. Student-centered planning takes into account the student's current situation, including school, community, and home life activities. Using this information, along with the student's own dreams and visions for the future, long-range goals are developed. These are then broken down into short-term and long-term steps to facilitate goal attainment. A major objective of student-centered planning is to find the community supports that will help students achieve their dreams and reach their goals. These supports can include community people, services, and agencies for friendship, support, and community networking.

Student-centered planning should not be confused with annual reviews or **Individualized Education Program** (IEP) meetings. Past practices have demonstrated a "deficit model," where IEP meetings frequently focused on the students' weaknesses rather than their strengths and how to capitalize on those strengths. Often students and families were either not involved in this process or had a minimal role. In contrast, the purpose of student-centered planning is to involve all persons important to the student and to focus on the student's strengths and interests.

The most important person on the student-centered planning team is, of course, the student. The other members of the team in student-centered planning should be those individuals who know the student best, such as the student's family, educational support personnel, and agency representatives. In addition, teams may also include employers, friends, and anyone who can support the student in pursuing her or his dream. These individuals can and should be invited to participate in the planning process by the student. It is important to note that although the case manager is required to attend the IEP meeting, he or she is not required to be present at a student-centered planning meeting. Teams that believe in student-centered planning understand that the most important person on the team is the individual they are supporting and commit to assisting that student.

The first step in student-centered planning is finding out what the student's strengths, interests, preferences, and vision for the future are. Once this vision is established, it should be used not only to guide the development of the IEP but also to make sure school experiences, both academic and extracurricular, address this vision. Student-centered planning is about the journey. One method that has been used extensively for this process is called MAPs or Making Action Plans (see Paul V. Sherlock Center on Disabilities n.d.).

Since the most important person in student-centered planning is the student, the individual needs to be taught and encouraged to actively participate and even to lead the planning meetings. One way for teams to help is to teach the student self-advocacy skills. Students who are effective self-advocates can articulate their own dreams, desires, passions, interests, and visions for the future. The team should then listen to the student and provide the support necessary for the student to achieve his or her goals. For example, one student classified with **Asperger's Syndrome** had difficulty socializing and relating to peers his own age, but was a college-bound "A" student. The child's study team tried to encourage him to get more involved in mainstream high school activities. During his planning meeting, he articulated his future goal in college of learning how to be a research librarian. The student's parents supported this goal wholeheartedly. Instead of trying to put the student in uncomfortable social situations, the team's responsibility was then to link the student with the appropriate resources, agencies, and supports that would assist him in finding an appropriate college match and aide in preparing for post-secondary schooling.

Student-centered planning is not an exclusive practice. The planning process is suitable for all students and adults with disabilities functioning at all levels. Student-centered planning is a process that extends through the lifetime of a person. It should be a continuous journey, not a once-a-year discussion at the student's annual IEP meeting.

Reference

Paul V. Sherlock Center on Disabilities. N.d. Making action plans: Student centered transitional planning. http://www.ric.edu/uap/publications/maps.pdf

Further Reading

Field, S. 1997. *A practical guide for teaching self-determination*. New York: Council for Exceptional Children, Division on Career Development and Transition.

Sands, D. J., and M. Wehmeyer. 1996. *Self-determination across the lifespan: Independence and choice for people with disabilities*. Baltimore: Brookes.

Wehmeyer, M., and D. J. Sands. 1998. *Making it happen: Student involvement in education planning, decision making, and instruction*. Baltimore: Brookes.

Websites

Cornell University, Employment and Disability Institute: http://www.ilr.cornell.edu/ped/tsal/pcp/courses.html

Inclusion.com: http://www.inclusion.com/

Training Resource Network: http://www.trninc.com/pcpresources.html

TRACY AMERMAN

Time-Out

Time-out is a behavior modification technique that involves the removal of an individual from sources of reinforcement (i.e., rewards that increase a particular behavior) for a specific period of time. Time-outs are utilized across various settings, particularly throughout the education system and with special education populations, as a means of reducing undesirable behavior. Depending on the degree to which a child's behavior is deemed inappropriate, she or he is placed in a different, less rewarding setting for a specified amount of time. Time-out is also commonly known as an "extinction procedure." During extinction, the desired activity is removed, with the hope that this will cause the misbehavior to stop. Opponents of the time-out argue that this is a form of punishment, whereby the child is denied the opportunity to remain in his or her current setting.

The time-out environment must be less reinforcing than the time-in environment. It is important that the environment or activity from which the learner is removed be a desirable one, because taking the child out of a disagreeable situation may be counterproductive. For example, if a student does not want to be in the classroom during a test and is displaying undesirable behaviors, removing the student (e.g., sending her or him to the office), may actually be reinforcing and could potentially increase the student's problem behavior. Since a time-out interrupts the child's instructional experience, it is a relatively aversive behavior reduction technique, especially when misused. Therefore, it should not be the only method used to reduce inappropriate behaviors.

It has been suggested that time-out periods for children in special education should be between two and eight minutes, using a rule of thumb of approximately one minute per year of age (e.g., age three = three minutes of time-out, but never exceeding eight minutes). It is essential to use a timer to ensure consistency in order for the time-out to be effective. There are several types of time-out procedures that can be categorized according to their level of restriction. When choosing a time-out procedure, it is important to select the option that allows the child to remain in the educational setting whenever possible.

Nonexclusion Time-out

In a nonexclusion time-out, the child remains in the instructional setting but is temporarily prevented from taking part in reinforcing activities. All attention and reinforcement are removed when the undesired behavior occurs. *Planned ignoring* is one type of nonexclusion time-out, in which all forms of social attention are removed. In planned ignoring, the teacher withholds reinforcement by refraining from physical, verbal, or visual interactions with the child. For example, a teacher may ignore a student for a short period of time directly after the inappropriate behavior occurs. Another type of nonexclusion time-out is the *removal of specific reinforcers* such as food, toys, or materials that the child finds pleasurable. For example, if a child is throwing candy, the caregiver can remove that candy for a specified period of time.

Exclusion Time-out

In an exclusion time-out, by contrast, the student is physically removed from a reinforcing environment and cannot otherwise participate in the activities. One example of an exclusion time-out is *contingent observation*. This procedure involves moving the student away from the activity in which the misbehavior occurred. The student continues to remain in the area of the activity, but is not otherwise allowed to participate. During this type of time-out, the student observes the other children behaving appropriately. After a short time, the student is allowed to return to the group. Another type of exclusionary time out is *exclusion*. In this procedure, the student is removed entirely from the activity and sent to a designated time-out area within the classroom but away from the group. The student is prohibited from both participating and watching the rest of the group. *Isolation/seclusion* is a third type of exclusionary time-out and is considered to be the most restrictive time-out procedure. In this type of time-out, the student is removed entirely from the setting to a separate time-out area. The time-out area should be a room or space entirely secluded from the group. An example of this would be to send the child to a designated area in the school that is less reinforcing, such as the hallway or an unoccupied classroom. The area should not be reinforcing, but neither should it be too confining, poorly ventilated, or inadequately lit. It is important to note that when utilizing either an exclusion or isolation/seclusion time-out procedure, an adult must supervise the student at all times without providing any reinforcement.

When implementing a time-out, there are several important guidelines to consider. First, it is important for the student to know the reason for the time-out and how long it will last. It is also important that all reinforcement be removed during this time, including attention from peers. The time-out area be neither reinforcing (e.g., next to a TV) nor excessively aversive (e.g., in a dark, scary, or isolated room). After the time-out procedure is complete, the child is free to resume activities. Be sure to praise the child if he or she stops the behavior *before* a time-out is imposed.

Second, use of time-outs should continue only if they are successful in reducing inappropriate behavior. The child's behavior should be monitored in order to determine the procedure's effectiveness, observing whether the undesirable behavior has increased, decreased, or stayed the same. It is important to note that, as with any behavior modification technique, the undesired behavior often increases before it decreases. Thus, it may be necessary to monitor a behavior for several days before making any necessary changes.

Finally, excessive and prolonged use of time-outs in an educational setting may violate the child's legal right to receiving an appropriate education. Teachers should always adhere to local and state policies regarding time-outs. This rather simple but powerful procedure must be utilized with great care and should be one of many child management techniques used to modify behavior.

Further Reading

Harlan, J. C., and S. T. Rowland. 2002. *Behavior management strategies for teachers: Achieving instructional effectiveness, student success, and student motivation: Every teacher and any student can!* 2nd ed. Springfield, IL: Thomas.

Schloss, P. J., and M. A. Smith. 1994. *Applied behavior analysis in the classroom*. Needham Heights, MA: Allyn & Bacon.

Wolfgang, C. H. 2005. *Solving discipline and classroom management problems: Methods and models for today's teachers*. 6th ed. New York: Wiley.

Yang, A., and R. S. Charney. N.d. Buddy teachers: Lending a hand to keep time-out positive and productive. *Responsive Classroom* 17 (1). Available at http://www.responsiveclassroom.org/newsletter/17_1NL_1.asp

Zirpoli, T. J. 2005. *Behavior management: Applications for teachers*. 4th ed. Upper Saddle River, NJ: Pearson Education.

Websites

Center for Effective Parenting: http://www.parenting-ed.org/
Intervention Central: http://www.interventioncentral.org/

STEPHANIE R. SINCO AND RIK CARL D'AMATO

Treatment of the Emotionally and Behaviorally Disturbed

The term *Emotionally and Behaviorally Disturbed* (EBD) is used by school systems to classify students who demonstrate an array of mental health problems and/or behavioral disorders. A child classified with EBD might experience difficulties maintaining friendships or progressing academically and may be perceived in a negative light by teachers or family members unaware that the child's maladaptive behavior is, indeed, a health problem. Treatment is one of the most challenging aspects of EBD and typically focuses on changing the problem behaviors to more appropriate ones.

With few exceptions, treatment of children with EBD usually takes place within the school. Selecting an appropriate treatment involves multiple factors, given the complexities inherent in the disorder and the many people involved in the treatment plan: family members, teachers, the school psychologist, pediatricians, psychiatrists, and so on. Currently, treatment usually involves a combination of interventions: individual and group counseling, social skills training, behavioral management interventions, consultation with families and agencies, medication, and/or modifications to the child's academic program. To ensure success, each individual involved in the treatment plan must be consistent and in agreement, the plan should be regularly monitored and evaluated to determine its effectiveness, and *changes must be made if necessary.*

Children classified with EBD are usually mandated for psychological or counseling services according to their **Individualized Educational Program**. Various types of therapies are used, including family, cognitive-behavioral, group, interpersonal, and supportive therapy. These therapies incorporate strategies for understanding feelings, thoughts, and behaviors; learning self-control; and improving self-esteem, mostly through a talking modality. Family therapy is used to address any problems within the family that may be contributing to the child's emotional or behavioral difficulties. Families also need to be made aware that emotions and behaviors are a reflection and response to their child's external world. Cognitive-behavioral therapy is proven to be highly effective for children with EBD by focusing on lessening negative thoughts, improving problem-solving skills, and controlling social behavior and aggression. Group counseling can be structured and theme-based; social skills groups are often used to provide opportunities to model, learn, and practice positive interactions with peers and adults. Alternative approaches are considered creative therapies, such as art, music, or play therapy, which are effective with young children possessing less-developed language skills and children having difficulties expressing feelings and thoughts verbally.

Since school-age children spend a majority of their time in school, educators and school administrators are responsible for providing academic and behavioral modifications to ensure that emotional or behavioral problems do not impede learning processes. Unfortunately, in spite of the programs and facilities, children with EBD generally have poor academic outcomes due to a number of components, including insufficient teacher training to manage specific behavioral problems within the EBD population, classrooms lacking in high expectations and instructional demands, and behavioral problems that affect teaching on a regular basis. When a child is frequently disruptive in a classroom, many educators unintentionally label the child as the "troublemaker," potentially exacerbating inappropriate behaviors in a number of ways. For example, the child might *enjoy* receiving negative attention or the educator's actions may create a sense of learned helplessness causing the child to feel "stuck" in the negative role.

Schools, however, do work to identify individual academic needs of students with EBD and to implement a variety of educational interventions. **Direct instruction** is an instructional strategy that uses a structured, fast-paced, sequenced, and participatory implementation, which has been found to be successful with students with EBD. Peer tutoring, also used in schools, increases academic engagement and gives students the opportunity to practice specific skills. Temporary placements in more structured environments, such as **self-contained classrooms** with smaller teacher-to-student ratios or **social inclusion in early childhood special education classrooms**, are also used to give further educational support. Many students receive counseling and supportive treatments while in regular education classrooms.

In schools and more specialized settings, numerous behavioral management interventions are part of the overall environment. Token economies give students the opportunity to receive tangible rewards or points for positive behaviors. Many times students are asked to read and sign behavioral contracts that specify what behaviors are deemed appropriate and inappropriate, making students aware of behavioral expectations and consequences. **Time-outs** offer students the time to practice and employ relaxation techniques to calm down while in a crisis and to address problem behaviors. Positive reinforcements can be tangible or verbal, including teacher praise, teacher attention, stickers, time to draw, recess, and the like. They are often decided based on an individual's preferences, age, and what he or she is willing to change in order to receive the reinforcement. The objective is to increase positive behaviors; however, research shows that intermittent reinforcement is the most effective. Any behavioral intervention needs to be measured and evaluated to assess its effectiveness on a particular behavior. If an intervention is found to be ineffective, then the intervention needs to be adjusted as needed. Some programs specifically designed for EBD students use systemwide interventions, such as **Life Space Intervention**, which uses a therapeutic, verbal method for dealing with a child in crisis to help her or him learn from the experience.

Medication has been proven to be an effective part of a treatment plan to address emotional, behavioral, and mental symptoms associated with EBD, as long as it is coupled with other interventions. Students meeting the criteria for EBD may also have other *Diagnostic and Statistical Manual of Mental Disorders* (DSM-IV) classifications such as **ADHD**, bipolar disorder, conduct disorder, or anxiety disorder that contribute to displays of the emotional and behavioral disability. There are several different types of psychotropic medications to treat the many variations and difficulties associated with EBD, such as stimulants, antidepressants, anti-anxiety drugs, mood stabilizers, and antipsychotics. Stimulants, for example, are primarily used to treat attention deficit disorders and are labeled for pediatric use. Any time medication is administered, it should preferably be closely checked and evaluated by a psychiatrist. Although many potential long-term side effects of psychotropic medications on young children are still unknown, medications are still prescribed with the belief that serious mental disorders left untreated can negatively alter the chemistry of the brain, also resulting in adverse long-term effects.

The effectiveness of any treatment plan is contingent on collaboration among schools, families, and community or outside therapeutic services. Research has found that family involvement in the treatment of a child with EBD gives families more control over treatment and increases the chances of successful outcomes. Involvement for parents might also include attending parent education classes to learn more effective behavioral management skills; oftentimes, parents can inadvertently reinforce negative behaviors by "giving in" to the child or using inappropriate punishments that may add to angry and resentful feelings in the child. If children with EBD are left untreated, many emotional and behavioral problems can continue throughout their life. As adults, people with EBD can be at high risk for substance abuse as well as aggressive and self-destructive behaviors. However, when treated effectively, many children can learn to control and manage their behaviors.

Further Reading

Dawson, C. 2003. A study on the effectiveness of life space crisis intervention for students identified with emotional disturbances. *Reclaiming Children and Youth* 11 (4): 223–30.

Falk, K., K. Lane, and J. Wehby. 2003. Academic instruction for students with emotional and behavioral disorders. *Journal of Emotional and Behavioral Disorders* 11 (4): 194–97.

Heward, W. 2003. *Exceptional children: An introduction to special education.* 7th ed. Columbus, OH: Merrill/Prentice Hall.

Kaufman, J., T. Landrum, and M. Tankersley. 2003. What is special about special education for students with emotional or behavioral disorders? *Journal of Special Education* 37 (3): 148–57.

National Institute of Mental Health. 2000. Treatment of children with mental disorders: Questions and answers. NIH Publication no. 00-4702. Bethesda, MD: National Institute of Mental Health, National Institutes of Health, and U.S. Department of Health and Human Services. Available at http://www.nimh.nih.gov/publicat/nimhchildqa. pdf.

Pacer Center. 2001. What is an emotional or behavioral disorder? http://www.pacer. org/parent/php/php-c81.pdf.

DANA FREED

Policies and Practices

Bilingual Special Education

Bilingual special education is "an individually designed program of special instruction that includes the use of the home language and culture along with English. Bilingual special education addresses the needs of students in an inclusive environment where their individual academic needs are addressed" (Baca and Valenzuela 1998, 21). In bilingual special education, the student's native language and culture are regarded as strengths and as avenues to assist the student to achieve.

The establishment of bilingual special education has its roots in **Public Law 94-142** of 1975 (the Education for All Handicapped Children Act) and in **Section 504 of the Rehabilitation Act** of 1973, which mandated that children with special needs were entitled to services to meet their needs. Due to the increasing number of minority students during the past decades, states were mandated to provide services for students with disabilities who were also English-language learners (ELLs). The **Individuals with Disabilities Education Act** (IDEA) of 1997, part B, establishes and clarifies the requirements of the law concerning services to ELLs. A limited-English-proficient (LEP—interchangeable with ELL and the term federal legislation uses to address these students) child with a disability may require special education and related services for those aspects of the educational program that address the development of English language skills and other aspects of the child's educational program. In addition, for an LEP child with a disability, the **Individualized Education Program** (IEP) must address whether the special education and related services that the child needs will be provided in a language other than English. (See the discussion of consideration of "special factors" when developing, reviewing, and revising the IEP in § 300.346(a)(2)(ii) and § 300.346(b) and (c) of IDEA, part B.)

Bilingual special education has grown alongside special education and bilingual education, and as such it has become a separate entity. Similar to bilingual education programs, bilingual special education programs feature a wide range of interventions using two languages, one of which is English. The model most frequently used in the United States is the *Transitional Model*. This model relies on both the students' native language and English for instruction until competence is achieved in English. When English competence is achieved, students are placed in English monolingual programs. All students in bilingual programs are required to have English as a Second Language (ESL). This is an educational approach in which LEP students are instructed in the use of the English language. Their instruction is based on a special curriculum that typically involves little or no use of the native language. Students who require bilingual instruction and do not receive this service are provided with ESL services. For the rest of the school day, the students are placed in mainstream classrooms, immersion programs, or bilingual programs.

Other program models such as *Maintenance Bilingual Education* (which provides native language instruction through the elementary grades, decreasing in intensity as English proficiency increases) or the *Two-Way Enrichment Bilingual Education* (where native English speakers are acquiring a second language in an integrated program with native speakers of a language other than English that are acquiring English as a second language) are not offered frequently in bilingual special education.

Mandates and regulations notwithstanding, there is still considerable discussion concerning the provision of bilingual special education programs. These questions are an extension of the ongoing inquiry in the field of bilingual education where there is still no agreement as to which programs provide the best type of services in relation to the heterogeneity of the population, the exit and entry criteria, and the equal protection of the law. Furthermore, the transition of a special bilingual student to a monolingual program is seen as a way to help to improve the student's problem, based on a general belief among educators that the additional pressures of bilingualism are an added burden for the bilingual special student. Overall, research on the use of bilingual education in the instruction of students with learning disabilities is extremely scarce.

Although one of the primary goals for most students with learning disabilities is to improve communication skills, teachers find this task overwhelming because bilingual students' language proficiency can vary significantly. The language proficiency of the teachers, in turn, can also vary drastically. The lack of trained professionals decreases the number of bilingual classrooms and the availability of bilingual services. As a result, some students that need services are placed in bilingual classrooms where there is a monolingual teacher and an assistant who speaks the native language of the child.

The decision to provide bilingual special education for students with disabilities who are English-language learners is made by the Committee on Special Education or by the IEP team. In general, the language delivery strategies chosen should be based on the student's language proficiency in both English and her or his native language.

Reference

Baca, L. M., and J. S. de Valenzuela. 1998. Development of the bilingual special education interface. In *The bilingual special education interface*, ed. L. M. Baca and H. T. Cervantes. 3rd ed. Upper Saddle River, NJ: Merrill.

Further Reading

Arreaga-Mayer, C. 1993. Ecobehavioral assessment of exceptional culturally and linguistically diverse students: Evaluating effective bilingual special education programs. In *Proceedings of the Third National Research Symposium on Limited English Proficient Student Issues: Focus on Middle and High School Issues*. Washington, DC: U.S. Department of Education, Office of Bilingual Education and Minority Languages Affairs.

Baker, C. 2001. *Foundations of bilingual education and bilingualism*. 3rd ed. Clevedon, England: Multilingual Matters.

Ortiz, A., and B. A. Ramirez. 1988. Schools and the culturally diverse exceptional student: Promising practices and future directions. Reston, VA: The Council for Exceptional Children/ERIC Clearinghouse on Handicapped and Gifted Children.

Ovando, C. J., and V. P. Collier. 1997. *Bilingual and ESL classrooms: Teaching in multicultural contexts*. 2nd ed. New York: McGraw-Hill.

U.S. General Accounting Office. 1994. *Limited English proficiency: A growing and costly educational challenge facing many school districts*. Washington, DC: GAO.

Valenzuela, J. S. de. 1998. Language acquisition and the exceptional child. In *The bilingual special education interface*, ed. L. M. Baca and H. T. Cervantes. 3rd ed. Upper Saddle River, NJ: Merrill.

Winzer, M. A., and K. Mazurek. 1998. *Special education in multicultural contexts*. Upper Saddle River, NJ: Merrill.

SARA G. NAHARI

Child Study Teams

The term *Child Study Team* is utilized to describe a multidisciplinary group of professionals whose main function is to assist teachers in designing and implementing research-based interventions within the regular education environment for a student exhibiting learning and/or behavioral difficulties. Through consultation and collaboration with the Child Study Team, general educators can create educational settings that are likely to improve a student's learning, thereby decreasing unnecessary referral or placement into special education.

The notion of child study began to flourish at a time when criticism was targeted against the school district practices relating to the high ratio of students being referred, evaluated, and subsequently placed into special education. In addition, an overrepresentation of students from culturally diverse backgrounds receiving special services had been a significant concern in the field for many years. In response to these criticisms, the conceptual framework of the "prereferral" intervention was established to explore instructional alternatives within the general education system prior to referral for special education. However, the prereferral intervention process was unsuccessful in significantly reducing the number of special education evaluations and placements because this practice had been viewed as a stepping-stone to special education placement.

The **No Child Left Behind Act** (NCLB) was created to ensure that every student reaps the benefits of well-trained teachers, evidence-based curricula, and safe learning environments. Furthermore, the Individuals with Disabilities Education Improvement Act (IDEIA)—an update of the **Individuals with Disabilities Education Act** (IDEA)—advocates for the provision of early interventions to enhance academic progress for all students within the general education population, especially for at-risk students. The intent of the Early Intervening Services section in IDEIA is to curtail overidentification and avoid unnecessary referrals to special education. The enactment of IDEIA also recommends increased consultation by related service personnel to support general education teachers in providing research-based interventions. Through this process of early intervention, education professionals will be able to distinguish between children that possess different learning challenges and those children who truly have disabilities. Therefore, the best practice would be to serve all children in regular education classrooms as much as possible with all supports deemed necessary. As a result, the prereferral intervention was renamed "child study," with a focus on preventative approaches in the regular classroom setting designed to reflect current thinking in service delivery.

The Child Study Team is also known as the Prereferral Intervention Team, Student Success Committee, Teacher Assistance Team, Instructional Support Team, and School-Based Intervention Assistance Team. The Child Study Team is comprised of a number of professionals, which may include, but is not limited to, the referring teacher, other general and special education teachers, the building administrator, the school psychologist, the school counselor, the school social worker, parents, and in some cases, the student. In other instances, based on the student's needs, additional special education professionals and community persons may be in attendance.

When a child struggles academically or socially in the general classroom, the teacher may request assistance from the Child Study Team. After receiving the request, the Child Study Team will convene to determine the problem, identify the educational needs, and plan for intervention. For the Child Study Team process, a collaborative problem-solving approach has been widely advocated to effectively meet the unique learning needs of every child. In order to exhaust all general education resources and alternatives prior to a special education referral, this collaborative problem-solving approach gathers expertise from its varied professional membership, encourages participation from all professionals involved, and compiles the data into an opportunity for collective decision making.

The collaborative problem-solving approach is comprised of four basic components: problem identification, intervention development, intervention implementation, and evaluation. *Problem identification* involves the collection and analysis of student data, which may include interviews, observations, samples of classwork, previous educational history, and possibly even medical records. Analysis of the data should yield a better understanding of the student's strengths and weaknesses. Moreover, the team members should be able to describe academic or behavioral difficulties in concrete and measurable terms and formulate hypotheses about why the problem is occurring.

Satisfactory progress toward intervention design and implementation can only be made after identifying particular skill or performance deficits and attempting to understand the underlying influences. Research-based interventions can be developed to enhance learning in different modalities and developmental stages. During this *intervention development* stage, the Child Study Team can assist the referring teacher in accessing a variety of materials and understanding how to provide adaptations and modifications appropriately.

During the *intervention implementation* phase, the Child Study Team members should collect data on student progress and document the strategies attempted. In this manner, quality and accountability will be ensured during the *evaluation* phase.

The advantages of having a Child Study Team process are threefold. First, the identified students are being assisted in the classroom, which ensures that regular education services are effectively explored for students prior to referral for comprehensive assessment. Second, the referring teacher gains additional knowledge and skills relating to early identification and intervention by participating in the Child Study Team process. The referring teacher will thus be better prepared to serve other children in the general education setting that exhibit similar difficulties in the future. Consequently, this process will ultimately reduce the number of students referred for special education services and increase the cost-effectiveness in serving all students in schools. Lastly, an effective Child Study Team will promote close collaboration and shared responsibility among personnel in general education, special education, and other related services.

Further Reading

Buck, G. H., K. C. Wilcox, E. A. Polloway, and A. Smith-Thomas. 2003. Prereferral intervention processes: A survey of state practices. *Exceptional Children* 69:349–60.

Burns, M. K., M. L. Vanderwood, and S. Ruby. 2005. Evaluating the readiness of prereferral intervention teams for use in problem-solving model. *School Psychology Quarterly* 20:89–105.

Friend, M., and L. Cook. 1997. Student-centered teams in schools: Still in search of an identity. *Journal of Educational and Psychological Consultation* 8:3–20.

LEESA HUANG

Gifted Education: Traditional and Emerging Approaches

Although there are numerous definitions of *gifted and talented*, there is a general consensus that individuals who are gifted and talented have either performed or have the capacity for performance at the top of the fields in which they are considered gifted.

One goal of gifted and talented education is to allow individuals to develop their innate talents to the fullest. A second goal is to maximize the human resources available to society, in the belief that appropriately educated gifted and talented individuals will make substantial contributions to the broader society in their talent domains.

Based on this notion of superior performance, approaches to gifted education can generally be divided into two major strands—*acceleration* and *enrichment*.

Acceleration approaches involve having students move through a curriculum or area of study at a faster-than-normal pace. Enrichment approaches involve either having students explore traditional subject matter in greater depth than in the typical educational setting or exposing students to additional disciplines than would normally be provided. Although discussed separately, acceleration and enrichment are not mutually exclusive, and both approaches may occur simultaneously.

Within both the acceleration and enrichment approaches, there are a variety of programs, ranging from modified curricula in the regular classroom and pullout programs to **self-contained classrooms** and special schools. Additionally, many gifted and talented programs are administered by universities and offered during hours outside of regular school, including the summer. Providing special programming for gifted and talented students is in keeping with the concept of a free and appropriate public education—a phrase more often used in describing the education of students with performance challenges rather than those with superior performance.

Federal law acknowledges that students can be gifted and talented in several areas, including intellectual, creative, leadership, and specific academic domains, as well as the performing and visual arts. However, programming for gifted and talented students typically occurs in school settings, and the majority of gifted and talented programming in the public schools is in specific academic domains. Thus, measures of cognitive functioning are heavily weighted toward identifying students, given the predictive validity of *intelligence* across academic domains. Additionally, in part due to the controversy around the construct of intelligence, measures of cognitive functioning have received tremendous research scrutiny and yield reliable and valid scores, whereas measures of creativity, leadership, and skills in the visual and performing arts are fewer and the scores on these constructs are not as psychometrically robust.

Acceleration Options

Acceleration in a talent area is an option that is usually suited for students who learn quickly, in that it requires the individual to move though a set of curricula or develop skills in a domain at a stepped-up pace. Acceleration can be grade based or subject based. Some students begin their formal schooling earlier than age 5, because they are already cognitively prepared for formal instruction. Other students may skip a grade, either in its entirety or in a particular subject area. For example, a student who is gifted in mathematics may be in third grade for most subjects, but attending ninth-grade mathematics classes.

In other instances, students may move through all of the grade levels, completing each in less than a year. Advanced Placement examinations offered by the College Board provide an opportunity for students not yet in college to demonstrate their mastery of college-level material, and Advanced Placement courses are offered both by public schools and university-based programs. Some university-based programs also provide the opportunity for students to complete a yearlong program of study, typically at the high school level, over the course of a few weeks during the summer.

The national talent search programs use the Scholastic Aptitude Test and other achievement-based assessment tools to identify students who can benefit from acceleration opportunities or advanced courses in an academic domain and provide programming options for these students. *Radical acceleration* is a term used to describe the education of students who complete high school graduation requirements three or more years early. In a two-volume report, Nicholas Colangelo, Susan G. Assouline, and Miraca U. M. Gross (2004) provided a comprehensive summary of the research support for the types and effects of acceleration.

Enrichment Approaches

Many of the ideas used in current enrichment approaches originate from Joseph Renzulli's work on the enrichment triad (Renzulli and Reis 1986). Renzulli conceptualized giftedness as consisting of three interlocking strands:

- above average, though not necessarily superior ability
- creativity
- task commitment

According to Renzulli, all three components are necessary for gifted performance.

A number of assumptions accompany this conceptualization. First, *giftedness* is neither absolute nor permanent. For example, individuals with superior measured ability at a given point in time may not always be identified as gifted subsequently, especially if they do not possess creativity and task commitment. Thus, it is not always possible to predict who will be gifted as an adult. Second, giftedness can be *cultivated* by developing task commitment and creativity. Therefore, it is important to provide enriched educational experiences to all individuals with above-average abilities, because they are *all* potentially gifted in this conceptualization.

The enrichment approach, then, is much broader based and can be implemented on a school-wide basis. In addition to allowing the greatest number of students to benefit from enriched educational opportunities, Renzulli and Sally M. Reis (1986) contended that this approach to gifted education is less likely to be opposed on the grounds that it is elitist; on the contrary, it is more likely to be supported by parents, teachers, and policy makers. Whereas traditional gifted and talented education programs, including accelerated options, are available to about 5 percent of the school population, enrichment approaches typically involve about 20 percent.

Enrichment activities can be divided into three levels. Level 1 activities involve exposing students to a wide range of disciplines outside the regular curriculum. The aim of this level is to stimulate general interests but also to maximize individuals finding talent domains in which they have above-average ability. Level 2 activities involve developing cognitive and affective skills within domains, including metacognitive, research, and communication skills. Finally, Level 3 enrichment involves developing talent-specific skills to an advanced level and producing authentic products.

Communities of Learning

In closing, it is important to highlight the role of communities in the development of talent (see Sosniak 1999). Some of the more obvious communities of learning are specialized schools and summer programs that cater to specific talent domains ranging in topic from academic subjects to the visual and performing arts to athletics. However, whenever we change the placement of a student, for example, through grade skipping or early entrance to college, we are also changing the talent community that interacts with the individual. Thus, we should not ignore the contributions of appropriate role models and the importance of interacting with others who are talented in the same domain. They are equally as likely to facilitate an individual's movement through the zone of proximal development as more formal models of programming.

References

Colangelo, N., S. G. Assouline, and M. U. M. Gross, eds. 2004. *A nation deceived: How schools hold back America's brightest students* (The Templeton National Report on Acceleration). 2 vols. West Conshohocken, PA: John Templeton Foundation.

Renzulli, J. S., and S. M. Reis. 1986. The enrichment triad/revolving door model: A schoolwide plan for the development of creative productivity. In *Systems and modes for developing programs for the gifted and talented*, ed. J. S. Renzulli, 216–66. Mansfield Center, CT: Creative Learning Press.

Sosniak, L. A. 1999. An everyday curriculum for the development of talent. *Journal of Secondary Gifted Education* 10:166–72.

Further Reading

Daniel, R. 2000. Performing and visual arts schools: A guide to characteristics, options, and successes. *Journal of Secondary Gifted Education* 12:43–48.

Nordby, S. M. 2004. *A glossary of gifted education.* http://members.aol.com/svennord/ed/GiftedGlossary.htm

Stephens, K. R. 1998/1999. Residential math and science high schools: A closer look. *Journal of Secondary Gifted Education* 10:85–92.

Websites

College of William and Mary, Center for Gifted Education: http://cfge.wm.edu/

Council for Exceptional Children, Information Center on Disabilities and Gifted Education: http://ericec.org/

National Association for Gifted Children: http://www.nagc.org/

Neag Center for Gifted Education and Talent Development: http://www.gifted.uconn.edu/

FRANK C. WORRELL

Giftedness in Diverse Populations

The concept of giftedness has expanded over the years from a narrow definition (e.g., Sir Francis Galton, Lewis Terman) mostly associated with high intelligence to a broader, multifaceted definition that encompasses social competence and diverse talents and abilities across individuals from diverse backgrounds. In 1972, Sydney Marland provided a broader definition of giftedness that included children of both genders who showed exceptional performance in specific areas or across intellectual, creative, academic, artistic, kinesthetic, or leadership domains. Special efforts were made by researchers in the study of gifted and creative characteristics that supported the **inclusion** of children from rural, low socioeconomic, and culturally diverse backgrounds into gifted programs.

Recently, prominent psychologists such as Joseph Renzulli, John Feldheusen, Robert Sternberg, and Howard Gardner have developed more expansive models of intelligence, giftedness, and creativity. These models emphasize the identification and development of strengths and talents in all children through varied opportunities at a school-wide level and beyond self-contained gifted programs. This enhanced perspective has implications for how educators, particularly those in the field of special education, can focus on the unique strengths of children who have traditionally been considered exceptional only in the negative sense of the word. This group includes culturally and linguistically diverse (CLD) children, underachieving students, and children with learning disabilities.

CLD students comprise children who are immigrant, second-language learners or whose background is influenced by the traditional values, languages, and customs of their native cultures. Giftedness in these children is valued, expressed, and reinforced in unique ways that may differ from those of the mainstream population. It is important to note that CLD students, particularly those from low-socioeconomic backgrounds, have been historically overrepresented in special education classes, yet overlooked in gifted programs. The lack of adequate identification of gifted abilities in these children could be attributed to the restrictive definition of giftedness, the lack of cultural sensitivity and competence in the identification process, and the limited range of opportunities offered by traditional self-contained gifted programs.

Children who are underachievers constitute another group of students whose talents and gifts have gone unrecognized by both educators and special educators in the school system. By definition, *underachievement* is a discrepancy between intellectual potential or ability and academic achievement. Underachievement is primarily caused by a combination of personal attributes and environmental factors. Examples of personal attributes can include an unidentified learning disability, an individual's belief that he or she cannot successfully accomplish a task or goal (low self-efficacy), and a limited ability to self-regulate behavior. Environmental variables may involve factors such as family size, low parental expectations and values, and a mismatch between a student's learning style and a teacher's instructional style. Often children who are underachieving may be highly creative or have special abilities that lead them to be bored with traditional text-based instruction, rote-memory learning tasks, and teacher-directed activities.

Another group of children who remain underidentified in terms of specific aptitudes, abilities, and talents are those with learning disabilities or children suspected of having attention and hyperactivity problems. Often these children may exhibit a "paradoxical combination" of characteristics; they may present varied problems academically, emotionally, behaviorally, and/or physically, while at the same time having exceptional abilities in other specific domains. As a result, teachers are less likely to nominate these students to gifted programs, and if nominated, they rarely qualify for both special education and gifted programs due to funding issues.

There are three types of students with a combination of learning abilities and gifted characteristics:

1. identified gifted students with subtle learning disabilities who demonstrate periods of underachievement

2. gifted students with severe learning disabilities who have not been identified as gifted

3. students who are not identified as both gifted and learning disabled—these children's high ability masks their disability, while their disability covers up their gifts and talents, often resulting in average abilities and lower achievement

Identification of these children is difficult due to the endless debates about the definitions of *giftedness* and *learning disability*, which are perceived as being mutually exclusive. In addition, overreliance on IQ tests, rigid cutoff scores, problems identifying the "masking phenomenon," and varying criteria among school districts also continue to hinder the identification of gifted strengths in these children.

The literature in the area of giftedness in diverse populations suggests that best practices in identification methods include a comprehensive philosophy of giftedness, adequate training for teachers in the nomination process, the development of flexible criteria, and the use of multiple methods of assessment. Selection should consider the influence of a learning and achievement difficulty, learning style, and cultural and linguistic differences. Interventions should move away from strict remediation of deficits to emphasizing strengths and interest-based activities. Approaches should focus on gifts, while using compensatory strategies and adaptations such as technology, graphic organizers, and learning through the arts for weaknesses. Learning environments should provide advanced-level and real-world problems, value diversity and individual differences, use multisensory approaches and individualized instruction, provide counseling, develop partnerships between special education and gifted programs, and promote parental participation and mentoring role opportunities from community members. Providing enhanced experiences in the classroom and special "pullout" or interest-based, small group enrichment or acceleration opportunities to foster creativity, talents, and special abilities would benefit all students.

Further Reading

Barkan, J. H., and E. Bernal. 1991. Gifted education for bilingual and limited English proficient students. *Gifted Child Quarterly* 35:144–47.

Baum, S. M., C. R. Cooper, and T. W. Neu. 2001. Dual differentiation: An approach for meeting curricular needs of gifted students with learning disabilities. *Psychology in the Schools* 38:477–90.

Esquivel, G. B., and J. C. Houtz, eds. 2000. *Creativity and giftedness in culturally diverse students.* Cresskill, NJ: Hampton Press.

Fancher, R. E. 1985. *The intelligence men: Makers of the IQ controversy.* New York: Norton.

McCoach, D. B., T. J. Kehle, M. A. Bray, and D. Siegle. 2001. Best practices in the identification of gifted students with learning disabilities. *Psychology in the Schools* 38:403–11.

Rayneri, L. J., L. B. Gerber, and L. P. Wiley. 2003. Gifted achievers and gifted underachievers: The impact of learning style preferences in the classroom. *Journal of Secondary Gifted Education* 14:197–204.

Reis, S. M., and D. B. McCoach. 2002. Underachievement in gifted and talented students with special needs. *Exceptionality* 10:113–25.

**GISELLE B. ESQUIVEL AND
GERALDINE OADES-SESE**

High-Stakes Testing

High-stakes testing is the practice by which the results of a student's large-scale assessment are used to determine her or his enrollment in tracked classes, grade retention or promotion, or conferral of a high school diploma. Both the **Individuals with Disabilities Education Act** (IDEA) and the **No Child Left Behind Act** (NCLB) require the **inclusion** of students with disabilities in state and local assessments, regardless of whether the assessment has attached high-stakes consequences. The goal of including students with disabilities in large-scale assessments is to ensure that they are included in all aspects of school reform and that schools are held accountable for the educational outcomes of students with disabilities. The assumption that students with disabilities could reach high academic standards is relatively new; in fact, it was not until the 1997 reauthorization of IDEA that students with disabilities were required to have access to the general education curriculum and that their progress toward achieving these academic standards was reported. In 2002, NCLB moved one step further by requiring that schools be held accountable for the academic achievement of students with disabilities in the form of large-scale assessments.

Federal responsibility for students meeting academic standards focuses on schools and school systems; however, the agent ultimately responsible for ensuring that students meet the standards varies from state to state. Some states hold schools accountable. Here, the school's progress on large-scale assessments dictates whether the school receives or loses money, receives support, or in some instances, is reconstituted by the state. Other states hold teachers accountable. In these cases, classroom large-scale assessment scores dictate whether a teacher receives bonus pay or a promotion. Many states hold the students themselves accountable.

States that hold students accountable for educational standards use large-scale assessment tests as one or the only means of evaluating student progress. Consequences attached to test results include placement in tracked classes, retention or promotion, and awarding or denying a high school diploma—with the latter being the most prevalent. The use of one single test score to make educational decisions is problematic, according to the American Psychological Association, as large-scale assessments are not developed for individual decision making, and decisions based on a single test score are not a valid use of a score on a large-scale assessment. That said, twenty-six states have or are in the process of making high school graduation contingent on passing a statewide exit exam, now referred to as "high-stakes tests."

While all students with disabilities are required to participate in state assessments, a small minority of students who have more significant disabilities may participate in an alternate assessment. This may take many forms—two examples are student portfolios, a collection of students' work evaluated by predetermined state criteria; and performance assessments, usually one-on-one assessments that measure predetermined skills.

Students with disabilities who take typical state assessments are by law allowed testing accommodations. Accommodations are meant to "level the playing field," that is, to minimize the impact of the student's disability and maximize the ability of a student to achieve academically. Administering a test in Braille for students who are blind and offering extended time on tests for students with disabilities that affect rates of reading are two examples of testing accommodations that seek to correct distortions caused by a disability. Testing accommodations are often separated into six categories: setting, timing, scheduling, presentation, response, and other. For example, an accommodation in a setting may refer to a child taking the test individually or in a small group; an accommodation in timing may refer to extending the student's time when the test is time specific. However, the effects of testing accommodations are mainly unknown and therefore educators cannot be sure that they are indeed "leveling the playing field" for students with disabilities.

There are limited empirical data on the effect of high-stakes testing on students with disabilities. In fact, there is a dearth of information on the effects of high-stakes testing on *any* student group. However, there is a great deal of conjecture. An important argument used to support high-stakes testing is that "social promotion" will end; students will no longer move through school or graduate without meeting the commensurate educational standards. However, this argument is difficult to substantiate, as social promotion is not well documented and there is uncertainty about its prevalence.

Proponents of high-stakes testing claim that attaching tangible rewards to a test will serve to motivate students to work in a more focused, more diligent manner. Similarly, there are claims that high-stakes testing will motivate teachers to provide students with the appropriate curriculum, thereby exposing them to high academic standards. Opponents, however, assert that the high stakes will decrease the students' and teachers' motivation, and in fact there is research that suggests that the pressure of high stakes motivates students and teachers negatively (Heubert and Hauser 1999).

Proponents also claim that high-stakes tests focused on standards will ensure that the curriculum is clear and based on the assessed standards. Opponents, on the other hand, believe that attaching high stakes to a large-scale assessment will limit the curriculum and require teachers to "teach to the test." Further, there is some research to suggest that even when the curriculum is aligned to the standards and to the assessment, students with disabilities may not be enrolled in classes that provide access to this curriculum (Katzman 2004).

The most somber claim opponents make is that attaching high stakes to large-scale assessments will lead to higher dropout rates. In fact, there is research suggesting that high-stakes testing and one of its consequences—retention at grade level—do lead to increased dropout rates (Heubert and Hauser 1999). There is also concern that the negative effects are higher for students with disabilities in minority groups, because the dropout rates for students of color are higher than for their white peers. Further, high stakes are an additional burden on an already struggling urban educational system.

The issues that arise for students with disabilities when attaching high-stakes consequences to standardized tests are complex. Consequently, there are no simple answers. Research shows that high-stakes testing may have detrimental effects on students with disabilities; indeed, a student can conceivably have success in school for twelve years and then, because of the results of one score on one test, not receive a high school diploma. At the same time, it is important that students with disabilities reach high academic standards. Without strong accountability measures, there is no process for knowing if students with disabilities are achieving success with a standards-based reform curriculum. Removing students with disabilities from the accountability measures may remove them from the school reform process itself. Until more is known, what is needed is a concerted effort to ensure the attainment of high standards, along with an equally strong effort to protect students with disabilities from the negative consequences that will in effect push them away from school.

Further Reading

Fuchs, L. S., and D. Fuchs. 2000. *Accountability and assessment in the twenty-first century for students with learning disabilities*. Philadelphia: Pew Charitable Trusts.

Heubert, J., and R. M. Hauser, eds. 1999. *High stakes: Testing for tracking, promotion, and graduation.* Washington, DC: National Academy Press.

Katzman, L. 2004. Students with disabilities and high stakes testing: What can the students tell us? Ph.D. diss., Harvard University.

Thurlow, M. L., J. L. Elliott, and J. E. Ysseldyke. 1998. *Testing students with disabilities: Practical strategies for complying with district and state requirements*. Thousand Oaks, CA: Corwin Press.

Websites

American Educational Research Association (AERA): http://www.aera.net/

The AERA has a Special Interest Group (SIG) on "Inclusion & Accommodation in Large-Scale Assessment" (formerly "Research on the Inclusion of Students With Disabilities and Limited English Proficient Students in Large-Scale Assessments") whose purpose is to promote research and disseminate information on activities and projects focusing on the inclusion of students with disabilities and LEP students in large-scale assessments.

Educational Policy Reform Research Institute: http://www.eprri.org/

EPRRI is a federally funded program that is increasing our knowledge and understanding of ways that students with disabilities can be fully included in educational accountability measures.

National Center on Educational Outcomes: http://education.umn.edu/nceo/

The NCEO provides national leadership in the participation of students with disabilities in national and state assessments, standards-setting efforts, and graduation requirements.

LAUREN KATZMAN

Inclusion

Inclusion is an educational philosophy that calls for schools to educate all learners— including students with disabilities and other special needs—together in high-quality, age-appropriate general education classrooms in their neighborhood schools. It seeks to create classrooms that offer all students access to appropriate, relevant, and challenging curricula and individualized instructional strategies addressing their unique academic, social, and behavioral strengths and challenges. Inclusive classrooms are structured to foster student friendships and the acceptance of individual differences. Rather than working in separate classrooms, educators work collaboratively to create a unified educational system to deliver a range of resources and related services within the confines of the general education classroom.

Schools use a variety of collaborative models to implement inclusion. These models are designed to lessen some of the difficulties associated with programs where students leave the general education classroom to receive services, such as students missing academic instruction, insufficient communication and coordination between professionals, scheduling problems, and fragmentation of the curriculum. In the **Collaborative Consultation** *Model*, teachers work together to implement strategies to address students' learning and behavioral challenges and to coordinate the instructional program. While general educators have primary responsibility for their students and the instructional program, the special educator and other ancillary support personnel deliver a range of individualized instructional accommodations and related services to students with disabilities in the general education setting.

Many school districts also are using *cooperative teaching*, where general education teachers and supportive service personnel such as special educators and speech/language therapists collaborate to teach students in inclusive settings. Educators involved in cooperative teaching seek to establish an equal status relationship by sharing responsibility and accountability for planning and delivering instruction, evaluating, grading, and disciplining students. Depending on the goals of the lesson, the nature of the material covered, and the needs of students, cooperative teaching teams use a variety of different instructional arrangements so that all members of the team perform relevant and meaningful instructional activities that promote student learning.

Inclusion was preceded by the concept of *mainstreaming*. However, although inclusion shares similar goals and implementation strategies with mainstreaming, inclusion and mainstreaming are different. Whereas inclusion provides all students with full-time access to general education classrooms, mainstreaming offers selected students part-time or full-time placements in general education classrooms based on their readiness as assessed by educators. While inclusion uses a "push-in" model to deliver a wide variety of supportive services within the general education classroom, mainstreaming often involves a "pullout" model where supportive services are delivered outside the general education classroom.

Inclusion grew out of the concept of the *least restrictive environment* (LRE)—the idea that students with disabilities should be educated with their nondisabled classmates as much as possible. The LRE concept also includes a preference for students attending school as close as possible to their homes so they can interact with other students from their neighborhood and participate in all aspects of the school program. Another important aspect of the LRE and inclusion is the principle of *natural proportions*, which means that the percentage of students with and without disabilities in a classroom should be consistent with their percentages in the larger school population.

The LRE for an individual student is based on the student's educational needs rather than his or her disability. While schools are encouraged to place students in inclusive settings, the LRE for some students can be shifted to less inclusive educational settings when their school performance indicates that even with supplementary aids and services, they cannot be educated satisfactorily in a general education classroom.

Further Reading

Kluth, P., R. A. Villa, and J. S. Thousand. 2002. Our school doesn't offer inclusion, and other legal blunders. *Educational Leadership* 59 (4): 24–27.

Salend, S. J. 2005. *Creating inclusive classrooms: Effective and reflective practices for all students.* 5th ed. Columbus, OH: Merrill/Prentice Hall.

Sapon-Shevin, M. 2003. Inclusion: A matter of social justice. *Educational Leadership* 61 (2): 25–28.

Snyder, L., P. Garriott, and M. W. Aylor. 2001. Inclusion confusion: Putting the pieces together. *Teacher Education and Special Education* 24:198–207.

Walther-Thomas, C., L. Korinek, V. L. McLaughlin, and B. T. Williams. 2000. *Collaboration for inclusive education: Developing successful programs.* Boston: Allyn & Bacon.

Websites

Inclusion Network: http://www.inclusion.org/
Inclusion Resources: http://www.uni.edu/coe/inclusion/resources/resources.html
Kids Together: http://www.kidstogether.org/

SPENCER J. SALEND

Individualized Education Programs

In 1975, **Public Law 94-142** was the first law to address the specific requirements of educational content, development, and implementation for individuals with disabilities. According to the law, educational content is to be developed by a team of people that includes a special education facilitator and/or general education teacher, related service providers (e.g., counselors; speech, physical, and occupational therapists), family members (e.g., legal guardian or parents), the student if appropriate, and others (e.g., administrators, advocates or lawyers, and medical professionals as needed). In order to establish the agreed-upon content, the team must abide by and document the outcome by creating an **Individualized Education Program** (IEP). The IEP is a legal document that outlines the specific learning needs of the student and consequent adaptations to the curriculum and physical environment that must be made to accommodate the child.

Due-process rights are procedural safeguards that protect civil rights. They are designed to maximize equal educational opportunities and ensure parental involvement and consent during the educational process—including written notifications in the parents' primary mode of communication throughout the whole process. By law, parents may challenge any of the school's decisions about the education of their child. The term *due process* with regard to special education is almost entirely associated with the IEP process.

Two other terms that are integral to the IEP process are *least restrictive environment* (LRE) and *free and appropriate education* (FAPE). The law mandates that individuals with disabilities be educated alongside nondisabled students in the LRE. The educational environment is judged on a continuum of settings that ranges from most restrictive (institutions, etc.) to restrictive (e.g., special education **self-contained classrooms** in a general education school) to least restrictive (the general education classroom). The LRE is currently considered the most favorable environment for children with disabilities; it provides the opportunity for social interactions with their nondisabled peers.

The law also stipulates that every child has the right to a free and appropriate education, which means that student's needs must be met to the extent that they cease to adversely impact the child's ability to learn. A FAPE entails evaluating and sometimes assessing students to determine their specific educational needs. The IEP is developed and implemented to assist the child in the school setting, at no cost to the family.

Currently, the IEP is designed for persons with disabilities up to the age of twenty-one and is the centerpiece of a student's education. The IEP is divided into three main parts:

- The Individualized Family Service Plan (IFSP) serves students and their families from birth through age three in early intervention programs.
- The IEP serves students ages three through twenty-one, which includes preschool educational services.
- The Individualized Transition Plan (ITP), which is actually an inclusive extension of the IEP, serves students ages fourteen through twenty-one to account for the transition from school to employment and independence.

In addition to the IEP, there are many types of plans that extend the details of the educational program but are not mandatory. One of the most common among them is the Behavioral Intervention Plan (BIP). Unlike the ITP, the BIP is not mandatory. All students by age fourteen will receive an ITP, but not all require a BIP. Where the ITP is mandated by age level, the BIP may be implemented at any age, for any duration of years, or never at all. It is developed as an addendum to the IEP on an "as-needed" basis.

The IEP process must be followed for every child referred and/or identified with a disability. The process includes the following steps:

1. Referral
2. Evaluation
3. Determination of eligibility
4. Development of the IEP
5. Implementation of the IEP
6. Annual review

The process begins when a child's teacher or parent recommends the child for services. Consequently, the school arranges a referral meeting, and it is there that evidence and reasons for the referral are presented and the parents are offered an opportunity to decide whether or not they would like to have their child evaluated. If the parent agrees, then an evaluation is conducted by an educational evaluator and a school psychologist. Using both formal and informal methods to observe and test a student's abilities, they must determine whether the child is eligible for special education.

If the child is determined eligible by a team of people that includes the teachers, parents, school psychologist, and others, then an IEP is developed. The IEP is tailored to the child's specific learning needs and may include accommodations, such as extended time on tests or the use of a scribe or computer, and goals for educational and social/emotional achievement. Once the IEP is in place, it is the special education facilitator and/or teacher's responsibility to follow and implement it in conjunction with other service providers (occupational therapists, speech therapists, physical therapists, etc.) to ensure that goals stated on the IEP are met.

The annual review requires a special education facilitator or teacher (along with the team of service providers and parents) to review the student's progress and determine how effective the previous recommendations were up to that point and are likely to be in the coming year. Steps 4 through 6 of the IEP process are repeated on a yearly basis. Every year a new IEP is developed, and every three years a student is reevaluated to determine if the child is still eligible to continue receiving services by repeating steps 2 through 4 of the IEP process. At every step, the student's parents or guardians must consent to proceeding to the next step, and they have the right to challenge any of the decisions made by the service team. Once the IEP has been formalized as a document, the special education facilitator and teacher hold the primary responsibility to implement it and coordinate services as outlined in step 5.

The IEP process serves some key objectives. Foremost among them, the process ensures continuous monitoring of the individual's level of performance in both social and academic areas. Second, it establishes a factual source of data regarding the student's long- and short-term educational goals. Finally, the IEP process forces educators to use methods such as rubrics to evaluate individual progress. The child's level of achievement acts as a feedback system, which in turn influences the goals and objectives for the following school year, that is, whether the level of expectations needs to be raised or lowered.

Implementing the IEP is probably the most complex task in the whole process because it involves an inordinate ability to multitask, which can be stressful. The burden of success depends heavily on the special education facilitator's ability to correctly observe the child's progress and motivate students to learn. In general, the facilitator must coordinate services to ensure that every detail of the IEP is being carefully followed. Daily, weekly, and monthly progress needs to be monitored in order to adjust short- and long-term goals and objectives via written documentation, portfolios, and correspondence with the student, parents, and other service providers.

Additionally, special adaptations and modifications are created to meet the curriculum demands outlined in the IEP. *Adaptations* are things used to help a student better engage in her or his environment and surroundings, while *modifications* are changes made to enhance the curriculum—both are used to help the student process information and learn. An example would be enlarging the print of the pages in a book written at a lower grade level that is age and grade appropriate for a student having difficulty reading. In general, the more severe the disability, the more critical the role of adaptations and modifications become.

Finally, considering that the IEP is a legal document, procedural safeguards include confidentiality practices. The Family Education Rights and Privacy Act addresses issues of confidentiality (e.g., access to educational records, parental right to inspect and review records, amendment of records, and destruction of records). In general, an educational agency may disclose personally identifiable information from the education records of a student without the written consent of the parent only under certain circumstances. For example, public school confidentiality practices require IEPs and other evaluative materials to be safely secured (e.g., in a lock-and-key file cabinet) by an administrator who is held accountable for the files, yet the files must be accessible to qualified staff within the school, from the district, or from the department of education. Copies may be provided to direct service providers who are involved with a student's educational program within a given school, but copies are not allowed to be given to agencies outside the school system, nor to anyone else not directly involved with the student's educational program, without proper consent forms signed and dated by the parent or guardian of the child. Service providers who obtain copies of an IEP also have a responsibility to ensure that the materials are secured in a safe place and are not allowed to share information with anyone not directly involved with the student's educational program.

Further Reading

Burns, E. 2001. *Developing and implementing IDEA-IEPs: An individualized education program (IEP) handbook for meeting Individuals with Disabilities Education Act (IDEA) requirements.* Springfield, IL: C. C. Thomas.

Kaff, M. S. 2004. Multitasking is multi-taxing: Why special educators are leaving the field. *Preventing School Failure* 48 (2): 10–17.

Meyen, E. L. 1995. Current and emerging instructional practices. In *Special education and student disability: An introduction*, ed. E. L. Meyen and T. M. Skrtic. 4th ed. Denver: Love.

Smith, D. D. 2001. The context of special education: The legacy of the twentieth century and the promise of the millennium. In *Introduction to special education: Teaching in an age of challenge*, 4th ed., 3–36. Boston: Allyn & Bacon.

U.S. Department of Education. 2005. Family Educational Rights and Privacy Act (FERPA). http://www.ed.gov/policy/gen/guid/fpco/ferpa/index.html

Winzer, Margret A. 1993. Approaching integration. In *The history of special education: From isolation to integration*, 381–85. Washington, DC: Gallaudet University Press.

Websites

Special Education in Plain Language: The IEP Process: http://www.cesa7.k12.wi.us/sped/Parents/pliepprocess.htm

JOSEPH VALENTIN

Life Space Interventions

Life Space Intervention (LSI) is a therapeutic, verbal intervention strategy used by adults with students in crisis who cannot manage their feelings and behaviors, as well as the reactions of others to the behaviors, without assistance. Adults trained in LSI techniques act as mediators for students, using strategies that are based on the in-depth clinical interviewing skills developed by Fritz Redl and later adapted by Nicholas J. Long and Mary M. Wood. According to Redl, the quality of the adult's interviewing skills and verbal intervention is the key to success or failure in achieving a therapeutic outcome of a crisis situation. LSI focuses on the crisis situation and the immediate life experience or "life space" of the student. The crisis becomes an optimal time for learning. Effective use of LSI can turn a crisis situation from a destructive event and experience into an instructional and insightful one. LSI is used in educational settings and programs, correctional facilities, and alternative living homes.

Many educators will, at some point in their work with children, find themselves faced with the responsibility to intervene in situations where the physical safety of students or adults is at risk. Educators may also be faced with situations that have the potential to reach a crisis level without quick and skillful intervention by the educator. Arguably, some of the most important skills teachers, administrators, or counselors must develop are those for defusing or deescalating emotionally charged incidents before they attain a crisis level, as well as the skills to work with students already in crisis.

A basic underpinning of successful use of LSI is an understanding of crisis situations and the Conflict Cycle. According to Redl, Long, and Wood, a crisis is the product of a series of events, beginning with a stressful situation that triggers the student's feelings, which in turn trigger defensive behaviors. While these behaviors are attempts by the student to protect or insulate himself or herself from the feelings and anxieties of the stressful incident, they often incite others or evoke hostile, counteraggressive, or defensive behaviors in others. Most often, the reactions of others create even more stress for the student and reinforce the initial thoughts and feelings. This is known as the Conflict Cycle.

Stressors can be emotional, psychosocial, developmental, or psychological in nature. Schools and classrooms produce many stressful situations, including, but not limited to, ridicule; bullying; failure with adults, classmates, and friends; marginalization; injustice; and physical threats to personal safety or basic needs. If the Conflict Cycle is not interrupted or redirected, it will spiral and gain intensity. As it intensifies, it becomes more difficult to resolve, due to the increasing complexity of the inner feelings, emotions, and behaviors that are unleashed.

Achieving a change in behavior becomes very difficult to consider for two reasons. First, when students are in highly charged conflict situations, their thoughts and actions are driven by emotions rather than rational thought. Second, adults engaged with students in such situations are often overcome by their own personal emotions of helplessness, fear, anger, or frustration that can arise when they are called upon to deescalate a serious crisis. Along with the original stressors, students in crisis often must face and deal with the added burden of an adult's anger, rejection, or insecurity. While the crisis may be resolved, the cycle is perpetuated and self-fulfilling mutual perceptions by adults and students as being hostile, aggressive, and not to be trusted are maintained.

LSI involves a six-step verbal process:

1. Discussing the crisis incident that brought about the need for LSI
2. Talking with the student to clarify and expand understanding of the incident and the student's personal involvement in it, and to decrease the student's emotional intensity
3. Exploring the student's feelings and anxieties in order to understand the central issue and to decide on a therapeutic goal
4. Exploring and selecting a solution proposed by the student, or by the adult if the student is unable to do so
5. Rehearsing with the student the actual steps that are to be taken next, including a discussion of the feelings and reactions that the student and others may have when the solution is enacted
6. Creating a transition plan for the student to follow as she or he returns to the setting or activity where the crisis occurred; this final step includes a respectful closure to the thoughts and feelings shared by the student during the intervention

Effective use of LSI requires adults to disconnect from the conflict and to display "dispassionate compassion" during the crisis. Adults who are skillful in LSI identify very clear roles and responsibilities for themselves during LSI. They must make connections for students between the child's feelings and behaviors. Students in crisis are very seldom able to recognize their feelings or speak about them. Yet these are essential abilities that students need to develop if learning and change are to occur. Adults who are effective in using LSI develop the ability to understand a student's behaviors as expressions of inner feelings and anxieties and can convey this to students. This connection is significant, because it fosters development of an important belief that if one can manage feelings and anxieties, one can independently self-manage behavior in positive ways. This ability is called "decoding" behavior and is the ability to observe body language, question, listen, reflect, and form hypotheses about anxieties, concerns, and issues. Over time and through the effective use of LSI by adults, students learn to decode their behaviors and that of others for themselves. Adults who are effective in using LSI understand that they have a responsibility for teaching this skill to students.

LSI requires that adults seek to bring about change in behavior not by exerting control, but through influence. This responsibility for bringing about change occurs through the use of motivation to engage students in active participation in LSI, through the use of friendship and the modeling of personal characteristics that develop trust, and through the sharing and teaching of skills for understanding events and triggers. All of these are essential abilities for solving crisis situations. Adults who are effective in using LSI know which of these influences to use with particular students. These abilities foster the development of trust that is necessary when working with students who will require many interactions with LSI before real change in behavior and self-management can occur.

To determine whether LSI is an appropriate strategy for specific children, educators should assess the students' skills and abilities in noncrisis situations for the presence of sufficient cognitive and communicative skills. The necessary skills and abilities include:

- attention and retention skills
- minimal verbal skills
- memory and reasoning skills to understand the sequence and essence of an incident, to share reasons the incident occurred, and to understand the related problems that the incident has produced for the student and others
- ability to trust an adult
- willingness and ability to share information with an adult

LSI can be used successfully with individuals and groups, with young children, and with students who have developmental delays.

LSI offers real opportunity for change as students, through mediation by adults, learn how to constructively manage stress, self-regulate behavior, and become agents in breaking their personal Conflict Cycle. When used skillfully, LSI creates opportunities for students to realistically solve problems and develop their ability to self-control, and for adults to understand a crisis through the eyes of their students while preserving—or even building—relationships, responsibility, caring, and learning. LSI is empowering for students because it uses students' reactions to stressful incidents to change behavior, enhance self-esteem, and expand understanding and insight into their own feelings and behaviors, as well as the feelings and behaviors of others' towards them. Skillful use of LSI with students shifts responsibility for change in behavior from external control by adults to self-regulation by students. LSI enables students to gain a greater understanding of the people and events in their lives that trigger stress and to trust adults to act as mediators. Adults skillful in LSI convey respect for students' feelings and their positive attributes. LSI enables students' to accept adults' guidance, to consider the choices and consequences that are available to them, and to choose positive resolutions for their crisis situation.

Further Reading

Long, N. J., and M. M. Wood. 1991. *Life space intervention: Talking with children and youth in crisis*. Austin, TX: Pro-ed.

Redl, F. 1959. Strategy and techniques of the life space interview. *American Journal of Orthopsychiatry* 29:1–18.

_____. 1963. The life space interview in the school setting. *American Journal of Orthopsychiatry* 33:717–19.

_____. 1966. *When we deal with children*. New York: Free Press.

Wood, M. M., and D. Weller. 1981. How come it's different with some children? A developmental approach to life space interviewing. *Pointe* 25:61–66.

KATHLEEN McSORLEY

Positive Psychology and Special Education

Positive psychology, a term coined by Martin Seligman, is the scientific study of positive emotions (e.g., pride, joy), positive individual traits (e.g., creativity, hope, optimism), and positive institutions (e.g., schools). It aims to shift the focus of psychology away from primarily examining the pathology of individuals to equally understanding and building positive qualities. In positive psychology, there is the fundamental assumption that all people have both strengths and weaknesses and that the strengths can serve as a buffer for the deficiencies. Positive psychology contends that psychology should not be just about fixing what is broken but also about nurturing unique talents and strengths to support greater overall well-being. Therefore, *positive school psychology* is the prevention-oriented practice of using empirically sound methods to enhance academic, social, and behavioral competencies of all students by focusing on the students' strengths and resources. The application of positive psychology to special education assessment and instruction could enhance the effectiveness of the special education system for children as well.

Special education relies on assessment practices to collect data for the purpose of making decisions regarding educational placements. School psychologists and diagnosticians typically perform these assessments, which focus on measuring educational and cognitive ability via a medical-model approach. Traditional or medical-model approaches to assessment tend to focus on treatment for individuals' deficits to the exclusion of equally assessing and addressing strengths and resources. Positive psychologists claim that special education assessment could be greatly enhanced by also systematically evaluating students' strengths. Research suggests that bolstering strengths and resources produces more positive outcomes than correcting deficits does. There are federal and state mandates set forth by the **Individuals with Disabilities Education Act** amendments of 1997 regarding the assessment of students' disabilities and deficits, but no equivalent mandates to assess their well-being and strengths. Researchers in school psychology are beginning to recognize the necessity to shift assessment and treatment from focusing on deficits and toward enhancing competencies and building strengths.

Michael Epstein, author of the only empirically validated, published assessment measure constructed from a strengths perspective, asserts that a strengths approach to assessment is based on four key beliefs. First, all children have strengths. If more time were devoted to identifying and enhancing these strengths, children would be in a better position to manage stress and adversity (e.g., challenging academic instruction). Second, children can be motivated by how teachers, parents, and others respond to them. Seligman argues that attention to strengths or positive aspects leads to increased motivation, more enjoyment in activities, and improved social behaviors. Third, failure to display a strength is not equivalent to a deficit; rather, it indicates that the child has not had the opportunity to learn specific skills that will build such strengths. Fourth, individuals are more likely to utilize their strengths and resources when these positive traits are recognized and supported. Additionally, other positive psychologists assert that it is through one's strengths that deficits are overcome. Thus, **Individualized Education Programs** should include coverage of one's strengths and resources, as well as goals devoted to reinforcing and building students' strengths in an effort to indirectly affect areas of deficiency.

Just as attention to students' strengths could positively affect special education assessment practices, positive psychologists believe that focusing on students' unique strengths could also enhance learning. Special education students, primarily those with a learning or behavior disorder, are flooded with negative messages because of their deficits. Through these messages, children construct meaning about themselves and their abilities, which influence their beliefs about themselves as learners and the purpose of education. Special education teachers, however, are in a position to help students develop positive perceptions of their academic abilities.

Positive psychologists suggest that teachers help students develop accurate beliefs about their academic competence. This can be done by giving specific feedback on which aspects of the work product were good (e.g., good introduction sentence, nice handwriting, excellent transition) and sending home notes at the end of the day reflecting specific praise or specific constructive criticism. Another suggestion is to provide students with challenging and novel tasks that they are capable of completing. A third suggestion is for teachers to praise students for working hard rather than praising students only for high grades or other performance indicators. Effort is changeable, whereas innate ability may not be. Research has shown that praising effort over performance helps to foster long-term learning goals in children and adolescents.

Positive psychology contends that education should be concerned with increasing positive emotion in children. According to Seligman, the "Father of Positive Psychology," providing opportunities for children to display their unique talents and strengths throughout the day and then rewarding them when they do can foster positive emotion. When individuals feel positive emotion, their thinking becomes more creative and diverse and their behavior more exploratory. This exploration then leads to new opportunities for a student to have "mastery experiences," which occur when students feel they have completed an activity successfully. Mastery experiences increase positive emotion, which leads to further exploration and discovery, exponentially increasing positive emotion. It is believed that happy people view their future as controllable. Even if they have endured negative past experiences (e.g, a failing grade), happy people believe that things will eventually work out. Children with learning disorders must be systematically given the opportunity to express their strengths, experience mastery, and feel the accompanying joy that results.

Further Reading

Chafouleas, S. M., and M. A. Bray. 2004. Introducing positive psychology: Finding a place within school psychology. *Psychology in the Schools* 4 (1): 1–5.

Clonan, S. M., S. M. Chafouleas, J. L. McDougal, and T. C. Riley-Tillman. 2004. Positive psychology goes to school: Are we there yet? *Psychology in the Schools* 41 (1): 101–10.

Epstein, M. H. 2004. *Behavioral and Emotional Rating Scale: A strength-based approach to assessment—examiner's manual.* Austin, TX: Pro-Ed.

Lopez, S. J., and C. R. Snyder. 2003. *Positive psychological assessment: Handbook of models and measures.* Washington, DC: American Psychological Association.

Rhee, S., M. J. Furlong, J. A. Turner, and I. Harari. 2001. Integrating strength-based perspectives in psychoeducational evaluations. *California School Psychologist* 6:5–17.

Seligman, M. E. P. 2002. *Authentic happiness: Using the new positive psychology to realize your potential for lasting fulfillment.* New York: Free Press.

Seligman, M. E. P., and M. Csikzentmihalyi. 2000. Positive psychology: An introduction. *American Psychologist* 55 (1): 5–14.

Website

Positive Psychology Center: http://www.positivepsychology.org/

BROOKE HERSH

Preschool Assessment

Preschool assessment is a process of examining the development of young children to determine if expected growth milestones are being met. The preschool years are generally considered to include ages three to five until a child enrolls in kindergarten. This period may also include ages three and younger, however, and assessment focused on the birth to age five time frame is often referred to as *early childhood assessment*.

There are a variety of reasons why young children may be assessed. Parents are often curious about the progress of their youngster's development, similar to checking their child's height and weight against growth charts at the pediatrician's office. Teachers may assess their preschoolers in the beginning of the school year and again at the end of the year as a means of tracking academic progress. Assessments may also be conducted due to concerns about a child's lack of developmental growth, emergence of emotional and behavioral problems, or other impairments. These assessments are generally conducted by school psychologists or related professionals with specialized training in early childhood assessment and development. Early childhood assessments have been increasing over the past few decades as parents and pediatricians become more aware of available services, along with the need to identify potential problems and offer early intervention before problems exacerbate.

Early childhood assessments are designed to evaluate the *whole child*. This means that all major domains of development are included in the comprehensive assessment battery, rather than focusing on only specific domain or area of delay. The reason for conducting a comprehensive assessment is that early childhood development is intricately hierarchical and interwoven. Delays that appear to fall in only one skill area may cause delays in other developmental areas or may have been precipitated by other, perhaps undetected skill delays. For instance, a child who appears to have delayed speech and language development may also have delayed fine-motor skills (which can also include difficulty manipulating the tongue and lips to form speech sounds) and delayed intelligence (such as difficulties with understanding concepts, vocabulary development, and comprehending directions). Although a problem may appear to be an isolated skill delay, there may be multiple causes to that delay or consequences resulting from it. Therefore, a comprehensive early childhood assessment is required, regardless of the reason for referral, to assess the development of the whole child and any isolated and interrelated developmental delays.

A comprehensive early childhood assessment typically includes the following five domains of development:

1. cognition
2. communication
3. daily living, self-help, or adaptive skills
4. social skills
5. motor skills

These areas are evaluated during an initial assessment to ascertain if delays exist and, in some cases, if further testing is warranted. Additional testing may involve referral to specialists for more extensive evaluation, such as a speech/language pathologist for communication concerns, audiologist for hearing concerns, physical therapist for gross motor concerns, occupational therapist for fine motor concerns, or neurologist for concerns regarding biologically mediated disorders.

In the *cognitive* area, a school psychologist with experience in early childhood assessment will test the youngster and interviews his or her family to evaluate cognitive functioning in a variety of skill areas. The assessment typically includes language or verbal components, such as listening and comprehension ability, vocabulary production, basic skill concepts (colors, shapes, counting, etc.), and simple, language-based logic problems. The battery also includes nonverbal, visual-spatial, or visual-perceptual tasks, such as copying block designs, completing puzzles, scanning pictures and completing matching tasks, using logical deduction to organize materials, drawing and copying shapes and letters, and completing sequenced problem-solving tasks in a visual-spatial medium.

Children with significant cognitive delays may be eligible to receive preschool special education services. This service may be delivered by an itinerant special education teacher, who travels to different preschools, day care centers, or the child's home to provide the instruction. The service can also be provided by more intensive, classroom-based instruction incorporating special education into the preschool curriculum. Children qualifying for the preschool special education classroom typically have more significant cognitive delays requiring more intensive instruction and teacher support.

Referrals for *communication* delays are conducted by a speech language pathologist, although the child may be first identified as having delayed speech and/or language during the cognitive evaluation and then referred to the speech language pathologist for additional testing. Children are assessed for their speech development after age three using measures of articulation and fluency. They are typically not assessed for speech clarity before age three because very young children produce numerous and frequent articulation errors that are developmentally appropriate. However, children as young as six to twelve months can be assessed for language development. Beginning at twelve months, most children are beginning to produce their first words, and by eighteen to twenty-four months they are combining words and using short sentences. Thus, children who haven't spoken by eighteen months or are still using single-word utterances at thirty months likely have delayed language.

Language is assessed in two domains: expressive and receptive language. *Expressive language* refers to the production of words and sentences in a meaningful way, while *receptive language* refers to understanding language. A child may have an expressive language disorder or a combined expressive and receptive language disorder; it is rare for a child to have a receptive language disorder in isolation, because if the child doesn't understand language that she is hearing (input), it is unlikely she will produce fluent and coherent expressive language (output).

Speech language therapy is usually provided by the therapist in a therapy room that contains the necessary materials for session and is soundproofed so that speech sounds and prompts are clear and audible. Some therapists work on an itinerant basis, traveling to the child's home or day care center to provide therapy. While it would be beneficial to provide services where the child is located, it is difficult to control for environmental variables and distractions in those situations. It is important that prior to the initiation of speech services, a complete audiological examination be conducted to ensure that the child is hearing normally. Young children may have hearing loss that goes unnoticed, particularly because they are susceptible to having excessive fluid and ear infections in their middle ears. While most pediatricians conduct perfunctory audiological screenings, a more thorough audiological evaluation using a soundproof booth and total ear examination by an audiologist is necessary to rule out hearing impairment that can affect speech and language.

The school psychologist usually conducts the assessment of *daily living skills*, also known as *self-help skills* or *adaptive skills*, although this can also be completed by a trained special educator. Typically, the parent is interviewed regarding the child's functioning at home in the areas of dressing, feeding, toileting, and the ability to follow rules, understand and avoid dangers, and learn ways to adapt successfully to their environment. Behavioral observations conducted during the assessment or in the child's home or classroom are used to augment the parent's report.

Children may have self-help skill delays for a variety of reasons, including lack of exposure to certain tasks and responsibilities, lack of opportunity to practice tasks, cultural customs limiting these opportunities, or developmental delays that affect the acquisition of self-help skills. As an example of the latter, children with fine motor weaknesses may have difficulty holding utensils and glasses properly, thus spilling their food often. They may also have difficulty dressing, especially tricky fine-motor tasks like fastening zippers and buttons or tying shoelaces. In addition, school psychologists examine the relation between the child's adaptive functioning and his or her cognitive functioning, which may indicate if a global delay is present. Alternatively, some children from intellectually impoverished environments may perform poorly on cognitive tests, but fall within or above age expectations on adaptive measures. This suggests that these children are functioning adequately at home in terms of self-care, but are not being exposed to educational enrichment on par with their age peers.

Social skills are assessed by the psychologist, who consults with the child's teacher and parents to better understand how successful the child is at navigating his social realm. Children who are successful at negotiation—obtaining wants and needs, initiating and building friendships, engaging in rewarding and exciting play with peers, and resolving interpersonal conflicts—are considered to be *socially competent*. Children with difficulties negotiating their social world are at risk for social failures and rejection, which may lead to harmful social, academic, and behavioral outcomes in the future. Parents complete rating forms that allow comparison of their child's social skills to those of similarly aged peers. The forms account for age and gender differences in socialization and behavior. Children with significant social skill and social competence delays may qualify for specialized training in these areas. Psychologists, social workers, special educators, or counselors conduct individual and group social skills training to ameliorate these deficits. In addition, behavior management plans can be crafted to instruct parents and teachers how to encourage and reward prosocial behaviors that will lead to an increase in social competence.

Finally, *motor skill* development is evaluated in multiple ways and times throughout the assessment. Motor skills are organized into two developmental domains: (1) fine-motor skills, which refers to the child's ability to produce finely tuned movements in the fingers, hands, tongue, and lips, and (2) gross motor skills, which consist of the movements of the larger muscle systems such as arms, legs, or the entire body and include balance, coordination, and muscle strength. The psychologist will conduct a screening of fine and gross motor areas to determine if the child exhibits difficulties performing age-appropriate tasks. Often simultaneously, the speech pathologist is examining the speech motor musculature and feeding skills to ascertain if motor coordination difficulties underlie any speech language problem. An example of this is a developmental disorder called *speech apraxia*, which refers to a difficulty in motor planning to execute speech motor movements. If these problems are evident, a referral is made to an occupational therapist for assessment of fine motor and attentional difficulties and/or to a physical therapist for further evaluation of gross motor difficulties. These evaluations, and the therapies that can ensue if a child qualifies for services, can be more easily conducted in a home or center-based environment, as the activities are game-like and children look forward to actively participating. On the other hand, it may be difficult to transport the materials used by occupational and physical therapists due to their unwieldy size, such as beach ball–size therapy balls, balance beams, tricycles, pegboards, and puzzles.

As young children are identified by their parents and pediatricians as possibly falling behind their peers on certain developmental milestones, the next step is *referral to assessment*. Although some families can afford and pursue private evaluations and therapies, most families rely on publicly supported programs to obtain assistance for their child. Children ages three to five are referred to the family school district's Committee on Preschool Special Education (CPSE). Younger children are referred to the Early Intervention (EI) program, which is coordinated through the county's department of health. Both the EI and CPSE systems set in motion the steps necessary to conduct the assessment: obtaining parental consent for assessment, requesting an updated medical evaluation, contacting service providers to conduct the necessary assessments, and so on.

While parents have the choice of providers, families are often referred to evaluation centers (typically found in preschools offering special education services) where multidisciplinary teams comprising school psychologists, special and/or regular preschool educators, speech pathologists, social workers, and physical and occupational therapists work together to coordinate the assessment, compare findings, and link recommendation strategies. The advantages of this coordinated approach include fewer visits for parents, synchronized evaluations in an "arena" style (more than one evaluation occurring simultaneously), and the ability to provide recommended services to the child and family after the evaluation is completed. Given the intertwined nature of development in early childhood, it is vital that assessment and intervention services be seamless and coordinated between home and school environments, which will maximize the intervention effectiveness.

Further Reading

Bracken, B., ed. 2004. *The psychoeducational assessment of preschool children*. 3rd ed. Mahwah, NJ: Lawrence Erlbaum Associates.

Bredekamp, S., and C. Copple, eds. 1997. *Developmentally appropriate practice in early childhood programs*. Rev. ed. Washington, DC: National Association for the Education of Young Children.

Epstein, A. S., L. J. Schweinhart, A. DeBruin-Parecki, and K. B. Robin. 2004. Preschool assessment: A guide to developing a balanced approach. In *NIEER Preschool Policy Matters*, no. 7 (July). Available at http://nieer.org/docs/index.php?DocID=104

Lidz, C. S. 2002. *Early childhood assessment*. New York: Wiley.

McAfee, O., D. J. Leong, and E. Bodrova. 2004. *Basics of assessment: A primer for early childhood educators*. Washington, DC: National Association for the Education of Young Children.

Meisels, S. J., and S. Atkins-Burnett. 2005. *Developmental screening in early childhood: A guide*. 5th ed. Washington, DC: National Association for the Education of Young Children.

Shonkoff, J. P., and S. J. Meisels, eds. 2000. *Handbook of early childhood intervention*. 2nd ed. Cambridge: Cambridge University Press.

Zero to Three (2005). *Diagnostic classification of mental health and developmental disorders of infancy and early childhood*. Rev. ed. Washington, DC: Zero to Three.

PAUL McCABE

Psychiatry and Special Education

The education of children and adolescents has long been a challenge for our society. Numerous problems can be found in the often underfunded educational enterprise, many of which are highlighted by the press, which tends to focus on school violence and the perennial shortage of qualified personnel. Simultaneously, more children and adolescents are developing mental health problems than at any other time in history.

To help with the increase of childhood mental health problems, the field of psychiatry has become a major component within special education. Psychiatry is the branch of medicine dealing with the treatment and prevention of mental, emotional, and behavioral problems. Psychiatrists are trained medical professionals whose care for individuals often includes prescribing medications and/or offering psychotherapy. When addressing students' learning and behavior problems, psychiatrists apply their knowledge of medicine and therapy to develop interventions or consult with a variety of professionals. In order to ensure effective treatment of many learners with disabilities in the schools, psychiatric intervention must be considered a crucial component for many children with particularly difficult-to-treat disorders, such as **depression**. Often, psychiatrists serve as a member of a team that meets to develop an appropriate **Individualized Education Program** for a child or adolescent.

The history of special education is relatively brief compared to that of general education. Through centuries of reform, proponents of fair and ethical treatment of students have helped shape how schools accommodate those who have difficulties in the school setting. Recent educational reform stemming from cases in the legal system has sought change in the treatment of children in special education, increased allocation of funds, and availability of appropriate educational opportunities. A variety of mental, emotional, and behavioral disorders affect students in schools and a select group of professionals—including school psychologists, school counselors, and special education teachers—are qualified to meet the needs of these learners.

There is a notable difference between disorders in the schools and those that are diagnosed from the field of medicine. In schools, children with disabilities must meet certain criteria according to education law. Medical professionals typically rely on the American Psychiatric Association's *Diagnostic and Statistical Manual of Mental Disorders* (DSM-IV) to diagnose mental, emotional, and behavioral disorders. However, the education system's definition does not encompass the requirements of the DSM-IV, nor is a DSM-IV diagnosis suitable for an individual child to receive special services in a school. A psychiatric diagnosis using the DSM-IV does not clearly translate into educational law and thus special education services. However, the criterion is similar across the education and medical fields. As a result, medical professionals must be sensitive in their reports to schools because the classification criterion varies across settings.

Whereas the DSM-IV sets the standards used to determine diagnoses and usually services in medical settings, the newly reauthorized **Individuals with Disabilities Education Act** (IDEA) dictates the classification of disability in the schools. Services and funding for those services are allocated according to IDEA and other educational laws.

Perhaps the best example of psychiatry in practice in the schools is the work done with students with emotional disturbance. This disorder, as explained in federal law, is a condition in which children cannot make or maintain relationships with peers. Students likely have inappropriate behaviors or feelings that socially impair them in normal circumstances. These youths experience difficulties in learning that cannot be explained by intellectual, sensory, or health factors. Students with emotional disabilities struggle in schools by having problems working with peers and following teacher instructions. Teachers and parents often feel frustrated and at a loss in working with these students. Fortunately, psychiatrists can assist teachers and parents in developing appropriate treatment of students with emotional disturbance.

In order to suitably serve children, psychiatrists and education professionals must work together as a team, each offering their specialized expertise. By bridging the gap between education and medicine, a psychiatric component in treatment ensures the most effective treatment of many disorders affecting children and enables them to cope with the rigors of their education and even thrive in the school setting.

With advances in brain-scanning technology, the biological basis of behavior has been uncovered more clearly in the last decade. Psychologists and the nurses that work with learners, families, and school personnel are becoming more involved in the schools because the educational system is often unprepared for dealing with the medical problems of students with significant emotional problems (e.g., depression, anxiety) and the way they can affect a child's school day.

Only by melding medical treatment with individualized psychological and educational services can we offer children and adolescents a productive educational experience. Advances in the use of a variety of medicines have enhanced treatment for learners with emotional and behavioral disorders. Traditional psychological treatments such as behavior support, group counseling, and individual psychotherapy and counseling, especially when coupled with medication, have proven useful in treating individuals with a wide variety of psychiatric problems in schools.

Further Reading

Gask, L. 2004. *A short introduction to psychiatry*. Thousand Oaks, CA: Sage.

Hardman, M. L., C. J. Drew, and M. W. Egan. 1999. *Human exceptionality*. 6th ed. Needham Heights, MA: Allyn & Bacon.

Heward, W. L. 1996. *Exceptional children: An introduction to special education*. 5th ed. Englewood Cliffs, NJ: Merrill.

National Dissemination Center for Children with Disabilities. 1996. Educating students with emotional/behavioral disorders. http://www.nichcy.org/pubs/bibliog/bib10txt.htm

Websites

American Psychiatric Association: http://www.psych.org/

Council for Exceptional Children: http://www.cec.sped.org/

IDEA 2004 Statute Changes: http://www.directionservice.org/cadre/stat_index_ideia.cfm

National Association of School Psychologists: http://www.nasponline.org/

National Institute of Mental Health, "Depression" resources: http://www.nimh.nih.gov/healthinformation/depressionmenu.cfm

National Mental Health Information Center: http://www.mentalhealth.samhsa.gov/publications/allpubs/CA%2D0006/

JUSTIN M. WALKER AND RIK CARL D'AMATO

Psychoeducational Assessment of Bilingual Learners

The psychoeducational assessment of bilingual learners for the purposes of educational intervention and placement should meet the same rigorous standards set for such assessments of children who speak English as their dominant language. In fact, this is a requirement of federal law. Unfortunately, in practice that standard is difficult to achieve. Tests that are commercially available and assessment procedures used in schools have been developed based on the performance of children whose native language is English and for whom familiarity with American values and culture is normative. Beyond the technical difficulties in developing adequate tests and procedures, assessment professionals who are fluent in the languages that children speak at home are not always accessible. Given the shortage of adequately trained bilingual assessors, translation of tests and use of interpreters are often employed to meet the demand for psychoeducational test data—rendering the clinical value of such assessments questionable. The concern about bilingual assessment quality grows and becomes more urgent as increasing numbers of English-language learners (ELLs) fail to meet **No Child Left Behind Act** benchmarks throughout the country.

Language diversity in schools presents a challenge to educators who overwhelmingly are fluent only in English. Faced with large numbers of children who speak a language other than English at home, local, state, and federal policies have sought to accelerate the acquisition of English among those students. Although since the 1980s there has been some support for bilingual education, in most cases these programs have used the native language only as a vehicle for improving English fluency rather than to support dual-language proficiency. The pressure on schools to bring these students to a level of competence that meets newly instituted local and national educational standards has resulted in large numbers of second-language learners being identified as potentially disabled.

Teachers reasonably expect that assessment professionals will be able to ascertain if an ELL's academic difficulties are rooted in cognitive dysfunction or are typical signs of acculturation stress or transition to another language. This assumption is grounded in the unquestioned acceptance of professional evaluators' knowledge and competence. Yet the psychological testing model practiced in schools systematically underestimates the unique strengths of bilingual children and highlights their difficulties in mastering the English language or becoming acculturated to mainstream American society. It has been argued that tests of cognitive ability administered in the English language are, for these children, tests of their language proficiency in English. Consequently, assessment results tend to confound limited English proficiency with limited cognitive ability or with a language disability. Even when assessment incorporates translated tests or utilizes interpreters, reliability and validity are inadequate for diagnostic purposes, leading to potentially biased conclusions.

In most cases, the designation of disability hinges on professional judgment rather than on reliable test results. While this practice may not be necessarily objectionable—many conditions, such as autism are based on clinical judgment due to lack of accurate testing procedures—the lack of familiarity with acculturation processes and second-language acquisition among clinicians places this population at great risk for misdiagnosis. Data from national studies indicate that, in the great majority of these cases, children who are referred for evaluation are indeed found to be disabled and are subsequently found eligible for special education supports and programs. This pattern of identification, referral, and placement is so prevalent that it has resulted in the disproportional placement of ELL children in programs for the mild to moderately disabled. ELL children are labeled "learning disabled," "speech impaired," or "emotionally handicapped" in greater numbers than would be expected by the size of their populations. Child advocates have characterized special education placements practices for ELL children as discriminatory. In several notable cases, the courts have agreed and have not only questioned assessment practices but also required corrective actions.

Standardized tests and most large-scale testing programs used in schools interpret differences in results among students as indications of individuals' learning capacity. However, that conclusion can be valid only if all children tested have had equal opportunities to learn the material included in the tests. This is never the case for ELLs; these students tend to have significantly different life experiences and lack exposure to the content tested, and therefore the differences in results cannot be interpreted as reflecting differences in abilities alone. Test results are just as likely to reflect limited exposure to the dominant culture and limited comprehension of the second language. For example, even when ELL students are in the same class with English-dominant peers learning a new mathematics concept, the learning task for the second-language learners is complicated by the tenuous nature of their comprehension in English. The mathematics lesson may not be completely understood—not because the children lack ability in mathematics but simply because they understood only half of the words spoken by the teacher. Despite this commonsense observation, teachers and clinicians tend to look for the origins of academic difficulty exclusively within the child and to interpret poor learning outcomes as symptoms of a disability. Lack of understanding of the second-language learning and acculturation processes places ELLs at greater risk for disability classification.

It stands to reason that some second-language learners do in fact have disabilities—in proportions similar to their English-dominant peers. Identifying these children's needs requires great familiarity with the child's language, culture, and acculturation experiences. Assessment professionals should reassess their reasons for suspecting a disability and reconsider the likely benefits of alternative educational placements or supports. Rather than identifying school failure as an expression of limitations within the child, clinicians and teachers need to explore the social, cultural, linguistic, and academic contexts that promote or inhibit learning.

Sound educational decision making hinges on the quality of information available. Testing data for ELLs tend to be flawed and should be interpreted with caution. A school-based assessment must extend beyond results obtained in a formal testing situation. Such an assessment should include comprehensive reviews of cognitive functioning and school performance conducted by clinicians who are fluent in the child's native culture and language and who are familiar with the challenges of second-language acquisition, acculturation, and the barriers present in the particular school environment.

Further Reading

Artiles, A., and S. C. Trent. 1994. Overrepresentation of minority students in special education: A continuing debate. *Journal of Special Education* 27 (4): 410–37.

Artiles, A., and G. Zamora-Duran. 1997. *Reducing the disproportionate representation of culturally diverse students in special and gifted education*. Reston, VA: Council for Exceptional Children.

Bursztyn, A. 2002. The path to academic disability: Javier's school experience. In *Rethinking multicultural education: Case studies in cultural transition*, ed. C. Korn and A. Bursztyn, 160–83. Westport, CT: Bergin & Garvey.

Cummins, J. 1986. Psychological assessment of minority students: Out of context, out of control? *Journal of Reading, Writing and Learning Disabilities International* 2:1–8.

Figueroa, R. A., and E. Garcia. 1994. Issues in testing students from culturally and linguistically diverse backgrounds. *Multicultural Education* 1:10–19.

Kincheloe, J. L., S. Steinberg, and P. H. Hinchey, eds. 1999. *The post-formal reader: Cognition and education*. New York: Falmer Press.

Losen, D. L., and G. Orfield. 2002. *Racial inequity and special education*. Cambridge, MA: Civil Rights Project at Harvard University and Harvard Education Press.

Websites

BUENO Center for Multicultural Education: http://www.colorado.edu/education/bueno/

National Association for Bilingual Education: http://www.nabe.org/

ALBERTO M. BURSZTYN

Social Inclusion in Early Childhood Special Education Classrooms

In the field of early childhood special education, **Individuals with Disabilities Education Act** (IDEA) legislation became a strong foundation for integrating young children with disabilities into programs designed for their typically developing peers. Many studies have indicated advantages to all the children in inclusive early childhood settings. Typically developing children have been observed to be more aware of other children's needs, more comfortable with disability, and more accepting of human differences. Also, children with disabilities have shown developmental gains in the areas of communication and social skills and have benefited from increased interactions with typically developing children in integrated settings.

While recognizing these benefits of inclusive environments, it is also critical to rethink the true notion of **inclusion** in the context of social experiences of children with disabilities and typically developing children. It goes beyond simply placing children with disabilities in the same physical space as their typically developing peers and providing modified instructional materials and curricula. Social experiences of children in inclusive settings should be examined beyond the quantitative aspects of social behaviors such as the frequency and duration of social interactions, types of play, and initiative and responsive behaviors. It is important to recognize the complex notion of children's social relationships and the power dynamics present in early childhood inclusion classrooms.

Although seldom associated with early childhood classrooms, power is central to all social relations among young children. Children sometimes don't get along and deliberately use their powers to include and exclude others. The power dynamics among young children have clearly emerged while examining the leadership skills of young children. More specifically, competent children, who are usually typically developing children with high cognitive and language competency, begin to emerge as leaders and often exclude other children, especially children with disabilities, from play. Here is a short exchange that illustrates power dynamics between a child with disabilities and typically developing children.

> Three preschool children are eating lunch at a table.
>
> "Calvin. Calvin. Calvin," Ira calls. "I'm talking to you, Calvin!"
>   Calvin does not respond to Ira. Instead, Calvin reaches over and takes a Spiderman cup from in front of Henry. Calvin smiles and puts it back. Henry smiles.
>   "Calvin. Calvin," Ira looks directly at Calvin, waving a large plastic bottle of orange juice in front of him while calling his name. Calvin does not look up. Instead he takes a plastic spoon and begins digging into a bowl of rice.
>   Calvin leans towards Henry, who is sitting on his right, and says something. Henry smiles as Calvin speaks. Calvin then leans back in his chair and says, "I just got it at camp."
>   Ira calls out again, "Calvin! Talk to me!"
>   Calvin replies quietly without looking up, "No."
>   "Yes," Ira says.
>   "No," Calvin replies again.
>   "Yes."
>   "No."
>   Ira asks Calvin, "Do you use the bathroom?"
>   "Stop it!" Calvin replies. "I don't want to talk to you." Calvin continues eating his rice.
>   "Ugh!" Ira grunts, then returns to eating his lunch.

In this example, Calvin, a typically developing child, continually ignores Ira, a child with special needs, while paying attention to another typically developing child, Henry. Even when Ira finally captures Calvin's attention, he does not have the cognitive ability to carry out an appropriate conversation. Instead, Ira asks Calvin a question that is out of context and receives negative response from Calvin. This example illustrates how a child with disabilities may face social rejection by peers when placed in an inclusive classroom with typically developing peers. Researchers have shown that children with disabilities are less successful in their social bids to peers, appear to take the lead in interactions less often, and tend to have more disruptive play when entering the play group. In an inclusive classroom, typically developing children are more likely to initiate and extend the play ideas, enhance the quality of play, and regulate social interaction. On the other hand, children with developmental delays may lack age-appropriate social understanding of complex interactions or have difficulty communicating effectively with peers.

Using their well-developed communicative competence, typically developing children may take over the position of power and exercise this power to marginalize children with disabilities. Even though children with disabilities are included in play with typically developing peers, it is more likely that typically developing children will be in charge of the play activities, regulating and directing others according to their agenda. Therefore, it is important to closely examine the quality of social experiences for children with disabilities. A critical issue is how children with disabilities are making meaningful social connections and relationships with typically developing children.

Even though it is hard to come up with quick-fix solutions, the key to unlock this complex issue is in the hands of teachers. The facilitative role of early childhood special education teachers within the natural context is critical. When looking at inclusive early childhood classrooms, one of the important elements for successful social integration is observant and sensitive teachers who are willing to take the time to build positive relationships with children. In terms of strengthening social relationships between children with disabilities and their typically developing peers, teachers need to not only help children with disabilities to optimize their ability to express themselves socially but also encourage typically developing peers to respond to them in more socially positive ways. Therefore, teachers' responsibilities go beyond providing curriculum adaptation and instruction; teachers also need to assume a complex role as facilitators of social experience, promoting the principles of "equity" and "social justice" when working with diverse groups of young children. Both general and special educators must pay close attention to the creation of a climate and set of opportunities that allow all children, regardless of their ability or disability, to flourish in ways that reflect each individual's strengths. Social inclusion at the early childhood level is not all about pushing for a political agenda, but is more importantly about building a social community where all children are valued and respected.

Further Reading

Guralnick, M. J., R. T. Conner, M. A. Hammond, J. M. Gottman, and K. Kinnish. 1996. The peer relations of preschool children with communication disorders. *Child Development* 67:471–89.

Recchia, S. L., and Y.-J. Lee. 2004. Troubling constructions of leadership in the early childhood classroom: Creating space for multiple voices. Paper presented at the Interdisciplinary Conference on Reconceptuallizing Early Childhood Education, Oslo, Norway.

Recchia, S. L., and E. Soucacou. 2004. Nurturing social experience in the early childhood special education classroom: Perspectives on three teachers. Paper presented at the American Education Research Association Annual Meeting, San Diego.

Walton, T. 2001. Why inclusion benefits everyone. *Child Care Information Exchange* 139:76–79.

YOON-JOO LEE

Social Skills Training in Inclusion Classrooms

Students receiving special education services encompass diverse groups of learners and include a wide array of disabilities. Regardless of the type of disability, most individuals learn to socialize within their families, in classroom settings, and eventually in the employment arena. Socialization is an important aspect of interpersonal relationships, and possessing the required skills to maintain healthy relationships during childhood and adolescence is considered a predictor of future adjustment. Many children classified with learning disabilities and emotional disturbances experience difficulties socializing and frequently find it difficult to make and keep friends. Having poor social skills has been shown to be associated with poor academic achievement and emotional distress. While not all children with disabilities are lacking in social skills, the number of those who are is significant enough to warrant attention and elicit suggestions from educational researchers for teaching social skills.

The 1997 version of the **Individuals with Disabilities Education Act** (IDEA) mandated that all children with disabilities be educated in the least restrictive environment (LRE) possible. While LRE has mostly been implemented by serving students with disabilities in **self-contained classrooms** in regular education schools, **inclusion** implies providing special education services in regular classrooms, regardless of the severity of the child's disability. As a result, the term *inclusion* describes a more uncompromising approach to integration.

One clear advantage of educating children with disabilities in inclusion classrooms is that children with disabilities have the opportunity to socialize with their nondisabled peers. The most appealing aspects of inclusion for children with disabilities in relation to their social experience is that they:

- are educated with their nondisabled peers as a heterogeneous group
- experience a sense of belonging to the group
- share activities with individualized outcomes
- make use of environments frequented by nondisabled peers
- receive a balanced educational experience (i.e., inclusive education represents an *individualized balance* between the academic, functional, and social/personal aspects of instruction)

This implies that educators within inclusion classrooms recognize the need to be concerned about the development of students' self-esteem and socialization, as well as their educational inadequacies. Attaining adequate skills for socialization in inclusion classrooms is a requirement that will lead to interpersonal success later in life.

As mentioned earlier, it has been observed that some children with disabilities manifest difficulties interacting with their peers beginning in preschool. Special education researchers now recognize that social skills training is an essential component of success in the development of peer relationships and educational achievement. General education teachers have also come to value appropriate social skills in their classrooms and have been encouraged to implement social skills training programs at the preschool, elementary, and high school levels.

Some research also suggests that some students with disabilities do not like to receive all of their education in the general education classroom. For example, one study (Lovitt, Plavins, and Cushing 1999) observed that some children with less severe disabilities demonstrated their partiality for special education classes because of negative experiences (i.e., being made fun of, put down, and picked on) in general education classes. Studies of students with more severe disabilities placed in full inclusion programs indicated that students felt more comfortable in classes with classmates that had comparable problems and interests.

General education and special education teachers are encouraged to adhere to the recommended guidelines for insuring appropriate socialization for children with disabilities at the school level. Educators now know that social skills training can be implemented through individual, small group, or entire classroom participation. Teachers may use a direct instructional approach in which the teacher illustrates examples and provides counterexamples to the students. Emphasis should also be placed on how to interact, how to guide thoughts and emotions, how to use problem-solving skills, and how to manifest trustworthiness for oneself and others.

When implementing social skills training, educators should recognize that social skills learned in one culture might be inappropriate in another. A bicultural competence and social skills training approach is also suggested for use with children from diverse backgrounds. This nonbiased training model focuses on a *situation-specific* approach that concentrates on the level of social skills needed for optimal socialization. In doing so, educators focus on the problem behavior, look at the specific differences between the individual's observed behavior and the behavior approved as effective, and conduct an analysis of socially competent behavior within the actual cultural setting. Educators' awareness of the idea of bicultural competence for socialization is important since many children with disabilities come from culturally and linguistically diverse backgrounds.

Although inclusion has received the support of many parents of children with special needs, other parents have strongly opposed this kind of integration. This view stems from parents' concern that their children would not receive the individualized education in an inclusion classroom that they would receive if they were in a more restrictive environment, such as a self-contained classroom for children with learning disabilities. Educators, school psychologists, and social workers know that placing a child with a disability in a general education classroom does not guarantee that the child will do well academically or be socially accepted by his or her nondisabled peers. In this regard, it is recognized that educators must teach appropriate social skills to children with disabilities as well as educate those children without disabilities about the difficulties of living with a disability.

References

LaFromboise, T. D., and W. Rowe. 1983. Skills training for bicultural competence: Rationale and application. *Journal of Counseling and Psychology* 30:589–95.

Lovitt, T. C., M. Plavins, and S. Cushing. 1999. What do pupils with disabilities have to say about their high school experience? *Remedial and Special Education* 20:67–76, 83.

Odom, S. I., S. R. McConnell, and M. A. McEvoy, eds. 1992. *Social competence of young children with disabilities: Nature, development, and intervention.* Baltimore: Brookes.

Palmer, D. S., K. Fuller, T. Arora, and M. Nelson. 2001. Taking sides: Parent views on inclusion for their children with severe disabilities. *Exceptional Children* 67:467–84.

Further Reading

Cartledge, G., and J. F. Milbrun. 1995. *Teaching social skills to children and youth: Innovative approaches.* 3rd ed. Boston: Allyn & Bacon.

Website

Social Skills Training: http://www.indiana.edu/~schpsy/sskills.html

DANIELLE MARTINES

Teacher Satisfaction and Retention in Special Education

Teacher turnover and retention have for some time been a focus of attention for those concerned with maintaining a high-quality teacher corps. Beginning in the early 1980s, reports predicted teacher shortages caused by increased enrollments, teacher retirements, and more stringent definitions of the "highly qualified teacher" mandated by the **No Child Left Behind Act** (NCLB). These shortages were predicted to be especially dire in high-needs areas such as math, science, and special education. Interestingly, research shows that it is in these fields where the greatest turnover occurs.

The satisfaction teachers have with their jobs is an important topic in education and is becoming even more important in special education. Teachers' satisfaction with their work is unique to every teacher, and it varies over time and setting. There are combinations of intrinsic and extrinsic sources of motivation relating to the satisfaction teachers have in their employment. Although no one condition ultimately leads to dissatisfaction with employment, there are some trends that identify common reasons for job dissatisfaction in special education. The general consensus among administrators is that teacher quality in the United States is high. However, the problem in the schools lies in keeping those quality teachers in their classrooms. Younger, early-career teachers are much more likely to leave than those in mid-career. One of the key demographic factors in job satisfaction is teacher experience and age; teachers who are more experienced and senior tend to be more satisfied and stable in their employment.

The primary reasons for the decreased satisfaction and turnover among teachers, including special education teachers, include inadequate support from school administration, student discipline problems, low salaries (especially when compared with available alternative careers), and the limited input afforded to faculty regarding school decision making. In fact, job dissatisfaction and burnout play a greater role in teacher turnover than does teacher retirement. The data also show that school characteristics and organizational conditions affect teacher satisfaction, burnout, and turnover. For example, small private schools have the highest rates of turnover.

In addition to these factors, special education teachers have a distinct set of factors that affect satisfaction with their work. For example, in contrast to regular classroom teachers, special educators deal with a unique and occasionally difficult population. These students are often not a high priority for the school administrators. In an era focused on testing, it is difficult to increase the scores of special needs students. Special education teachers' work sometimes has a more emotional component—a factor readily associated with mental exhaustion and burnout. They are likely to have more meetings with concerned parents. Special education teachers tend to be a minority in the school, resulting in a smaller social support network. Collaboration with regular classroom teachers is lacking because the regular classroom teachers are often not trained to work with the special education teacher; they are more than willing to relinquish the special needs child to the special needs teacher, despite the push toward **inclusion**. Also, special education teachers have increased paperwork requirements. All of these stressful situations contribute to burnout and consequential problems in lower satisfaction and high turnover. Regardless of the motivation for leaving a position, vacant teaching positions are often filled by less experienced or less qualified teachers. The result is that students receive less quality education.

The causes of job satisfaction, dissatisfaction, and burnout and their consequences (e.g., decreased performance and turnover) are well researched. Schools and school districts are aware of these causes and are working to increase teacher satisfaction in order to decrease burnout and turnover; there are specific strategies that address these issues.

Perhaps the most effective way to enhance teacher competence and teacher job satisfaction is through professional development. This is especially needed by beginning special education teachers who are setting out on a teaching career. With the initiation of the NCLB, schools had to quickly respond to accountability by enacting support, mentor, guidance, and orientation programs—also referred to as induction—to keep newer teachers in their buildings. Sometimes these programs have focused on upgrading teacher skills so that they are in accordance with the law. For example, teachers need to have taken a minimum amount of coursework in an area to be "highly qualified." Other programs focus on such needed topics as classroom management, writing Individual Education Programs, meeting with parents, and so on. Such mentoring programs provide the experience new teachers need to feel comfortable and supported in their work.

Additionally, both decision-making support and support from administrators contribute to retention and job satisfaction. Thus, training programs for principals to serve as instructional leaders and to recognize the particular needs of special education teachers can help improve the job satisfaction of these teachers.

Another suggested way to improve teacher retention is to recognize their work by increasing teacher salaries, often by a substantial amount. Research indicates that teachers with higher salaries have a lower rate of leaving their schools than those who are paid less. This may not be caused by the satisfaction of a materialistic need, but rather by a sense of reward and value for their performance. Some school districts provide teachers in high-needs areas, including special education, with salary adjustments. However, it is unlikely that most districts can afford to pay teachers more than they currently do without reducing other resources.

Special education teachers engage in a variety of nonteaching activities each day. One of the many demands—in addition to meetings, consultation, and planning—is paperwork, which many special education teachers agree is excessive. Special education teachers have rigorous requirements that may place extra stress on them, leading to lowered satisfaction. With new educational laws and **high-stakes testing**, a brief and busy school year is shortened even more by preparing for exams and accounting for student progress. An extended school year could allow for more class time to complete units and reduce the stress of having too much work to complete in a short amount of time. Furthermore, assistance with the paperwork would go a long way to relieving the stress that comes with meeting administrative deadlines.

Special education teachers work with a difficult and diverse population. Without support, the many needs of special education students can lead to lower job satisfaction for special education teachers. Teachers who find motivation and satisfaction in their employment are more effective in helping their students. Teachers with a strong efficacy for their jobs frequently help boost job satisfaction for others in their building. Through empowerment and decision making, teachers become more effective and satisfied with their work. Students and their parents receive better educational services when teachers are satisfied with their jobs.

Further Reading

Boe, E. E., S. A. Bobbitt, L. H. Cook, S. D. Whitener, and A. L. Weber. 1997. Why didst thou go? Predictors of retention, transfer, and attrition of special and general education teachers from a national perspective. *Journal of Special Education* 30:390–411.

Ingersoll, R. M. 2001. *Teacher turnover, teacher shortages, and the organization of schools.* Seattle: Center for the Study of Teaching and Policy, University of Washington.

Latham, A. S. 1998. Teacher satisfaction. *Educational Leadership* 55:82–83.

Reyes, P., and D. Hoyle. 1992. Teachers' satisfaction with principals' communication. *Journal of Educational Research* 85:163–68.

Websites

About Special Education: http://specialed.about.com/
Internet Special Education Resources: http://www.iser.com/
No Child Left Behind: www.nochildleftbehind.gov/

EUGENE P. SHEEHAN AND
JUSTIN M. WALKER

Transition Services in Special Education

Transition services are necessary to assist special education students in achieving their future goals. This process should result in goals that not only are realistic and achievable but also lead to full-time employment or success in postsecondary education, independent living, and gainful participation in the community. Self-determination is a key component of the transition process, and as a result, students need to be aware of their preferences and become proactive in the planning process. It is a dynamic and fluid process that responds to the abilities, service needs, and determination of the individual.

Educating children with disabilities was not widely addressed until compulsory education was declared a human right in 1948. Prior to this time, there were only limited services available to students with disabilities, and so most students with disabilities were educated with the mainstream population as long as they were able to meet an "expected level of achievement." From after World War II and through the 1970s, the main service delivery model was educating students with disabilities in **self-contained classrooms** and segregated programs, such as schools for the blind. During this time, minimal services consisted of a modified curriculum that would allow students to work at their ability level.

Starting in the late 1970s, laws providing more extensive services began to surface, three of which were essential in changing the face of special education services. The first pertinent law was **Public Law 94-142**, the Education for All Handicapped Children Act of 1975, which stated that all children with disabilities were to be afforded a free and appropriate public education in the least restrictive environment. Under this law, students in primary and secondary schools were to be offered access to all programs and services that were available to students without disabilities, such as vocational training and home economics.

Around this time, research began to show that there was a lack of focus on services for postsecondary students concerning employment opportunities and independent living. The next important law enacted was the Education of the Handicapped Act amendments of 1983, which provided $6.6 million to create model programs that fostered school-to-work transitions for students with disabilities, funded research in this area, and promoted personnel development.

The last law, and perhaps most crucial of all, was the **Individuals with Disabilities Education Act** of 1990 (IDEA, PL 101-476) which mandated that a statement of transition be included in students' **Individualized Education Programs** (IEPs) by the age of 16. With this law, special educators were now required to spend a portion of their time planning postsecondary services and to include this information, along with the specific agencies responsible for providing the services, within the statement of transition.

When IDEA was first reauthorized in 1997, changes included:

1. providing additional services such as transportation, speech therapy, counseling, and occupational therapy as part of transition planning
2. requiring a transition statement in a student's IEP by the age of fourteen
3. allowing students with disabilities to participate in statewide testing
4. including general education teachers as IEP team members
5. requiring IEP teams to consider the use of **assistive technology** devices (technological equipment utilized to allow students to work to their potential)

In 2004, IDEA was reauthorized for a second time and renamed the Individuals with Disabilities Education Improvement Act (PL 108-446). The new IDEA upheld prior mandates for transition services and provided a slightly changed definition of transition services. *Transition services* are now defined as a coordinated set of activities for a child with disabilities that are based on a *results-oriented process*—rather than an *outcome-oriented* one—that takes into account a student's strengths. Additional changes require that transition services include services that will assist students in meeting their goals and a statement that the student has been informed of his or her rights one year before reaching age of majority (the age at which rights are transferred to the student). The statement of transition by the age of 14 has been removed and replaced with appropriate measurable postsecondary goals that will assist the student in a successful transition.

Transition services address a student's independent living, employment skills, career exploration, and employment continuity in the community upon graduation from their academic program. The transition process, also referred to as **student-centered planning**, involves transition screening (i.e., discovering the student's interests, preferences, and needs), academic planning such that coursework is in alignment with career goals, and organizing community supports and subsequent job placement in local businesses. An assessment of the student's needs and life goals also needs to be conducted. The identification of transition needs for a student can begin with helping the student focus on her interests. Through educational planning, classes can be identified for students that highlight their interests and can help them focus on future choices. In addition, the process of transition services involves the identification of the services available to students such as vocational training and job placement services.

Career goals must be incorporated within the IEP. The IEP serves as a tool to establish both long- and short-term goals toward that career path. A collaborative effort is necessary in this planning process, because the IEP team consists of the student, his parent/guardian, his teachers, his **child study team** members, related services individuals (e.g., speech therapists, occupational therapists), and transitional agency representatives (e.g., personnel from a state's division of vocational rehabilitation). This collaborative effort is also essential in identifying the supports and accommodations that the student will need in the community, since transition occurs in both school and community environments. Identification of the academic program, vocational training programs, community supports, and postschool supports that are available pursuant to her interests should all be included in a student's IEP.

At the age of fourteen, students' transition needs are identified and their IEPs are developed. Students are invited to attend their IEP meeting and become an integral part of the decision-making process. The IEP meeting provides students with the opportunity to express their interests and preferences. At the age of sixteen, transitional services may be linked with agency support; such agencies may include the state division of vocational rehabilitation and the state division of developmental disabilities. The student's IEP should focus on adult-life skills as well as meeting her academic needs. Students are encouraged to explore career opportunities through work-study, vocational technical programs, community employment experiences, and academic coursework. When students graduate from high school, they are no longer entitled to special education services. Therefore, it is essential that the students have access to secondary education curricula and programs to prepare them for appropriate transition objectives.

Students' self-determination, as well as effective decision making by all members of the collaborative process, provides the context for goal-setting and planning for successful transitions. Schools do not always have the human resources and expertise for effective planning; in such cases, parental involvement and advocacy become critical for successful outcomes. Many of the services now in place are run by charity and not-for-profit organizations; the quality of their services varies widely across the nation. Most authorities agree that better planning and resources need to be made available for successful transitions to occur for all students with disabilities.

Beyond the uneven work of schools and agencies, young people with disabilities encounter other significant obstacles. In order for transition to work well, employers and the society at large need to become more tolerant and accepting. People with disabilities continue to be marginalized in the workplace and the community.

Further Reading

Clark, G. M., and P. L. Sitlington. 2006. *Transition education and services for students with disabilities*. Boston: Allyn & Bacon.

Dowdy, C. A. 1996. Vocational rehabilitation and special education: Partners in transition for individuals with learning disabilities. *Journal of Learning Disabilities* 29 (2): 137–47.

Johnson, D. R., R. A. Stodden, E. J. Emanuel, R. Luecking, and M. Mack. 2002. Current challenges facing secondary education and transition services: What research tells us. *Council for Exceptional Children* 68 (4): 519–31.

Kohler, P. D., and S. Field. 2003. Transition-focused education: Foundation for the future. *Journal of Special Education* 37 (3): 174–83.

Lehman, C. M., H. B. Clark, M. Bullis, J. Rinkin, and L. A. Castellanos. 2002. Transition from school to adult life: Empowering youth through community ownership and accountability. *Journal of Child and Family Studies* 11 (1): 127–41.

Lohrmann-O'Rourke, S., and O. Gomez. 2001. Integrating preference assessment within the transition process to create meaningful school to life outcomes. *Exceptionality* 9 (3): 157–74.

Neubert, D. A. 2003. The role of assessment in the transition to adult life: Process for students with disabilities. *Exceptionality* 11 (2): 63–75.

Websites

National Center on Secondary Education and Transition: http://www.ncset.org/
U.S. Department of Education: http://www.ed.gov/

ARLEEN RIOS AND JENNIFER FOSTER

Families and Disability

Child Abuse and Children with Disabilities

Child abuse and maltreatment in all of its forms—neglect, physical, sexual, emotional—continues to be an area of concern around the world in both industrialized and developing countries, despite significant attempts to put into place preventative legislation, interventions, and procedures. Difficulties in appropriately identifying abuse and investigating, prosecuting, and providing treatment to perpetrators, victims, and families remain the key issues in being able to permanently eradicate child abuse in most communities. In addition, as a result of multiple attempts to stop the maltreatment of children, professionals have come to face the reality that there is no simple, cause-and-effect framework in which child abuse can be prevented. The problem is multidimensional, requiring the understanding of a particular child, a family, the community, and systems that influence these individuals and the broader cultural context in which all of this interaction occurs. Add disability to these dimensions, and the picture is further complicated.

Work has been done in the field of child abuse to achieve greater clarity in terms of what actually constitutes abuse and maltreatment. However, these attempts vary across states and countries, not only complicating the gathering of statistical data in any one category but also preventing adequate research that could validate or advance greater understanding in critical areas. The key U.S. federal legislation addressing child abuse and neglect is the Child Abuse Prevention and Treatment Act (CAPTA), which was originally enacted in 1974 (PL 93-247). This Act has been amended several times, most recently being reauthorized on June 25, 2003 (as the Keeping Children and Families Safe Act of 2003, PL 108-36). CAPTA provides federal funding to states in support of prevention, assessment, investigation, prosecution, and treatment activities and also provides grants to public agencies and nonprofit organizations for demonstration programs and projects. Additionally, it identifies the federal role in supporting research, evaluation, technical assistance, and data collection activities. This legislation also sets forth a minimum definition of child abuse and maltreatment, which is then incorporated into laws within individual states:

> An abused child means a child under eighteen years of age (... unless designated as disabled and therefore, protected until end of state-approved school age ...) who is defined as abused by the Family Court Act and whose parent or other person legally responsible for his/her care: inflicts or allows to be inflicted upon such child physical injury by other than accidental means; creates or allows to be created a substantial risk of physical injury; commits, or allows to be committed, a sex offense; creates or allows to be created a state of substantially diminished psychological or intellectual functioning. (New York State Social Services Law, § 412; § 1012(e) of the Family Court Act)

Legislation has helped to increase the amount of substantive research and evaluation in this area, along with key media-exposed child abuse cases that have focused attention on the issues (e.g., Lisa Steinberg in New York City in 1987). Strong advocacy and societal responses as a result of some of these horrific events have increased the focus on providing mandated training for key professionals (teachers, social workers, psychologists, etc.) and strengthened efforts to coordinate investigative procedures.

Disability-related child abuse research and training, however, continues to lag behind developments involving typical children. Adequate statistics documenting numbers of children with disabilities who have been abused continue to be hard to interpret, given the ongoing problems with definitions of disabilities, inadequate reporting for many reasons (e.g., fear, dependency on caretakers, difficulty in communicating or being "believed," inadequate training of child protective workers and investigators), and confusion on the part of many professionals as to whether behaviors that evidence a "reasonable cause to suspect" are a result of abuse or the nature of the disability itself. However, despite the inadequacies, researchers continue to document higher numbers of children with disabilities having been abused as compared to their nondisabled peers. For example, of more than fifty thousand children in grades K–12 surveyed, of which approximately 15 percent were children with disabilities (all disability types represented), 31 percent of the children with disabilities had been abused, compared to 11 percent within the population of nondisabled students.

Similar to child abuse in general, the issue of abuse among children with disabilities is complicated by multiple factors. A high-profile, media-driven abuse case in the 1989—a rape trial in Glen Ridge, New Jersey—heightened overall awareness nationally and significantly advanced the understanding of the vulnerability of some individuals. The Glen Ridge case involved a seventeen-year-old girl with mental retardation who attended a local high school and was part of an **inclusion** program. She was gang-raped by members of the high school football team who knew her well. The case raised broad general issues in terms of consent, responsibility, and gender/social-class privileges, but was specifically relevant for people with disabilities. Cases such as these called into question the important role education plays, not only for individuals with disability, but to society at large and its "perception" of individuals in a society and their rights. This case dramatically demonstrated that the abuse of children with disabilities extends far beyond families and strangers, and includes also peers, sometimes in a way that is more difficult to control or prevent.

Children with disabilities represent a very heterogeneous population. How to adequately develop training materials for both children and the multidisciplinary teams supporting them (e.g., child protective workers, law enforcement, the judiciary, educators, court-appointed advocates) that are representative of such diversity of need continues to be a challenge, but is an area of current focus. Many different types of educational programs have been developed and implemented in schools for various populations of children and young adults (e.g., No-Go-Tell! [Krents and Brenner 1991]) with some success. Focus continues to be on improving problem solving, **self-advocacy**, and empowerment strategies for children with disabilities related to situations they may encounter within areas of potential victimization. Simultaneously, efforts are also under way to enhance the skills of investigators in communicating more effectively with these children and to adapt procedures (interview time and location, questioning strategies, etc.) so that potential abuse cases involving children with disabilities can be appropriately handled and not dismissed out of hand as has oftentimes been the practice.

Future work on the subject of child abuse and disabilities is being directed toward understanding the impact of victimization on children who are already dealing with an array of developmental, communication, perceptual, and social-emotional issues. Does this added trauma manifest itself in greater delays or additional handicaps that may further mask the abuse itself and make it more difficult to recognize or treat? A greater understanding in this area may provide improved protection for this particular population of children. Additionally, it is questionable whether focus really needs to continue in terms of establishing just how many or what types of children with disabilities have suffered or might be more vulnerable to abuse.

All children are vulnerable. Just as with any child, the degree to which they may be more vulnerable to abuse is related more to the intertwining of child–family–society interactions than to any other factor. Perhaps greater progress would be made in eradicating child abuse if the focus were shifted from the individual to the development of a society that values children and seeks to protect them from harm at all costs.

Reference

Krents, E., and S. Brenner. 1991. No-Go-Tell! Santa Barbara, CA: James Stanfield.

Further Reading

Committee on Child Abuse and Neglect and Committee on Children with Disabilities. 2001. Assessment of maltreatment of children with disabilities. *American Academy of Pediatrics* 108:508–12.

Debbaudt, D. 2002. *Autism, advocates, and law enforcement professionals: Recognizing and reducing risk situations for people with autism spectrum disorders*. Philadelphia: Jessica Kingsley.

Khemka, I., L. Hickson, and G. Reynolds. 2005. Evaluation of a decision-making curriculum designed to empower women with mental retardation to resist abuse. *American Journal on Mental Retardation* 110 (3): 193–204.

Lefkowitz, B. 1997. *Our guys: The Glen Ridge rape and the secret life of the Perfect Suburb*. Berkeley: University of California Press.

Little, L. 2004. Victimization of children with disabilities. In *Health consequences of abuse in the family: A clinical guide for evidence-based practice*, ed. K. A. Kendall-Tackett, 95–108. Washington, DC: American Psychological Association.

Sullivan, P. M., and J. F. Knutson. 2000. Maltreatment and disabilities: A population-based epidemiological study. *Child Abuse and Neglect* 24:1257–73.

Websites

Child Welfare Information Gateway: http://www.childwelfare.gov/

Reducing the Risk: Safety Strategies for People Who Use AAC (augmentative and alternative communication): http://www.accpc.ca/reducingtherisk.htm

CHRISTINE E. PAWELSKI

Families and Special Education

Families have played a central role in the development of contemporary special education in public schools. In fact, parental advocacy for access to free and appropriate education for their children with disabilities in the 1960s culminated in the landmark legislation that established special education services as a right in the mid-1970s. Shaped in the controversial climate of struggle for access to education, the relationship between schools and parents of children with disabilities is now regulated by federal law and court mandates. Currently, parents of children with disabilities are granted rights and a degree of control over their children's education that extend beyond those available to other parents. Despite the legal declarations and protections, however, parents of children with disabilities and schools are often at odds over expectations, educational placements, and the quality and quantity of services. The level of involvement in the education process ranges widely across families and schools, from hard-to-reach families who fail to participate in legally required educational planning meetings to families who monitor school services closely and do not hesitate to take legal action, when necessary, to demand specific interventions for their children. Most families fall between these two extremes.

Research suggests that active and constructive parental participation in school matters is most beneficial for children with special needs. Legislation that extended services for young children and their families in the 1990s emphasizes active collaboration in place of passive consent. Likewise, the latest reenactment of the federal law affecting school-age students expands parents' rights and promotes their engagement in all aspects of the educational process. Yet establishing and maintaining collaborative relationships between schools and families remain elusive goals. Investigations into the sources of conflict and disengagement between families and schools reveal complex and diverse roots. These include, but are not limited to, disparate views of the child's needs or potential, access to and quality of the accommodations in regular education or private schools, and access to specific treatments and services.

From the school's perspective, parental demands may appear costly, unrealistic, or impractical; as a rule, school administrators prioritize institutional needs over individual needs. On the other hand, parents may feel that their children are not being served adequately by the district and by their tax dollars. The presence of these differences is anticipated in the law, which provides ample guidance for legal disputes. Parents who are most savvy about their legal rights and seek legal representation are best able to win these disputes. Those who are ill informed or unable to access adequate representation tend to become quietly dispirited and withdraw from the educational planning process when they disagree with school actions.

Parents' relationships with schools may be described in terms of the emotions associated with the services being received. This implies that the relationship may either be mostly positive and harmonious or negative and rejecting. For example, a family's overall feeling about the school their child attends may be tinged with positive or negative associations. Similarly, relationships may be classified along an *engaged–disengaged* continuum, independent of emotionality. For example, families may be actively in conflict or in close collaboration with their school; in either case, the relationship may be described as engaged. Other families who have minimal contact with school staff would be described as disengaged.

Setting up these two variables in a grid yields four distinct types of relationships (see table). This framework could be used to explore the nature of parent–school relations. Families in quadrant A are involved in a positive, collaborative way, while those in quadrant B may be described as satisfied but unengaged. Families in quadrant C are engaged but dissatisfied, and those in quadrant D are both dissatisfied and disengaged.

Types of Relationships between Schools and Parents

	Engaged	Disengaged
Positive relationship	A Collaborative	B Passively consenting
Negative relationship	C In conflict	D Resigned

Families whose relationship with their school falls in quadrant A (collaborative) are positively engaged. These families work together with school staff and have developed a constructive and positive attitude toward the school and its services. This relationship enacts the type of collaboration anticipated in federal laws and sustains an approach that researchers consider most beneficial for children. Typically, these parents are readily available when approached by school staff and may initiate contact with the school in order to plan, monitor, and enhance their children's education. Differences are negotiated smoothly and successfully.

Families in quadrant B (passive consent) tend to voice satisfaction with school services, but typically do not attend meetings and do not contribute to the educational planning or monitor the services provided. Many of these families point to other responsibilities and/or a lack of time or resources that precludes their active involvement. While this may not be the most beneficial relationship for children's academic progress, educators tend to prefer it because it is a more traditional pattern of school–parent relationships that allows the school to proceed unhindered with educational plans. Parents who are uninvolved give tacit approval to school practices and are least likely to challenge school decisions.

Quadrant C (conflict) implies that parents are dissatisfied with school services and are actively demanding resolution of the conflicts in their favor. The nature of the differences may be personal and immediate, such as the parent who demands to meet with the principal and won't leave the school building until an audience is granted. Or the conflict may be more detached and calculated, such as with the parent who retains a lawyer to press for private school tuition for her child.

Finally, quadrant D (resigned) represents relationships where parents have largely given up and accepted the view that schools will not provide adequate services for their children. While these parents may still harbor hopes and optimism for their children, they have lost faith in the school system and school personnel. These families may feel impotent in the face of an unresponsive or blaming system. Researchers have found that families who are poor and members of minority groups are overrepresented in this quadrant. Many of these disaffected parents may lack knowledge of their rights, may not be fluent in English, or may fear school authorities—as is the case with undocumented immigrant families. Unfortunately, overrepresentation of children from diverse cultural and linguistic backgrounds in special education classes means that there is a disproportionate number of disaffected families from these populations.

While this framework is useful as a tool to classify families' relationships with schools, these relationships must be understood as dynamic processes subject to change. The fluid nature of these interactions is clearly evidenced by the changes in rapport with schools that families experience as children move from school to school or from grade to grade. Moreover, these complex human interactions *should not be oversimplified*. For example, a parent might be dissatisfied with a service provider, yet pleased with the classroom teacher; over the course of a school year, the same parent may come to respect the service provider based on the teacher's skilled implementation of services. Nevertheless, mapping out specific relationships and seeking ways to increase the proportion of families in quadrant A could benefit children with disabilities and the families who care for them.

Helping parents and schools develop cooperative relations requires initiative to challenge the status quo, as well as efforts from one or both parties to sustain communication. Possible avenues for facilitating change include improved communication, empathy, and access to advocates and information. Trust in parent–school relations has been identified as a building block for collaboration; to the extent that trust can be developed and deepened, family–school relations may improve—to the benefit of children with special needs.

Further Reading

Harry, B., M. Kalyanpur, and M. Day. 1999. Building cultural reciprocity with families: Case studies in special education. Baltimore: Brookes.

Meier, D. 2003. In schools we trust: Creating communities of learning in an era of testing and standardization. Boston: Beacon Press.

Noddings, N. 1992. The challenge to care in schools: An alternative approach to education. New York: Teachers College Press.

Stone, J. H., ed. 2005. *Culture and disability: Providing culturally competent services.* Thousand Oaks, CA: Sage.

Webb, N. B. 2001. *Culturally diverse parent–child and family relationships: A guide for social workers and other practitioners.* New York: Columbia University Press.

Websites

Advocates for Children of New York: http://www.advocatesforchildren.org/

Curry School of Education, University of Virginia: http://curry.edschool.virginia.edu/sped/projects/ose/resources/legal.html

School Psychology Resources Online: http://www.schoolpsychology.net/

ALBERTO M. BURSZTYN

Family Roles and Rights in Early Intervention

Families and, in particular, children's relationships with their primary caregivers are powerful influences on children's healthy development and learning. Families serve many important roles, from providing for children's physical growth to stimulating their development in important cognitive, language, and emotional domains. For young children with disabilities, families are an invaluable resource in the early intervention process. Their active involvement expands opportunities for providing interventions to children. Moreover, their involvement in planning can ensure that early intervention services are consistent with the values and routines inherent in young children's lives. For these reasons, caregivers serve as valuable members of the multidisciplinary teams that identify children's needs and plan early intervention services. Formulating genuine partnerships with caregivers in the team process, however, is challenging, requiring an understanding of how families support children's development, cultural sensitivity, and flexible solutions for engaging families' active involvement.

Individual Family Service Plans

The context for family involvement in the provision of early intervention services to children with disabilities is created by the Individual Family Service Plan (IFSP), which is required by the 2004 changes to the **Individuals with Disabilities Education Act**. The IFSP is the culminating document of collaboration among caregivers, early intervention educators, and other service providers (e.g., physical or occupational therapists, speech pathologists). It presents a comprehensive understanding of the child's needs, identification of services, and plans for service delivery and monitoring.

Two major assessments are fundamental to the IFSP. The first is a comprehensive assessment of the child, which presents a balanced perspective of competencies and needs. This assessment examines children's abilities across major developmental domains, including the language and communication, cognitive, social and emotional, and physical realms. The identification of early intervention goals and services for the child is based upon this multidisciplinary assessment.

Recognizing that the family system and home environment are crucial influences on children's development, the IFSP is also developed in accordance with a family-directed assessment of the home environment. This assessment entails identification of families' goals for their children, in addition to their personal resources and limitations for achieving these goals. By incorporating a family assessment into planning the IFSP, early intervention services can be family centered; that is, they can include specific supports and services that enable caregivers to meet their children's developmental needs.

The IFSP serves the central role of linking the direct assessment of the child and family environment to the provision of effective early intervention services. Based upon the assessment information, the IFSP delineates goals promoting children's development and a plan for providing services and interventions. In order to enable monitoring and evaluation of children's progress, anticipated and measurable outcomes for each goal are identified. A unique component of early intervention is the provision of services in children's natural environments. Unlike children who attend early childhood programs or school, young children below the age of three may spend their days in various environments, most often home or childcare facilities. Therefore, an important function of the IFSP is to specify where children will receive services.

A crucial component of the IFSP is the identification of a service coordinator. Given the broad developmental scope of early intervention services, children may receive services from a variety of professionals. Managing and coordinating this array of services can be confusing and stressful for families. Service coordinators can facilitate routine communication and collaboration among the various service providers to ensure that children's and their families' needs are sufficiently met through early intervention. Additionally, service coordinators can provide ongoing support to families by assisting them in understanding the benefits of the various services available and fostering their involvement in the services provided for their children.

Caregivers serve dual roles in developing and implementing the IFSP. Caregivers are members of the multidisciplinary team that determines children's needs and services. In this role, caregivers are *collaborators* in developing the IFSP. Moreover, caregivers are the primary *decision makers*. Informed parental consent is required for the IFSP to be implemented. Thus, caregivers' granting or withholding of consent determines the services utilized and the methods by which schools and supporting agencies will provide these services. Due-process procedures may be enlisted by either the caregivers or the early intervention service providers to resolve disputes concerning identification of children's needs or services. The IFSP is reviewed annually to ensure adequate monitoring of children's progress and the appropriateness of the intervention plan and service delivery approach.

Formulating Family Partnerships

Ideally, the team approach to developing the IFSP should result in a genuine, productive partnership among caregivers and early intervention service providers. Early intervention service providers' approach to working with families largely determines whether this outcome will be achieved. Too often, education and health care systems operate from a *delegation* model when involving families. According to this model, caregivers are expected to fulfill roles and responsibilities as determined by the early intervention professionals; for example, caregivers may be limited to receiving and responding to recommendations from the multidisciplinary team in the determination of the IFSP. In contrast, a *partnership* approach for involving families relies upon mutual respect, honest communication, active collaboration, and shared responsibility among family members and professionals. Here, caregivers are co-constructors of the IFSP.

Partnering with families in devising the IFSP is likely to enhance both the implementation of services and their effectiveness in improving children's outcomes. When caregivers are involved as partners in intervention planning, they are likely to formulate favorable perceptions of the services provided and their child's progress.

Although operating from a partnership rather than delegation approach is advantageous, it poses unique considerations and challenges for early intervention service providers. Caregivers need to be prepared to fully function as partners with other members of the multidisciplinary team. A fundamental first step to preparing them for this is to ensure that they are sufficiently educated about the process and procedures involved in devising an IFSP. Specifically, the steps of the classification and service delivery process, assessment procedures, services, and evaluation methods need to be adequately discussed with them. Preparation to serve as partners, however, has to extend beyond education to include empowerment. Empowering caregivers to serve as partners means that they must see themselves as competent and valuable team members, feel connected to the other team members, and be provided with means for becoming actively involved in advocating for their children. Professionals can facilitate the empowerment process by listening attentively to caregivers, affirming the worth of their contributions, and communicating honestly and respectfully with them.

Respect of individual and cultural differences among families is another vital component of establishing partnerships with caregivers. Team collaboration in establishing the IFSP is an interpersonal process; families will vary in what they regard as salient qualities in their working relationships with professional team members. For example, some studies have shown that many African-American families value professionals' genuine concern for their children. In contrast, Caucasian families may emphasize credentials and professional experiences among the team members. Certainly, professionals need to strike a balance between demonstrating their expertise and personal concern for children and families when partnering with caregivers.

Determining the goals and services also requires professional team members' sensitivity and responsiveness to families' individual and cultural values. Establishing goals that are mutually valued by both family members and early intervention professionals is a necessary starting point for ascertaining that families will welcome and be supportive of the subsequent services. Moreover, the emphasis on family-centered and home-based services in early intervention requires professionals to learn about each particular family rather than base service delivery approaches on conventional perspectives of family structure. For example, extended family members, such as grandparents, may be actively involved in caring for the child and could be beneficial to include in intervention plans.

Perhaps the most significant challenge in engaging families as partners in early intervention is coping with what professionals often define as *resistance*. Sadly, when family members do not do what is expected or needed to provide early intervention services, the tendency is for professionals to view them as resistant. Alternatively, we need to question the match of our services to families' values and realities. This requires us to embrace resistance rather than ignore it. Embracing resistance requires persistence, flexibility, and a deep understanding of the families' values and needs. Moreover, it requires honest communication with families to discern and respond to their preferences and dislikes throughout the early intervention process.

Further Reading

Christenson, S. L., and S. M. Sheridan. 2001. *Schools and families: Creating essential connections for learning*. New York: Guilford Press.

Epps, S., and B. J. Jackson. 2000. *Empowered families, successful children*. Washington, DC: American Psychological Association.

Harry, B., M. Kalyanpur, and M. Day. 1999. *Building cultural reciprocity with families*. Baltimore: Brookes.

Websites

National Association for the Education of Young Children: http://www.naeyc.org/

U.S. Department of Education, IDEA 2004 News, Information, and Resources: http://www.ed.gov/policy/speced/guid/idea/idea2004.html

PATRICIA H. MANZ

Family Stress and Autism

Over the last few years, the prevalence rate of autism, both nationwide and world-wide, has increased over previously reported rates. As a result, there has also been an increase in the general public's awareness of the disorder, and efforts are being made to provide parents and families with increased support. New classrooms and programs that attempt to meet the needs of children with autism are being developed within public schools. In addition, professionals who have specialized training in working with autistic children are being employed by school districts as consultants to provide support to teachers and auxiliary staff. However, support services for families to assist in comprehending what a diagnosis of autism means, maneuvering through the special education system, understanding student and parental rights, identifying effective treatments and interventions, securing services, and coping with and adapting to what lies ahead are lacking.

Autism is a developmental disorder where the individual is delayed in several areas. A diagnosis of autism is generally made before the age of three and is characterized by severe and pervasive impairment in the areas of social interactions, communication, and the presence of restricted, repetitive, and stereotyped patterns of behavior, interests, and activities. In addition, delays are also identified in social interactions, language use in social situations, and symbolic or imaginative play. The notification of a diagnosis of autism, or any other disability for that matter, is nothing less than devastating to parents. Unfortunately, the process a family must endure during the diagnostic phase is generally long, frustrating, and fraught with uncertainties.

Researchers have reported that the degree to which a family experiences stress and acceptance is largely dependent on the diagnostic process. Parents who detect delays in their child and seek diagnosis at an early age are more likely to cope and adapt better to the situation. By contrast, parents that experience a delay in diagnosis—or even worse, a misdiagnosis—often experience elevated levels of stress and frustration, marital problems, isolation from family and friends, and higher levels of depression. Interestingly, research has supported the notion that once a diagnosis of autism is given, parents are initially relieved because they now are able to understand their child's behavior, move toward acceptance, and begin to develop a course of intervention.

After a diagnosis of autism is given, parents begin to feel what was once referred to as the "burden of care." With the words "Your child has autism," the future that parents and other family members were working toward immediately and completely changes. Instead of spending savings on vacations, music lessons, sports, and college, money is quickly diverted to intervention services, medical needs, and long-term care. Time that was spent with a spouse and other children quickly diminishes as parents put all their attention, energy, and resources into caring for their child with autism. It is important to keep in mind that while all of this is occurring, parents are trying to cope with the reality that their child is disabled, the guilt that perhaps they did something wrong, their anger and frustration, and feelings of isolation and depression.

In addition to emotional stress, parents and families also experience stress related to what the future will hold, choosing and pursuing the right interventions, being emotionally isolated from their child, maintaining a "normal" family life, and increased financial burdens. In relation to the future, parents worry most often about how and whether their child will function in the real world and who will care for their child when they become too old to provide care.

There are generally three phases that parents experience with a child with autism. The first is considered a period of diagnosis and adjustment in which parents are consumed with stress related to interacting with professionals, obtaining a correct diagnosis, determining successful interventions, and securing services.

Deciding on appropriate interventions alone is a daunting task. There are multiple interventions and treatments available, and parents feel a great deal of stress when trying to figure out what would be the best course for their child. Along with this, parents also spend a large portion of their time and energy on researching options and providing care, and as a result they often develop additional monetary concerns due to loss of time at work or the need to stop working altogether. As a child moves through this phase, their issues become more pronounced, further increasing parental stress. Once a correct diagnosis is made, parents can develop an appropriate treatment plan and begin to adjust to their new lifestyle. Towards the end of this phase, parents generally experience a time period of growth and progress. Improvements in their child's communication skills and social capabilities play a role in the family's life becoming more typical.

The second phase is an increased time of stress as the onset of adolescence begins and the child's problems appear to worsen. Most often an increase in the child's physical and sexual maturity leads to emotional exhaustion for parents. During this phase, there may also be a need to change or modify an individual's treatment plan, because the child may have developmentally outgrown the current plan.

The third phase is adulthood, which brings an entirely new set of problems for parents to cope with. These problems may include locating a suitable residential living facility and the availability of employment opportunities. Overall, none of the aforementioned phases are easy for any parent to maneuver through.

In addition to the problems parents face during each phase, another source of anxiety for parents is the characteristics that a child with autism possesses. These characteristics may include verbal expressive difficulties, cognitive irregularities, difficulty with transitions and adapting to new environments, aggressive tendencies, and high levels of distractibility. There is also evidence that supports the notion that behavioral problems and the severity of a child's impairment are predictors of parental stress. For many parents, the inability to relate and communicate with their child, in and of itself, is a primary source of tension.

On a more positive note, parental education has been associated with assisting families in reducing their stress and depression. One way to do this is to teach parents naturalistic ways to increase their child's communication abilities. In addition, giving parents access to behavioral training has also been shown to decrease worry and increase parental self-efficacy. Interestingly, there is evidence to support the negative effect that parental stress can have on the level of success of any given intervention. However, it has been documented that lower levels of parental anxiety are associated with improvement and progress in a child's abilities.

Unfortunately, the harsh reality is that there is no cure for autism, and since each child with autism is completely different from the next, there is no one prescribed method of treatment or intervention. All services are generally dependent on the severity of the diagnosis and the child's ability levels. Therefore, there is no way to tell parents exactly what services their child will need or, more importantly, will benefit from. In this capacity, social workers, school psychologists, and educators can play a major role in assisting parents in choosing services, developing an academic program that meets the child's specific needs, and if necessary, locating a suitable out-of-district placement. In addition, school psychologists can also provide outside resources for parents, such as recommended family service agencies, parent support groups, trainings and workshops, physicians and specialists, respite care providers, and mental health agencies for individual and family counseling.

Further Reading

Baker-Ericzen, M. J., L. Brookman-Frazee, and A. Stahmer. 2005. Stress levels and adaptability in parents of toddlers with and without autism spectrum disorders. *Research and Practice for Persons with Severe Disabilities* 30 (4): 94–204.

Boyd, B. A. 2002. Examining the relationship between stress and lack of social support in mothers of children with autism. *Focus on Autism and Other Developmental Disabilities* 17 (4): 208–15.

Gray, D. E. 2002. Ten years on: A longitudinal study of families of children with autism. *Journal of Intellectual and Developmental Disabilities* 27 (3): 215–22.

Horowitz, A. N.d. Stress on families. http://www.autism-society.org/site/PageServer?pagename=livingfamily

Hutton, A. M., and S. L. Caron. 2005. Experiences of families with children with autism in rural New England. *Focus on Autism and Other Developmental Disabilities* 20 (3): 180–89.

National Autistic Society. 2005. The impact of autism on the family. http://www.nas.org.uk/nas/jsp/polopoly.jsp?d=307&a=3342

Website

Autism Today: http://www.autismtoday.com/

JENNIFER FOSTER

Research in Special Education

Action Research

Action research refers to investigations, conducted by teachers and other educators, that generally focus on problems or issues pertinent to immediate practice in the classroom or school. This approach to research differs from more traditional methods of investigation; the focus is typically on the participants and the scenario being studied rather than on generalizing the results to a larger population. The educator who conducts the investigation typically uses the results of action research studies immediately in the classroom. Action research is similar to *formative evaluation*, which is a method of assessing the quality of an ongoing program. Formative evaluation, along with action research, provides practitioners with information that can be used in making improvements to a particular educational setting.

Action research involves the collection of data by someone who is actively involved in the setting that is being studied. This intimate relationship between the researcher and the participants provides for a potentially deeper understanding of the unique problems in the environment under study. Unfortunately, having the investigator involved in the research also makes it difficult to generalize the results to other classrooms. On the other hand, because the focus of action research is limited to a specific situation, this is not considered to be a problem.

Generally, an action research study begins when an educator has unanswered questions about some aspect of her or his practice in the classroom. Such questions can arise as the result of a chronic problem identified by the teacher (difficulties in instruction, behavioral issues, etc.), by interested parties in the school (parents, administrators, etc.), or as the result of a new educational intervention (e.g., reading program) being introduced into the classroom.

Action researchers can develop questions by considering what issues in their daily practice are unresolved or potentially need improvement. Examples of such questions might be:

- What is the impact of a new method for teaching reading on students with Learning Disabilities (LD) in a third-grade classroom?
- How can the teacher help students who are having difficulty grasping basic academic concepts?

In the early stages of action research, the questions of interest serve mainly to guide the investigator through the next steps of the study. The questions must have relevance for the researcher and should pertain to some immediate issue of concern or interest.

Once the focus of the study has been identified, the action researcher typically conducts a review of the pertinent literature that has been published on the topic of interest in order to find out what other researchers have reported regarding similar issues. The literature search will also help to narrow down the scope of the investigation so that the research questions can be more easily answered. Indeed, the first attempt at developing a study typically results in questions that are far too broad to be answered in a single study.

As an example, if the teacher is interested in the impact of a new method of teaching students with LD to read, the literature search will reveal what previous investigations in this area have already uncovered. A teacher may discover that other action researchers have had success in employing a specific alternative method of teaching orthographic processing to children with nonverbal learning disabilities. The literature review will focus attention on new issues that are more relevant to the teacher's classroom practice and allow him or her to incorporate previous research into instruction. Furthermore, a reading of the literature will also provide the researcher with tips on how to conduct the study, based on methods used in previous research. To find relevant educational studies, the action researcher should use the Education Resources Information Center (ERIC) and PsycINFO databases, both of which can generally be accessed through any university library system.

The most important part of the action study is the development of a research plan, which is the step typically following a literature review. The researcher must identify precisely what data need to be collected in order to answer the research questions. Often, though not always, the sample to be studied is children in an existing classroom or some other group readily available and of immediate interest to the researcher. There are several broad categories of data collection that can be used, including direct observation, interviews, questionnaires/surveys, and measures of academic performance (test scores, grades on in-class assignments, etc.). Often, two or more of these types of data are used in action research so that the investigator can view the situation under study from multiple vantage points.

Direct observation involves the action researcher observing the relevant situation and recording pertinent information. Typically, the investigator will need to keep a written account of what is observed in the form of field notes. To preserve accuracy, notes should be taken as the observations occur or, if that is not possible, immediately following. Very soon after the observation, the researcher should go through the notes to ensure that they are readable and complete for future use.

Interviews of subjects represent another qualitative approach to action research. Most often the interview questions are written out in some detail and are asked exactly the same way to each interviewee. In some cases, however, less structured interviews can be conducted, particularly when the nature of the phenomenon under study is not well understood. This type of interview includes broad, general topics for discussion, but does not have specific questions to be asked. Results of the interviews should be recorded electronically (e.g., on a tape recorder) as well as by hand, thus ensuring that all of the responses are captured.

Questionnaires and surveys are useful when there is insufficient time to interview a large number of subjects or if the researcher would like to ask many questions. The development of a useful survey instrument is not a trivial task and must be undertaken with a great deal of care. The researcher should keep in mind that respondents might misunderstand items if they are not very clearly written. Survey development should involve a careful creation of question items, followed by (at the least) a review by colleagues who have not taken part in the initial survey writing. Ideally, the quality of the questions could be studied with a small sample in a *pilot study*. A pilot study involves giving the survey to a small group of individuals who are like those to be included in the actual data collection effort in order to identify potential problems and needed changes in the items. Thus, if parents are the intended targets of the survey, then the researcher might give the survey to a few parents and elicit feedback on the clarity of the items.

Finally, existing *academic data* can be used in action research. Such data can include scores on **high-stakes tests**, performance on teacher-made exams, homework grades, or any other naturally occurring measures of academic achievement. These scores can provide the researcher with quantitative information regarding student performance and can be very useful in identifying the impact of academic interventions on student learning.

The analysis of data in an action research study is similar to other research contexts, with the methods depending upon the nature of the information collected. Data collected using qualitative research methods such as direct observation and interviews will typically involve the search for common patterns in the data. This involves the identification of similar themes in observational notes and interviews across multiple subjects. Conversely, **quantitative research** methods such as questionnaires and study of academic data will typically be addressed using a variety of forms of quantitative analysis, some fairly simple and others more complex. The choice of analysis strategy is totally dependent on the nature of the data collected. In general, these statistical methods allow for a deeper understanding of quantitative information, allowing the researcher to identify patterns in the numbers that might help to better understand the phenomena under study.

Since the purpose of action research is to evaluate (and potentially improve) teaching practice, reporting of results is normally geared toward other practitioners who could benefit from the results of the study. The focus of the report is on what the results reveal about current practice or the impact of some intervention on the education of a particular group of students. These results of the action study should provide the teacher/researcher with information that can be directly applied in the classroom to improve some aspect of the education process. Therefore, the report should focus primarily on the situation under study and how these results can be used by practitioners in similar situations. Furthermore, because of the formative nature of action research, the study findings should also include recommendations for future action in the classroom, providing guidance for other practitioners.

Further Reading

Johnson, A. P. 2004. *A short guide to action research*. 2nd ed. Boston: Allyn & Bacon.
Mills, G. E. 2000. *Action research: A guide for the teacher researcher*. Upper Saddle River, NJ: Merrill.

Websites

Action Research Resources: http://www.scu.edu.au/schools/gcm/ar/arhome.html
Educational Action Research: http://www.tandf.co.uk/journals/titles/09650792.asp
Martin Ryder, University of Colorado at Denver, "Action Research": http://carbon.cudenver.edu/~mryder/itc_data/act_res.html
Qualitative Report, Qualitative Research Resources on the Internet: http://www.nova.edu/ssss/QR/qualres.html

W. HOLMES FINCH AND ANDREW S. DAVIS

Case Study

Many disciplines use the term *case study*, but it holds a different meaning for each. In general, a *case* is an example that is representative of a group or a concept. For law students, a case study consists of a court case that is now used to set precedent for judicial proceedings or the formulation of a law; for medical students, a case study depicts the symptoms or prognosis of a physical illness or abnormality. Special educators and psychologists derive case studies about the human condition, the learning process, and educational systems from quantitative instruments and qualitative observations. Early psychologists such as Alexander R. Luria used case study as their primary means of first evaluating and then individually intervening with patients. All of these uses of the term *case* are unique to their field, yet they are alike in the universal endeavor to uncover a greater truth about our world through the experiences of its inhabitants.

Since case study can be used to help understand an individual and that person's world, it includes a variety of contexts, variables, and multifaceted layers of understanding. By presenting the details of an individual's experience or the dynamics of a systemic relationship, a case study serves to make clear the complexity of situations that would otherwise remain unexamined. Case study is a unique form of research because it offers a compelling story that allows its readers to understand what life is like for the participants.

Educational case study has its roots in sociology and anthropology. A natural outcome of **ethnography** may be a case study that represents the larger population. Case study is a form of qualitative research, which means that data for the study are gathered by less structured instruments than those used in **quantitative research**. It is distinguished from other forms of qualitative research by being a unit, an entity of one. This does not mean that there is only one participant, though. While one participant may be studied, this is not the only type of case study that exists.

The following are all examples of cases that may be used in Special Education: one student, one teacher, a student and a teacher, one classroom, all the special education classrooms at one school, or the entire **inclusion** program in one school district. All of these are case studies of one that include from one to hundreds of people. This means the study needs to be designed in the best way possible to gather relevant details. The small amount of cases allows for a greater depth of data collection. In case study, data are gathered through observation, interviews, and document and record collection. Then, the information is integrated and analyzed to produce, distribute, and preserve new knowledge.

Case studies may be designed in a variety of ways. A case is usually examined because it has what Robert Stake has termed an *intrinsic interest* or an *instrumental interest*. Intrinsic interest means that something inherent about the specific case is of interest to the reader. Instrumental cases, however, are chosen to illustrate a topic of interest to the researcher. A *multiple* or *collective* case study might be designed where a number of cases are examined and common themes are drawn out by the researcher to illustrate the issues that unify or distinguish the cases from one another. For example, multiple special education classrooms may be examined within one school or across districts to determine how effective the curriculum and instruction are in each setting. *Case within case* is a design where a larger case is explored by examining smaller cases within it. For example, a special education classroom of interest may be explored by an in-depth study of three children within the class along with an overall study of all of the features of the classroom such as the teacher, parents, and curriculum.

Case study research has a long history of varying levels of acceptance in the field of research in general. In educational research, case study is currently seeing a revival. The scientific community's critique of case study is based on the concept of *generalization*, that is, how well the findings of a study hold up when applied to other situations. In quantitative research, it is commonly accepted that larger numbers of participants produce results that are more representative of the overall population. However, qualitative research is less concerned with the number of participants and more focused on the content of their responses. Since case study is qualitative in nature and is centered on one unit, the validity of its results is an ongoing issue in the field of educational research.

There is a continuum of opinions on this issue. Some researchers believe that the ability to generalize results is not the goal of case study. Others feel that case studies can generalize to the larger population if they closely follow scientific procedures. Most case study researchers are not caught up in this debate, as they believe that the detailed, in-depth, holistic, rich, and descriptive information their studies provide allows the readers to determine to what extent the case generalizes to their own situation. Stake has referred to this as *naturalistic generalization*.

Case study research is a through examination of a naturally bounded unit. The boundary may be of a person, place, or experience; it may also be bounded by time. The case is naturally occurring and tied to its context, allowing the study of people in their natural context. The particular nature of the case is what is of interest to the researcher.

Further Reading

Creswell, J. W. 1998. *Qualitative inquiry and research design: Choosing among five traditions.* Thousand Oaks, CA: Sage.

Gomm, R., M. Hammersley, and P. Foster, eds. 2000. *Case study method.* London: Sage.

Hamel, J., S. Dufour, and D. Fortin. 1995. *Case study methods.* Qualitative Research Methods, ed. J. Van Maanen, vol. 32. London: Sage.

Merriam, S. B. 1998. *Qualitative research and case study applications in education.* Rev. and exp. ed. San Francisco: Jossey-Bass.

Stake, R. E. 1995. *The art of case study research.* Thousand Oaks, CA: Sage.

_____. 2005. Case studies. In *Handbook of qualitative research*, 3rd ed., ed. N. K. Denzin and Y. S. Lincoln, 443–66. Thousand Oaks, CA: Sage.

Tellis, W. 1997. Application of a case study methodology. *Qualitative Report* 3 (3). http://www.nova.edu/ssss/QR/QR3-3/tellis2.html

Yin, R. K. 1993. *Applications of case study research.* Newbury Park, CA: Sage.

_____. 1994. *Case study research: Design and methods.* 2nd ed. Thousand Oaks, CA: Sage.

MARIA K. E. LAHMAN AND RIK CARL D'AMATO

Current Research on the Causes of Autism

Although autism was first identified more than sixty years ago, research into the neurological basis of autism is still in its infancy. The origin of autism is still very much in question today and ranges from outdated (and untrue) claims of poor or indifferent parenting to brain anomalies to a belief that the upsurge in the diagnosis of autism is the result of childhood vaccinations. Confounding the issue of accurately identifying a cause of autism is the wide variety of symptoms that children with autism express, as well as the confusion of autism with other Pervasive Developmental Disorders. An additional problem in uncovering the cause or basis of autism is the coexisting, or comorbid, disorders that children with autism experience. For example, it is not uncommon for children with autism to have Attention-Deficit/Hyperactivity Disorder (ADHD), Mental Retardation (MR), or Learning Disabilities (LD). Neurological markers have been proposed for each of these disorders, and some of them are similar to the markers for autism.

Autism is characterized by deficits in communication and social skills and by stereotypical, repetitive motor movements. However, each of these behaviors can differ dramatically from individual to individual. Clear genetic and developmental evidence exists to support the hypothesis that autism has a biological basis. For example, siblings of children with autism are much more likely than the general population to have autism. Research has identified that children with autism express social developmental anomalies in the first year of life. This early indicator of social dysfunction supports a biological predisposition towards autism. Thus, it is important for researchers to find biological and neurological markers of autism, since early identification of autism can lead to more successful interventions.

One of the most interesting current lines of research into the cause of autism is focusing on the differential brain volume between children with and without autism. Brain volume is usually measured in cubic centimeters. Researchers have indicated that children with autism have the same brain volume at birth as do children without autism. Then, from the ages of two to four, 90 percent of autistic children have *larger* brain volumes than their same-age peers, while by adolescence the children with autism have *smaller* brain volumes. It has been concluded that rapid brain growth in the first few years of life interferes with the acquisition of appropriate developmental skills, while the deceleration of brain growth as the child approaches adolescence interferes with the acquisition of higher-order brain functions. Adolescence is a time for the development of *executive functions*, the higher-order cognitive processing skills such as reasoning, planning, judgment, and abstract thought. Thus, the gradual decrease in brain growth during this critical period could partially account for the paucity of advanced cognitive functions seen in autistic adolescents.

Other neurological differences have also been noted in children with autism when compared to their same-age peers. These include areas of the *limbic system* (an area of the brain associated with emotional processing and memory) such as the *hippocampus* and *amygdala*, as well as areas in the *temporal lobes* and the *basal ganglia* (an area of the brain associated with movement). For example, in one study, individuals with autism and their parents had larger hippocampal volumes than did a group of control subjects (Rojas et al. 2004). Researchers have also noted that children with **Fragile X Syndrome** (the leading genetic cause of mental retardation) also have larger hippocampal volumes than controls do, and many children with Fragile X Syndrome demonstrate a number of autistic tendencies. There has also been an upsurge in interest regarding theories of intrauterine hormone development which claim that babies in the womb who produce more testosterone are predisposed to developmental abnormalities associated with autism. However, this is a new theory that is still being investigated.

There is a growing controversy regarding environmental influences on the recent upsurge seen in autism diagnoses. While many may argue that the increase is due to improved understanding and better diagnostic tools, others postulate that childhood vaccinations and other environmental factors are causing autism or autistic tendencies in children. The research on this theory is mixed, although much empirical evidence discounts the *acquired autism* theory—the idea that a child can acquire autism after birth from environmental conditions. For example, researchers found that withdrawal of the MMR (measles/mumps/rubella) vaccination did not decrease the incidence of autism, and they concluded that the vaccination was not related to the recent increase in diagnoses of autism (Honda, Shimizu, and Rutter 2005). In addition, a large-scale study investigated Thimerosal in vaccinations and concluded that it did not contribute to the development of autism (Andrews et al. 2004). Acquired autism is an issue that has recently been raised by some members of the U.S. Senate and will likely continue to be investigated. In sum, the current research on autism largely indicates that genetic and neurological factors are predictors of autism, although more research is needed on this topic.

References

Andrews, N., E. Miller, A. Grant, J. Stowe, V. Osborne, and B. Taylor. 2004. Thimerosal exposure in infants and developmental disorders: A retrospective cohort study in the United Kingdom does not support a causal association. *Pediatrics* 114:584–91.

Honda, H., Y. Shimizu, and M. Rutter. 2005. No effect of MMR withdrawal on the incidence of autism: A total population study. *Journal of Child Psychology and Psychiatry* 46:572–79.

Rojas, D. C., J. A. Smith, T. L. Benkers, S. L. Camou, M. L. Reite, and S. J. Rogers. 2004. Hippocampus and amygdala volumes in parents of children with Autistic Disorder. *American Journal of Psychiatry* 161:2038–44.

Further Reading

Acosta, M. T., and P. L. Pearl. 2004. Imaging data in autism: From structure to malfunction. *Seminars in Pediatric Neurology* 11:205–13.

Dawson, G., S. J. Webb, L. Carver, H. Panagiotides, and J. McPartland. 2004. Young children with autism show atypical brain responses to fearful versus neutral facial expressions of emotion. *Developmental Science* 7:340–59.

Website

Autism Society of America: http://www.autism-society.org/

ANDREW S. DAVIS AND JAIME S. ANDERSON

Ethnography

Ethnography is an approach to research that utilizes long-term study in the field and participant observation to understand the culture of the topic of interest. It is literally defined as people (*ethno-*) writing (*-graphy*). Ethnography has its roots in anthropology but may now be seen in all areas of social science research, from sports to communication to education. In order to understand ethnography, one needs to understand the use of the term *culture* and the method of participant observation.

Culture is not a concept that can be easily summarized, comprehended, or appreciated. It is defined as the shared beliefs and values of a group of people that are thought about and acted on. Culture includes traditions, ways of life, and customs. Ethnography attempts to understand the culture under study by observing a group of people interacting in their native environment. "Participant observation" is the method ethnographers believe allows the researcher to best capture a sense of what it means to be a part of a given culture. The term *participant observer* signifies the unique dual role of the ethnographer. Simultaneously, the ethnographer must be both participant at the research site and observer—they participate *in order to* observe. For example, in a special education public school classroom, the researcher might take the role of an assistant teacher in order to become integrated into the classroom and interact naturally as data are collected.

Educational ethnography is the examination of the culture of schools. The father of educational ethnography, George Spindler, brought ethnography to the educational setting, and his student Harry Wolcott further pioneered the field with famous educational studies such as *The Man in the Principal's Office* and multiple books on how to conduct and write educational ethnography. Through the years, educational ethnography has also been referred to as "classroom inquiry," the "ethnography of schooling," "anthropology and education," and "school ethnography."

Interest first developed in this area of anthropology because schools were seen as a central setting where culture was transmitted from generation to generation. For example, in the United States, schools attempt to incorporate a civics curriculum that is believed to produce educated and responsible voters, thus preserving the country's democratic culture. As educational ethnography continued to develop, the concept of *cultural transmission* was challenged as emphasis on the role of individuals in creating their own cultures increased. Thus, contemporary educational ethnography is interested in *both* the role of the individual and his or her relationship to the development of culture, which is now viewed as *cultural acquisition*.

In qualitative research, ethnography is seen as one of the finest research methods. This is due to the long period of time spent in the field, which is considered a reliable technique for enhancing the validity of qualitative research. It is thought that greater and more valid inferences can be drawn from the repeated incidents that extended field exposure uniquely provides. Long lengths of time in the field are defined as at least one cycle of the phenomena of interest. In special education, this may be one school year, a university semester, a seasonal year, or a report card period, depending on what topic is being researched.

One type of ethnography that is of particular interest to the field of special education is *team ethnography*, also referred to as *group* or *collaborative* ethnography. As ethnography moved from anthropological study into the educational arenas, it became increasingly clear that grant writers, universities, and busy researchers would need to form teams that could examine issues in multifaceted and varied ways. Ethnographic research teams occur when ethnographers join together at the same site or at similar sites and share their data. The simplest definition of ethnographic team research is two or more researchers—at least one of them an ethnographer—participating in research together.

In the history of ethnographic research, teams have included wife-and-husband teams, interdisciplinary teams, insider-outsider teams, **action research** teams, and ethnographic research teams. Examples of famous *husband-and-wife teams* include the Spindlers and the Adlers. *Interdisciplinary teams* involve ethnographers from different traditions and disciplines working in collaboration. *Insider-outsider teams* have members who are part of the group being studied and others who are external to the group. *Action research teams* are groups of ethnographers who are engaged in research with the belief that newly discovered data will offer solutions to problematic social issues. This technique is recommended for its efficiency, since most educators or researchers cannot spend long periods of time in the field. Today, the number of individuals that work alone is about equal to the number that work in teams. Therefore, developing experience with and skills at working in a "research group" may be a way of enhancing a study's validity, reliability, and overall rigor.

In many ways, ethnography is an ideal tool that can be used to help gain insight and understanding about the special educational enterprise, although it is not without criticism. One shortcoming of the participant observer role is that the observer is inherently unable to be objective, since they must participate and therefore assimilate, to some extent, to the culture they are observing. A criticism of educational ethnography, in particular, is that researchers typically use information from a single site as a **case study**. This does not allow the examination of educational issues through multiple venues and may neglect connections to larger cultural concepts.

Further Reading

Atkinson, P., A. Coffey, S. Delamont, J. Lofland, and L. Lofland, eds. 2001. *Handbook of ethnography*. London: Sage.

Emerson, R., R. Fretz, and L. Shaw. 1995. *Writing ethnographic field notes*. Chicago: University of Chicago Press.

Erikson, K., and D. Stull. 1997. *Doing team ethnography*. Qualitative Research Methods, ed. J. Van Maanen, vol. 42. London: Sage.

Garson, G. D. N.d. Ethnographic research. http://www2.chass.ncsu.edu/garson/pa765/ethno.htm

Hallcom, F. N.d. An urban ethnography of Latino street gangs. http://www.csun.edu/~hcchs006/gang.html

LeCompte, M. D., and J. Preissle, with R. Tesch. 1993. *Ethnography and qualitative design in educational research*. 2nd ed. San Diego: Academic Press.

Markham, A. N. 2003. Writing ethnography: A brief overview of assumptions. Appendix A of Going online: An ethnographic narrative, Ph.D. diss., Purdue University, 1997. Available at http://faculty.uvi.edu/users/amarkha/writing/dissappendixB. htm

Schensul, J., ed. 1999. *Ethnographer's toolkit*. 7 vols. Walnut Creek, CA: AltaMira Press.

Spindler, G., ed. 1982. *Doing the ethnography of schooling: Educational anthropology in action*. New York: Holt, Rinehart and Winston.

Van Maanen, J. 1988. *Tales of the field: On writing ethnography*. Chicago: University of Chicago Press.

Wolcott, H. 1984. *The man in the principal's office: An ethnography*. Prospect Heights, IL: Waveland Press.

_____. 1995. *The art of fieldwork*. Walnut Creek, CA: AltaMira Press.

Website

Center for the Ethnography of Everyday Life: http://ceel.psc.isr.umich.edu/

MARIA K. E. LAHMAN AND
RIK CARL D'AMATO

Quantitative Research

Quantitative research is a term descriptive of a broad array of research methodologies, all with a focus on numeric measures that address questions about a particular topic. Such numeric measures can take multiple forms, including scores on standardized or teacher-made tests, ratings given for performance of academic tasks or behavioral attributes, responses to survey questions, or frequency counts of some variable of interest. The reliance on numeric variables typically necessitates the use of statistical analyses, which can in turn be divided into two broad classifications, descriptive statistics and inferential statistics. Furthermore, quantitative research methods can take a variety of guises, including the most basic descriptive design, more sophisticated correlation and causal comparative research designs, and true experimental research. Each of these will be briefly discussed below.

Descriptive statistics are used to characterize a sample in terms of central tendency (e.g., the mean or median), variation (e.g., range, variance, or standard deviation), and frequencies of observed values. In addition, descriptive methods also include graphical procedures such as bar charts, pie graphs, scatter plots, and histograms, among many others. As a whole, descriptive statistics are used to present an overview of collected data. For example, a teacher may note that students learned a mean of six words a week with a new computerized spelling program, or that 90 percent of students passed a standardized achievement test.

In contrast to descriptive statistics, *inferential methods* are used to draw conclusions about a broad population from a sample of that population. Since often a researcher can never realistically obtain data from the entire population, a sample that is thought to be representative of the population being studied is selected. For example, a researcher may wish to study the performance on a standardized measure of reading achievement of students with reading disabilities. Since there are thousands of children across the country with reading disabilities, the investigator can gather data on only a sample representing the entire population of these children. After the researcher administers the test, the mean score can be calculated to determine the central, or typical, level of performance. Using inferential statistics, the researcher could take these results and generalize the performance of the sample to the population of all children with reading disabilities, and thereby gain a greater understanding of typical performance in the population for this reading achievement test. In order for such a generalization to be valid, of course, the data must truly be representative of the population as a whole. Most often, this goal is sought through the use of random selection of subjects to be included in the sample.

Researchers have available many inferential statistical analyses, which allow for the comparison of population means and the determination of the nature of the relationship between quantitative measures. For example, perhaps the researcher described above believes that children with Attention-Deficit/Hyperactivity Disorder (ADHD) will have higher reading scores than those with reading disabilities. The researcher can draw random samples from both populations and then use inferential analysis to ascertain whether the group means are indeed different. For example, suppose that the mean reading achievement score from a sample of fifty children diagnosed with ADHD is 87, while the mean for a sample of fifty children with reading disabilities is 80. Using inferential statistics, the researcher can determine whether these apparent differences in the sample will generalize to actual differences in performance between the two populations.

Quantitative methods also provide for the investigation of relationships between variables. These techniques allow the researcher to determine whether two measurements made on individuals seem to be related to one another or not. For example, an educational researcher might want to know whether the number of minutes spent on homework each week is related to academic performance. Inferential statistics allow the investigator to make conclusions regarding the nature of such relationships in the populations of interest.

In addition to the different statistical methodologies used to answer research questions, there are different research designs used to collect data. In the simplest case, a *descriptive design*, the goal of the study is simply to describe a particular population of interest. No effort is made to compare groups or find relationships between measured variables. Often researchers are interested in going beyond mere description, however, and would like to examine the nature of relationships between two or more variables or determine whether two or more populations differ. When this is the case, three research designs are commonly used. These designs differ in terms of the amount of control the researcher has in sampling the subjects to be studied and, where appropriate, assigning them to specific treatment conditions.

The research design that provides the most generalizable information is known as a *true experimental design*. This approach to quantitative research allows for the assessment of causation from one variable to another. The researcher has complete control over both the sampling of individuals for the study and the assignment of these individuals to one of several treatment groups. For example, consider a study in which an educational researcher wants to compare the efficacy of three methods for teaching addition to first graders diagnosed with a learning disability. In an experimental study, the researcher will be able to randomly select study participants from the population of children with learning disabilities, and these children can be assigned to one of the three treatment conditions. After the children undergo their respective treatments, the researcher, using inferential statistics, can compare their performance and make causal conclusions regarding the efficacy of each method.

Often it is not feasible to randomly assign individuals to different treatment conditions, such as in the comparison of genders or when intact classrooms are used. In these cases, the researcher may still wish to address questions that involve causal inference. Although this is not really possible outside of a true experimental study, a *causal comparative* research design can be used in an attempt to address such questions. Causal comparative research typically involves the use of statistical methods to control for factors that could not be controlled for through random assignment to treatment conditions. For example, imagine a researcher who is interested in studying the impact of a new behavioral intervention on the number of discipline referrals for fifth-grade students. The new intervention is to be conducted by the teacher, and all children in the class will receive the treatment. In order to compare the new method with individuals who did not receive the intervention, a second intact classroom must be compared with the first. Statistical methods can be used to account for any inherent differences in the students from the two classrooms, controlling for such factors as previous number of discipline referrals, age, gender, or any other factors that are believed to have an impact on students' behavior. While the causal comparative method does not allow for the same strong causal statements the experimental design does, it is perhaps the most commonly used approach to research because of the exigencies of the research environment.

The final quantitative design to be addressed here is called *correlational research*. This research design involves the collection of data as it appears in nature, and it is limited to measuring the relationships between two or more variables. No statistical controls are used as in the causal comparative approach. For example, a psychologist might gather performance data on a linguistic memory task and on a measure of verbal aptitude for a sample of twenty children in a special education class. The researcher would like to measure the strength and nature of the relationship between these two variables using a statistic known as the *correlation coefficient*. In this instance, the psychologist has no control over the makeup of the sample (they are twenty students in an intact classroom), nor can the researcher manipulate the values of either of the variables. Thus, only a relationship between variables can be discussed, but not true differences or causation.

While quantitative methods have proven very useful in studying educational and psychological issues, they do have inherent limitations that must be taken into account when interpreting results. First of all, all inferential statistics rely on various assumptions about the nature of the data being analyzed. When these assumptions hold true for the data, the statistics are reliable and provide useful information to researchers. On the other hand, when these assumptions are not met, the results of the inferential statistics are very possibly inaccurate and cannot be reliably interpreted. Another concern with quantitative methods is that they require the researcher to ask very specific, focused questions. Broad, far-reaching questions cannot typically be addressed in the context of statistical testing because it requires all hypotheses that it tests to be put into dichotomies. And, obviously, quantitative methods require that variables be measurable or at least able to be categorized into discrete groups. When this is not possible, quantitative methods are not truly applicable. In some cases, it is difficult to isolate the many factors that influence a phenomenon under study in the social sciences. In such instances, quantitative methods may be unable to isolate the causes of interest. Despite these concerns, when the assumptions underlying the inferential techniques are met and the questions of interest are specific in nature, quantitative methods can provide the researcher with definitive answers to questions of interest and have proven useful in a variety of contexts.

Further Reading

Coladarci, T., C. D. Cobb, E. W. Minium, and R. C. Clarke. 2004. *Fundamentals of statistical reasoning in education*. Hoboken, NJ: Wiley Jossey-Bass.

Joppe, M. N.d. Quantitative research techniques. http://www.ryerson.ca/~mjoppe/ResearchProcess/QuantitativeResearch.htm

Kaplan, D. 2004. *The Sage handbook of quantitative methodology for the social sciences*. Thousand Oaks, CA: Sage.

Ross, J. 1999. Ways of approaching research: Quantitative designs. http://www.fortunecity.com/greenfield/grizzly/432/rra2.htm

W. HOLMES FINCH AND ANDREW S. DAVIS

Teacher Research and Special Education

Teacher research refers to teachers studying their own classrooms in the interest of understanding and furthering the learning needs of their students. This has particular importance in special education, where instruction is differentiated, with teaching approaches tailored to the specific learning needs of students. Approaches that prove effective in working with particular children can become part of students' **Individualized Educational Programs** (IEPs), providing continuity to children when they move to a new grade or class. When special education teachers research their own classrooms, they often study a new program or approach they are trying with their children. For example, teachers might study a new method of teaching children to read or a new approach to furthering cooperation in the classroom.

Teachers' research efforts provide evidence of their efforts in such areas as curriculum development and interpersonal approaches with specific children and provide documentation of children's work. Teachers document their work though formal and informal observations of the class and by including detailed descriptions of their efforts with the children. They include work samples of the children's productions such as examples of their writing and artwork. Often, teachers choose to study a specific child whose behavior is puzzling or problematic or whose learning style presents challenges. This type of research, referred to as a *case study*, serves two purposes. It helps to further the understanding of children's needs and abilities, and it provides teachers with a framework for planning curricula and individualized approaches to instruction.

In researching their classrooms, special education teachers examine their own teaching practices. They observe the children they teach and critically reflect on their teaching methods and styles. The process of studying one's own classroom and scrutinizing one's own approaches to teaching provides opportunities for teachers to observe the multiple influences on classroom life (Jalongo and Isenberg 1995). The tools that special education teachers use to conduct teacher research are typically regular observations of their classrooms, often of specific children, and surveys and interviews with teachers, administrators, children, and families of the children they teach. This method of researching a classroom by drawing on multiple research tools is referred to as *triangulation* (Lincoln and Guba 1985).

Triangulation enhances the validity of the research study, providing a check for researchers that they are actually studying what they intended to research. It also pushes teacher thinking toward gaining critical understanding of how teacher practice, children's learning, and classroom dynamics interact in complicated ways. The emphasis on triangulation guides teacher thinking in the direction of encountering multiple perspectives and uncovering the underlying curricular, affective or social-emotional, and policy/organizational frameworks that operate beneath the surface of daily classroom life. Each framework provides a focal point through which to consider classroom practice.

The curricular framework describes the context in which teaching and learning take place. It includes the content and structure of curriculum development and instructional approaches, as well as their impact on individual children. The affective or social-emotional framework provides an alternate lens through which to study classroom practice. It provides a window into how the classroom environment encourages, or possibly subverts, teacher intentions to further children's social and emotional growth. The policy/organizational framework provides the structural context in which schooling takes place, including administrative and legal requirements as well as professional national, state, and local standards.

Narrow emphasis on a single framework can prove misleading. One teacher researcher, acknowledging the familial and affective frameworks at work in her classroom, became better able to focus on the curricular frame and worked more effectively with her first-grade class. Another explored different perspectives and considered how he might make room for diverse cultural frames in his special education classroom. Occasionally, cultural and familial frames are at odds with accepted educational practice. For example, as she conducted home visits, observed the children, and interviewed parents and colleagues, a teacher uncovered some fundamental tensions between the cultural expectations of the home and of the school, specifically around gender-role expectations. In one instance in which a father specifically requested that the teacher prohibit his son from playing with dolls, the teacher explained her nonsexist approach to education, as supported by professional teaching organizations, and maintained her stance in the face of the father's displeasure.

When teachers talk and write about their research, their stories often reveal how approaches to curriculum development and instruction shape the classroom environment. Their stories also reveal how a child's social and emotional development is addressed—or neglected—in classroom life. Similarly, teacher research stories often reveal family and cultural influences on children's lives and on the life of the classroom, as well. Finally, stories about teacher research suggest how organizational frameworks, such as school administration and governance bodies, and educational policies at the local, state, and federal levels impact on children with special needs.

When studying their own classrooms, special education teachers gain greater understanding of how these complex frameworks operate in the classroom. They become more critically aware of their own classroom-based choices and actions and the impact of these on the children they teach. Because it is focused on the practical implications of classroom life, teacher research has direct impact on student outcomes. When teachers study children's specific learning needs and styles and develop approaches to helping children learn effectively, the results of their research can be translated immediately into differentiated instruction, in which teaching approaches are tailored to the needs of specific children. These approaches are then formalized in the children's IEP goals.

References

Jalongo, M. R., and J. Isenberg. 1995. *Teachers' stories: From personal narrative to professional insight*. San Francisco: Jossey-Bass.

Lincoln, Y., and E. Guba. 1985. *Naturalistic inquiry*. Beverly Hills, CA: Sage.

Further Reading

Kincheloe, J. 1991. *Teachers as researchers: Qualitative inquiry as a path to empowerment*. London: Falmer Press.

Schon, D. A., ed. 1991. *The reflective turn: Case studies in and on educational practice*. New York: Teachers College Press.

Websites

Midlands Writing Project: http://www.ed.sc.edu/mwp/research.html

Teacher Research: http://ucerc.edu/teacherresearch/teacherresearch.html

CAROL KORN-BURSZTYN

About the Contributors

Tracy Amerman is an assistant professor of special education at New Jersey City University. She is a former special education teacher specializing in transition to postsecondary life for students with disabilities. She has also researched and published articles on inclusion and assistive technology.

Jaime S. Anderson is a student in Ball State University's school psychology doctoral program. She currently conducts autism assessments for the university's School Psychology Clinic.

David C. Bloomfield is head of the Educational Leadership Program at Brooklyn College, City University of New York. He is a graduate of Columbia University (J.D.) and Princeton University (M.P.A.) and was formerly general counsel to the New York City Board of Education.

Alberto M. Bursztyn is a professor of school psychology and special education at Brooklyn College and at the Ph.D. program in urban education of the Graduate Center, City University of New York. His current scholarship focuses on urban children and families, children in special education programs, multicultural assessment, and qualitative research methods. Dr. Bursztyn's recent publications include *Rethinking Multicultural Education* (with Carol Korn, 2002) and *Teaching Teachers: Building a Quality School of Urban Education* (with J. Kincheloe and S. Steinberg, 2004).

Jan Carr-Jones has been an advocate for persons with disabilities for more than twenty years. Having begun in vocational rehabilitation, she now works on issues related to transition from school to adult life.

Jennifer A. Chiriboga is an assistant professor at Duquesne University in the Department of Counseling, Psychology, and Special Education. Her research interests primarily include the psychosocial and academic experiences of children with chronic conditions.

Rik Carl D'Amato has a B.A. in secondary education from the University of Wisconsin–Whitewater, an M.S. in educational psychology/school psychology from the University of Wisconsin–Madison, and a Ph.D. in school psychology-neuropsychology from Ball State University. He serves as director of the Center for Collaboration Research in Education in the College of Education and Behavioral Sciences at the University of Northern Colorado (UNC). A former Fulbright scholar to Latvia, Dr. D'Amato currently serves as editor-in-chief of *School Psychology Quarterly*, the American Psychological Association's school psychology journal. He is an A. M. and Jo Winchester Distinguished University Scholar and an M. Lucile Harrison Distinguished Professor at UNC.

Andrew S. Davis is an assistant professor at Ball State University. He has written multiple articles and book chapters and has presented at several national conferences on pediatric neuropsychology.

Beth Doll is a professor in the School Psychology Program at the University of Nebraska at Lincoln. She serves as associate editor of *School Psychology Quarterly* and president of the Council for Directors of School Psychology Programs, and she is a frequent speaker on topics related to effective classroom learning environments. Her research addresses models of school mental health that foster resilience and enhance the well-being of students, as well as program evaluation strategies that demonstrate the impact and accountability of school mental health services.

Timothy G. Dowd is a visiting assistant professor of psychology at Miami University of Ohio. He teaches an undergraduate seminar in psychosocial aspects of physical disability and has received the Psi Chi Psychology Professor of the Year Award four times.

Graciela Elizalde-Utnick is an assistant professor and the coordinator of the Bilingual Specializations in School Psychology and School Counseling Program at Brooklyn College, City University of New York. She is also director of the Brooklyn College satellite of the Bilingual Psychological and Educational Assessment Support Center. A New York State–certified bilingual school psychologist, Dr. Elizalde-Utnick has expertise in culturally and linguistically diverse infants, toddlers, and preschoolers with special needs and their families. Her scholarly interests and research include selective mutism, language proficiency assessment, differentiating learning differences from disorders in English-language learners, home-school collaboration, and the relationship between the individualism–collectivism continuum and personal identity formation.

Patricia English-Sand is a faculty member of literacy and special education at Fordham University. She developed a course for differentiating instruction and has taught differentiated instruction for many years.

Giselle B. Esquivel is a professor, the current director of the School Psychology Programs, and past chair of the Division of Psychological and Educational Services in the Graduate School of Education at Fordham University. She is a nationally certified school psychologist, a licensed psychologist, a diplomate of the American Board of Professional Psychology, a fellow of the American Academy of School Psychology, and a fellow of the American Psychological Association. Dr. Esquivel has done extensive research and mentoring in the area of bilingual school psychology and cultural diversity. She is also involved in resiliency research, including spirituality and creativity as protective factors among children at risk.

W. Holmes Finch is an assistant professor at Ball State University. He conducts research in psychometrics and statistical analysis and has written articles on these subjects for a number of national journals. He teaches courses in statistics, research methods, and tests and measurements.

Namulundah Florence received her Ph.D. in education administration from Fordham University. Her research and teaching interests explore the impact of conceptions of self and society on education policy and practice—for example, cultural assimilation and exclusion within the academy and beyond. Recent publications include *bell hooks' Engaged Pedagogy: A Transgressive Education for Critical Consciousness* (1998) and *From Our Mothers' Hearths: Bukusu Folktales and Proverbs* (2005).

Jennifer Foster is a school psychologist. She received her M.S. in education and advanced certification from Brooklyn College. Her research interests include exploring how families cope with having a child with a disability; addressing barriers to family, school, and community collaboration; and investigating issues faced by students living in urban environments.

Dana Freed received an M.S. in education and an advanced degree in school psychology from Brooklyn College, City University of New York. Her interests include assessment, academic intervention, and treatment for children with emotional and behavioral disturbances.

S. Andrew Garbacz is a doctoral student in the School Psychology Program at the University of Nebraska at Lincoln. He is president of Student Affiliates in School Psychology, the national student organization of Division 16 of the American Psychological Association. His research interests include behavioral and academic interventions as delivered through a consultation model that emphasizes home-school partnerships, as well as international issues related to children's rights and education.

Michelle W. Greenberg is a doctoral student in school psychology at the University of Texas at Austin. Her research interests include depression among children, family interactions, and peer relations.

Gail B. Gurland is professor and director of the program in speech-language pathology and audiology at Brooklyn College, City University of New York (CUNY), where she has been a member of the faculty for more than thirty years. She has published several articles and presented extensively on the topic of language-based learning disabilities. She earned her B.A. and M.S. in speech-language pathology from Brooklyn College and her Ph.D. in speech and hearing sciences from the Graduate School of CUNY.

M. Kelly Haack is a doctoral student in the School Psychology Program at the University of Nebraska at Lincoln, and a predoctoral intern in psychology at the Munroe-Meyer Institute of Omaha, Nebraska. Her research addresses attributions for parents' participation in children's schooling.

J. Joshua Hall is a student in Ball State University's school psychology doctoral program. He is currently exploring sensory-motor skills in patients with multiple sclerosis and the relationship between executive functions and intelligence.

Brooke Hersh is a doctoral student in the school psychology program at the University of Texas at Austin. Her primary research interest is in developing positive psychological methods to enhance resilience in at-risk youth.

Leesa Huang is a nationally certified school psychologist and an assistant professor of psychology at California State University at Chico.

J. Patrick Jones is a doctoral student at Ball State University, completing a degree in school psychology with a cognate in special education. He has provided school psychological services for a public school (K–12) and guest-lectured for courses in behavior analysis.

Lauren Katzman is an associate professor in the Department of Curriculum and Teaching's special education program at Boston University. Her research has focused on students with disabilities' perspectives of the effects of high-stakes testing. She conducts evaluations of state and district implementation of the Individuals with Disabilities Education Act, most recently for the New York City

Department of Education, and provides professional development to schools to support their move to a more inclusive environment. Dr. Katzman was a special education teacher for fourteen years.

Carol Korn-Bursztyn is professor of education at Brooklyn College and the Graduate Center of the City University of New York. She holds a doctorate in child psychology and postdoctoral certification in psychotherapy/psychoanalysis from New York University. She is faculty director of the Early Childhood Center at Brooklyn College, coeditor of *Rethinking Multicultural Education* (2002), and series editor for Making Sense of Psychology (Greenwood). She is currently at work on a book, *Arts and the Early Years: Creativity, Imagination, and Reflective Teaching.*

Maria K. E. Lahman has a B.A. and an M.S. in early childhood education and a Ph.D. in child development. She taught early childhood education in public school and laboratory schools for ten years. Currently she is an assistant professor in applied statistics and research methods at the University of Northern Colorado in the College of Education and Behavioral Sciences. There she teaches graduate students primarily from education and other social science fields how to conduct qualitative research. Dr. Lahman's personal research focus is on educational research that uses ethnographic methods, and case study. She was the recipient of her college's 2002 Outstanding Teacher Award.

Yoon-Joo Lee is an assistant professor of special education at Brooklyn College, City University of New York. Her scholarly interests are social experiences of young children with special needs in inclusive settings and the use of action research to improve classroom practice.

Lakisha Lewis is currently a doctoral student in Arizona State University's school psychology program. She has conducted research and therapy with preschool-age children with autism at the University of Nebraska Medical Center in Nebraska. Her research interests include augmentative and alternative communication systems and behavioral interventions for young children with autism.

Sandra L. López is a doctoral student in school psychology at the University of Texas at Austin. Her academic and research interests include the treatment of depression among children in various ethnic groups and multicultural counseling.

Patricia H. Manz is an assistant professor of school psychology at Lehigh University. Her research and scholarship has concentrated on the roles of low-income, ethnic minority families in early childhood education. She has received recognition of her early career research through the National Institute for Disability Research and Society for the Study of School Psychology.

Kathleen M. Marker is a student in Ball State University's school psychology doctoral program. She is currently exploring hemispheric lateralization and pediatric depression, and the neurological basis of other childhood disorders.

Danielle Martines is director of the School Psychology Program at Montclair State University and a trilingual psychologist whose professional practice focuses on applying multiculturally focused assessments in schools, consultations, and individual counseling. Dr. Martines received a master's degree in school/community counseling from Long Island University and a Ph.D. in psychology from Fordham University, with a specialization in bilingual school psychology. She is currently completing a guidebook on multicultural school competencies.

Paul McCabe is an associate professor, a New York State–certified school psychologist, a New York State–licensed psychologist, a nationally certified school psychologist, and the president of the School Psychology Educators Council of New York State. He received his Ph.D. from Hofstra University. A specialist in early childhood social, behavioral, and language development and concomitant problems, Dr. McCabe is a consultant to early childhood centers and preschools, as well as a contributing editor to *NASP Communiqué, Applied Developmental Science*, and *Journal of Early Childhood and Infant Psychology*. His current research interests include examining the interaction between language impairment and socialization problems in early childhood; early childhood social competence; developmental psychopathology; and pediatric school psychology (including neuropsychology).

Paula J. McCall is currently a doctoral student in the school psychology program at Arizona State University, where she also earned a B.A.E. in special education and a M.Ed. in curriculum and instruction. She has worked with individuals with mental retardation for more than ten years, including four years as a public high school special education teacher. She currently serves as a special education director for a charter middle school and also has been employed in this position at an online charter high school. Her current research is in the area of depression in adolescents with mild mental retardation. She also is a member of the American Association on Mental Retardation, the National Association of School Psychologists, and the American Psychological Association.

Kathleen McSorley is an assistant dean at Brooklyn College, City University of New York. Her research interests include the preparation of educators to work in inclusive schools, systems change in middle school education, and responsibility-based behavioral strategies for working with students experiencing emotional conflict.

Sara G. Nahari is an associate professor in the Graduate School of Education and Psychology at Touro College and an adjunct associate professor in the Graduate Program in School Psychology at Queens College, City University of New York. She received her doctorate from Fordham University, where she also received a professional diploma in bilingual school psychology, and is a nationally certified school psychologist. Her entire career as teacher, guidance counselor, and psychologist in the New York City Public Schools was devoted to multicultural and bilingual issues.

Tiffany J. Neal is a student in the school psychology doctoral program at Ball State University. She is currently investigating gender differences in sensory-motor functioning and has previously presented on pediatric neuropsychology at national conferences.

Chad A. Noggle is a student in Ball State University's school psychology doctoral program and the associate director of the Ball State University Neuropsychology Laboratory. He is currently researching sensory-motor and cognitive differences in depression and Alzheimer's Disease.

Julia Nyberg is director of educational outreach at the Beall Center for Art and Technology, a research and exhibition center that explores new relationships among the arts, sciences, and engineering, promoting new forms of creation and expression using digital technologies.

Geraldine Oades-Sese is a Ph.D. candidate in the school psychology program and a 2004–2006 Holmes Scholar at Fordham University. She has extensive supervised clinical and assessment experience. She has contributed a book chapter on the identification of gifted and talented culturally and linguistically diverse children and adolescents and is currently working on her dissertation on resilience among at-risk preschool children. She is also involved in resilience research among maltreated children and medically fragile and multiply handicapped children at the New York Foundling Hospital.

Christine E. Pawelski is an educational program developer and an adjunct associate professor in the special education department at Teachers College, Columbia University. Her current program development focus involves the production of multimedia training materials for use in professional development in the areas of inclusion, alternative and complementary practices, global special education initiatives, and child abuse involving children with disabilities. Recent projects have included CD-ROMs and Web sites as well as the publication *Child Abuse and Children with Disabilities: A New York State Perspective, 2004.*

Terry L. Reese is a doctoral candidate at Ball State University. She has written several articles and presented at a national conference on neuropsychology.

Matthew R. Reynolds is a doctoral student in educational psychology at the University of Texas at Austin with a dual specialization in school psychology and quantitative methods. His interests are in the areas of pervasive developmental disorders, intelligence, and educational and psychological measurement.

Arleen Rios is a school psychologist in the Perth Amboy (New Jersey) School District. She is a member of Kappa Delta Pi, the education honor society. She has worked with children of the middle school level involving transition issues for the past five years.

Florence Rubinson is an associate professor of education at Brooklyn College, City University of New York. A major theme of her writing is the study of collaborative environments in schools as a means of educational reform.

Spencer J. Salend is a professor of special education at the State University of New York at New Paltz. A recipient of the Chancellor's Research Recognition Award, he has written extensively on educating all students in general education classrooms.

Maryann Santos de Barona currently is a professor and the interim associate dean for academic programs and personnel at Arizona State University. A graduate of the School Psychology Doctoral Training Program at the University of Texas at Austin, she has been active in addressing the need for culturally appropriate practices in assessment, treatment, and research activities and to increase Latino representation in the psychological community. Dr. Santos de Barona has served as president of the National Hispanic Psychological Association, editor of *El Boletín*, and a member of the APA Minority Fellowship Program Advisory Panel. She is currently the chair of the Arizona Board of Psychologist Examiners.

Elizabeth Scanlon is a school psychologist at an elementary school in the suburbs of Seattle. She earned her B.A. from the University of Pennsylvania and M.Ed. from Brooklyn College. Scanlon's interests include the response to intervention model, crisis management, working with at-risk populations, and brainstorming and implementing creative behavioral interventions.

Amy N. Scott is a doctoral candidate in educational psychology at Arizona State University, where she also earned her master's degree in educational psychology. She completed her internship in school psychology at the Louisiana School Psychology Internship Consortium and is now a certified school psychologist working in the Gilbert Public Schools. As an undergraduate, she attended the University of California at Berkeley, double majoring in psychology and religious studies.

Aubrey Sewell is an undergraduate psychology major at Miami University of Ohio. Her research and career interests include examining the social factors that influence violence against women.

Eugene P. Sheehan is dean of the College of Education and Behavioral Sciences at the University of Northern Colorado. A social psychologist, he has published articles on employee turnover and job satisfaction. He received the university's Distinguished Scholar Award and the Provost's Award for Leadership Excellence in Service.

Erin Siemers is a doctoral student in the School Psychology Program at the University of Nebraska at Lincoln and a predoctoral intern in behavioral pediatric psychology at the Kennedy Krieger Institute, part of the Johns Hopkins School of Medicine. She has served on the student editorial board for *School Psychology Quarterly* and as an ad-hoc editor for *School Psychology Review*. Her dissertation research addresses children's aggression within elementary school playgrounds, playground environments, and student reports of victimization worries.

Stephanie R. Sinco is a graduate student in the school psychology Ph.D. program at the University of Northern Colorado (UNC). Her research interests include neuropsychology in the schools, learning styles, classroom management, and evidence-based interventions. She serves as a graduate assistant in the College of Education and Behavioral Sciences at UNC.

Amanda H. Stoeckel has a B.A. from Gustavus Adolphus College and is a graduate student pursuing her Ph.D. in school psychology at the University of Northern Colorado. Her interests are in health promotion in psychology, serving children with post-traumatic stress disorders, school transition, and neuropsychological aspects of trauma. She has presented papers at various state and national conferences, is involved in a variety of research projects, and serves on the Student Review Board of *School Psychology Quarterly*.

Jonathan Titley is a doctoral candidate in the school psychology program at the University of Northern Colorado. His research interests include neuropsychology, learning disabilities, ADHD, depression, and using strength-based approaches in the schools. He serves on the editorial staff of *School Psychology Quarterly*.

David Trend is a professor of studio art at the University of California at Irvine. He is the author of *Welcome to Cyberschool: Education at the Crossroads in the Information Age* (2001).

James M. Trinkle II is a student in Ball State University's school psychology doctoral program. He is currently exploring the relationship between perinatal functioning and childhood social-emotional functioning.

Katherine L. Truesdell is an undergraduate psychology major at Miami University of Ohio. Her research and career interests include art therapy and sexuality.

Joseph Valentin is currently a facilitator serving students with disabilities in a New York City middle school in Brooklyn and an adjunct instructor for the graduate program in special education at Brooklyn College. He has a decade of experience grounded in early childhood, alternative elementary, and middle school inclusion settings servicing children with autism, behavioral disorders/emotional disturbances, developmental delays, and learning disabilities. He is a doctoral candidate pursuing a Ph.D. at the City University of New York Graduate Center in Urban Education with a research interest in pedagogical ontology. His most recent article voices the need for teachers in special education to critically reassess their identity as urban facilitators and agents of hope.

Howard B. Wakkinen is a graduate student in the school psychology Ph.D. program at the University of Northern Colorado (UNC). His research interests include professional issues in school psychology, models of consultation, positive psychology and resilience, neuropsychology in the schools, and evidence-based interventions. He serves as a graduate and teaching assistant in the College of Education and Behavioral Sciences at UNC.

Justin M. Walker has a B.A. from Michigan State University and is pursuing his Ph.D. in school psychology at the University of Northern Colorado. His interests are in assessment, alternative school settings, and the juvenile justice system, as well as in academia and bridging the gap between theory and practice. He has presented papers at various state and national conferences, is involved in a variety of research projects, and serves on the Student Review Board of *School Psychology Quarterly*.

Frank C. Worrell is director of the School Psychology Program and the faculty director of the Academic Talent Development Program at the University of California at Berkeley. His research interests include the role of psychosocial variables in academic achievement and the reliability and validity of instruments used to measure psychosocial constructs.

Chun Zhang is a faculty member of special education at Fordham University. She has published widely on topics such as culturally and linguistically appropriate practices and overrepresentation of children from culturally and linguistically diverse backgrounds in special education.

Index

Page numbers in **bold** type refer to main entries.